*The Planters of the Commonwealth*

# THE PLANTERS
# OF THE COMMONWEALTH

A *Study* of the *Emigrants* and *Emigration* in
COLONIAL TIMES: to which are added *Lists*
*of Passengers* to BOSTON and to the
BAY COLONY; the SHIPS which brought
them; their *English Homes*, and the *Places*
of their *Settlement* in MASSACHUSETTS

1620—1640

*By*

CHARLES EDWARD BANKS

*Member of the* MASSACHUSETTS HISTORICAL SOCIETY
*and of the* AMERICAN ANTIQUARIAN SOCIETY

Originally published: Boston, 1930
Reprinted: Genealogical Publishing Co., Inc.
Baltimore, 1961, 1967, 1972, 1975, 1979, 1984, 1991, 1997
Library of Congress Catalogue Card Number 67-30794
International Standard Book Number 0-8063-0018-3
*Made in the United States of America*

SCOTLAND

NORTHUMBERLAND
27

CUMBERLAND
1

WESTMORE
LAND
0

DURHAM
2

LANCASTER
39

YORK
70

WALES

CHESTER
12

DERBY
33

NOTTS
28

LINCOLN
63

STAFFORD
14

SALOP
14

LEICESTER
42

RUTL
9

NORFOLK
160

WARWICK
58

NORTHAMPTON
67

BEDFORD
49

CAMBRIDGE
29

SUFFOLK
266

WORCESTER
22

HEREFORD
7

OXFORD
27

BUCKS
75

HERTS
96

ESSEX
244

GLOUCESTER
68

BERKS
28

MIDD
78

WILTS
97

SURREY
47

KENT
188

SOMERSET
134

HANTS
67

SUSSEX
31

DEVON
161

DORSET
119

CORNWALL
10

MAP OF ENGLAND
Showing the number of emigrants from each county of 2646 emigrants traced

# PREFACE

WHEN Englishmen left their island to emigrate to the North American continent, to begin a new life in the unexplored wilderness, they adopted a name for themselves by which they were generally known in the first century of their experiment. The places to which they went were called 'plantations.' Bradford's 'History' is of the 'Plimmoth Plantation' — not the Plymouth Colony — and the various settlements in Virginia bore the name of plantations until within the memory of the present generation. From Maine on the extreme north to Virginia on the south the men who came to settle in this newly acquired territory adopted the name of 'planters' to distinguish themselves as men who had come to fulfill a national obligation. They were not planters in the agricultural sense, but in its spiritual significance. They came, not to plant crops for subsistence, but to plant on this virgin soil a new nation to perpetuate under other skies the cultural development of Anglo-Saxon civilization.[1]

This title of planter came to have a new and specific value in the English language and the earliest records of New England and the Southern Colonies justify this conclusion.[2] It is with respect to this term, chosen by themselves, that the following record of emigrants and emigration to Massachusetts is given the title of the 'Planters of the Commonwealth' and to their descendants it is dedicated.

The

---

[1] English local records have occasional references to the burial of persons from Virginia or New England designated as 'planters.'

[2] In the land records of Maine practically every settler is designated as a 'planter' in official documents, in preference to stating his trade.

The story of the planting of an English colony in the Massachusetts Bay in the first half of the seventeenth century becomes in its last analysis a study of its individual emigrants and their origins. Out of the little parishes of England came nearly twenty-five thousand persons sprung from the loins of the yeomanry. This emigration amounted to an exodus hitherto unexampled in the history of modern civilization, and it marked an epoch in the world's history that has not yet ceased to affect profoundly the destiny of mankind. These adventurers, scarcely known outside of their parochial boundaries, almost unconscious of the ultimate importance of their acts, began to plant on this portion of the North American continent the seeds of a new nation whose fruit should become another England, with its traditions, culture, and laws. They had few of the educated or social classes to guide them in this movement and with no historic examples to aid them in their problems. They were not entirely wise in their generation nor were they without the usual defects of their inherited qualities. Their names are as much a part of the foundation of Massachusetts and New England as are the records of their collective deeds. To know them by name and to learn of them in their former surroundings is to obtain a better knowledge of the beginnings of this Commonwealth.

The names of many of these emigrants who took part in this religious and economic hegira are to be found recorded in official depositories widely scattered in England and America in a variety of documentary collections, where they may be painfully recovered, one by one, in diaries, letters, court proceedings, and in modern books that relate to traditions of our colonial families. The prime, as well as the greatest, source of our knowledge of those who tempted fate in the great adventure of emigration to New England is the
collection

collection of Custom-House records of the various ports of England, now in the custody of the Master of the Rolls in the Public Record Office, Chancery Lane, London. They were formerly accumulated in several like depositories, such as the Tower of London, the Rolls Chapel, the State Paper Office, and a half-dozen smaller public collections, including the British Museum. These documents consist of lists of passengers permitted to travel to New England, certified by the customs officials principally of London, Ipswich, and Southampton. Unfortunately, these shipping lists are confined, with few exceptions, to the year 1635. The earliest list is dated March 1631/2 and gives the names of sixteen adult males with the name of the ship omitted. A note in Winthrop's 'Journal' supplies this omission. Two others exist for the same year. None exist for 1633 and six for the following year. What became of the missing lists of the other years which were required to be kept by Order in Council is a puzzle in the problem of disappearances. Since the centralization of these records, no new lists have been found, and it is believed that only unsuspected local depositories will ever disclose further original lists to these scanty contributions to the story of emigration to New England in the first half of the seventeenth century.

In 1842 the late James Savage, President of the Massachusetts Historical Society, visited England for the purpose of examining and transcribing such of these lists as were then available, and published his transcripts, under the title of 'Gleanings for New England History,' in the 'Collections' of that Society.[1] During the three years, 1858–60, while residing in London, the late Samuel Gardiner Drake also examined and copied these same lists, and printed his transcripts in 1860 in a small quarto volume, long out of print

and

---

[1] Third Series, volumes VIII and X. (Boston, 1843.)

and scarce. They had been previously issued serially in the
'New England Historic and Genealogical Register,' of which
his volume was a reprint.[1] These two pioneers in English
research were natural enemies in the historical world and
wasted much time and ink in criticizing the other's readings
of these names. In 1874, John Camden Hotten, a prolific
English writer on historical and biographical subjects, made
the third and last known general examination of these lists
after they had been assembled in one collection in the present
Public Record Office. They were then classified as 'Exchequer
K.R.' in the division scheme of the Deputy Keeper. Mr. Hotten published these lists of emigrants to the various American colonies, combined with much miscellaneous related material, in a large quarto volume.[2] This work is now out of print,
scarce, and highly priced by booksellers. Copies now to be
found in public libraries are generally badly worn through
continued use, as the poor paper on which it is printed
requires constant patching to withstand the rough handling
which a reference book of this character must suffer.

The compiler of the lists which follow in this volume, during a residence of nearly five years in England has examined
personally the originals of all the lists heretofore printed by
Drake, Savage, and Hotten, and subjected them to analytical
study with a view of presenting them in an intelligible form.
These three compilers transcribed and published these
passenger lists *verbatim et literatim*, which, of course, has its
value, but as originally recorded they appear to be copies
made without reference to connecting family groups. Children are separated from their parents in numerous cases,
wives

---

[1] *Result of Some Researches Among the British Archives for Information Relative to the Founders of New England.* (4to. 131 pp. Boston, 1860.)

[2] *Original Lists of Emigrants.* (Royal 4to. 580 pp. Chatto & Windus, London, 1874.)

wives and husbands officially divided, while their kinsmen and servants are similarly dislocated. As an example, the volume in which the emigrants of the ship *Planter* (1635) are entered gives six several lists of her passengers in as many places under dates March 22, April 2, April 6, April 8, April 10, and April 11, interspersed with lists of passengers booked for five other ships. Another excellent illustration of the almost hopeless jumble of families, where husbands, wives and children are separated, is to be seen in the lists of the *Abigail*, May–July, 1635.[1] The passengers are divided into fifteen separate groups, interspersed between the lists of five other vessels, evidently as they were entered from time to time. These dislocations have been restored, as far as possible, to an orderly arrangement. This adhesion to a literal reproduction of the record is not only confusing, but it perpetuates the separation of family groups and prevents a clear presentation of those who sailed in this particular ship. They will now appear all together in reconstructed order, and the same plan has been followed in other like instances wherever they occur.

And this raises a somewhat important practical question as to the original character of these lists, which has not been discussed by Drake, Savage, or Hotten. It will be apparent from an examination of the reproductions of the few lists which are shown in this volume, for 1632 and 1635, that they are in one handwriting and are remarkably uniform in appearance. In fact, the whole collection exhibits this same characteristic, and leads to the inevitable conclusion that they are not the originals, turned in from time to time by the Custom-House searchers, but fair copies of their notes made on the docks and consolidated in this office transcript for record. This gives them a certain secondary value,

[1] Hotten, pp. 73, 87, 88, 89, 90, 91, 92, 96, 97, 98, 99, 100, and Drake, 28, 31–38.

value, because of the chances for mistakes in transcribing, and may explain some obvious errors in names and ages of passengers which have puzzled many in the use of the printed lists.

Outside of these lists to be found in England, occasional names of emigrants are to be picked out of the great variety of documents in the Public Record Office in the Chancery Division and in the almost untouched records of the High Court of Admiralty. From both these sources I have obtained some valuable material which will be indicated in the reference to sources. In the archives of the several New England colonies it has been possible to find scattered references to emigrants and emigrant ships in the course of litigations recorded in the various local courts. Private records like the Trelawney Papers have yielded much material of value relating to Maine settlers and the ships in which they arrived.[1] The Wyllys Papers have furnished what little can be found about the earliest direct emigration to Connecticut.[2] Private diaries, such as Winthrop's 'Journal,' Higginson's 'Letter,' Shepard's 'Relation' and Mather's 'Diary,' have furnished information of unique interest explaining the means employed by the suspended Puritan clergymen to escape arrest when embarking for New England under assumed names. Winthrop's 'Journal' has proved a valuable check list for the ships arriving before 1640 with passengers.

In addition to these positive sources, a special feature of this work will be found in what may be called synthetic lists of emigrants, such as the passengers of the Winthrop Fleet of 1630, the *Mary and John* and the *Lyon* of the same year, reconstructed from evidences found in every available source

too

[1] 2 Maine Historical Society, III.
[2] Connecticut Historical Society, vol. 21.

too numerous to catalogue. As they were the earliest arrivals in the first settled town of Massachusetts, their identity could be established by church, town, and colony records. Similar lists have been reconstructed from like material in several other instances, which are indicated in each case and based on the same process of elimination. In this way it is possible to restore the picture of the emigrants and the ships in which they came with some degree of accuracy and probability without violating the rules of evidence.

Additions of this kind have been made to a number of the ships' lists, particularly in cases like the Hingham, Massachusetts, emigrants in the Cushing MSS., and the Hercules passengers of 1634 and 1637. In these lists the number of children and servants were originally published in figures. The names of these have been supplied by the compiler from various sources to make the lists complete.

With this explanation the student of our early history will have for the first time a comprehensive view of what was happening in New England from 1620 to 1640 when English ships were bringing Englishmen to our shores.

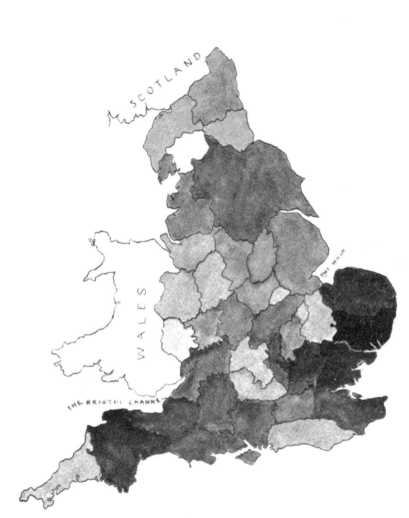

MAP OF ENGLAND

The heaviest emigration took place from the counties in the darkest shades

# CONTENTS

## PART I

A STUDY OF EMIGRATION TO NEW ENGLAND IN COLONIAL
  TIMES      I

## PART II

LISTS OF PASSENGERS AND THE SHIPS WHICH BROUGHT THEM   45

| | |
|---|---|
| 1620 | 47 |
| 1621 | 50 |
| 1622 | 52 |
| 1623 | 52 |
| 1624 | 57 |
| 1625 | 58 |
| 1628 | 59 |
| 1629 | 60 |
| 1630 | 65 |
| 1631 | 92 |
| 1632 | 95 |
| 1633 | 102 |
| 1634 | 107 |
| 1635 | 125 |
| 1636 | 179 |
| 1637 | 180 |
| 1638 | 190 |
| 1639 | 201 |
| 1640 | 202 |

APPENDIX   207

INDEX   209

# The Planters of the Commonwealth

∴

## PART I

### A Study of Emigration to New England In Colonial Times

# KEY TO ABBREVIATIONS

Banks MSS.  Collections of the Author
Winthrop    Journal (edition 1908)
M.C.R.      Massachusetts Colonial Records
S.P. Dom.   State Papers Domestic, Public Record Office
P.R.O.      Public Record Office, London
L.L.W.      Life and Letters of John Winthrop
Gen. Reg.   New England Genealogical and Historical Register

# THE PLANTERS OF THE
# COMMONWEALTH

· ·

## PART I

*A Study of Emigration to New England in Colonial Times*

WHEN the *Sarah Constant*, the *Discovery*, and the
*Goodspeed* housed their hawsers at Blackwall in the
Thames in December, 1607, and floated down the
river headed for Virginia, and the *Mary and John* and the
*Gift of God* pushed off from Falmouth Harbor in Cornwall,
in June of the same year, bound for the Maine   *The first*
coast, both to begin a colony, then and there be-   *ocean 'liners'*
gan the Atlantic passenger service which has vexed the 'vast
and furious ocean' for over three centuries. From these five
little vessels picking their lonely course across the Atlantic
there have developed great fleets of 'liners,' each one over a
hundred times larger than the largest of these two convoys.
If shallops of the size of the *Gift of God* started on a like trip
to-day, it would make the first page of every metropolitan
daily. The venturesome mariners of 1607 knew no other
method of traversing these three thousand miles to reach our
coast, and few are the records left to tell the tales of those
little boats tossed on mountainous seas for weeks out of sight
of land, trying to live in the relentless pounding of their
fragile hulks. The Southern Colony, which settled on the
James River, held its own from the first, favored by a mild
climate and a fertile soil, but the Northern Colony which selected

lected the rocky promontory of Sabino, at the mouth of the Kennebec River, languished after a peculiarly cold winter and was abandoned for a time to be renewed under more inviting conditions. To both of these places ships came and went, yearly, but as this account does not comprise the story of emigrants and emigration to the Southern Colonies there will be no further consideration given to that part of the passenger traffic which built up Virginia and the Southern States.

The maritime interests of England at the beginning of the period under discussion were entirely concerned with exports *Development* and imports of merchandise. These were the *of ocean* Alpha and Omega of their foreign trade and pas- *traffic* senger travel was merely incidental to this extensive business. Ships were not built to accommodate travelers, and those who desired to visit foreign countries had to adjust themselves to the inconveniences of a freighter. No European country provided such means of transportation nor had there been any demand for such facilities up to this time. True to her traditions of maritime adventure, England was the first nation to meet this demand, and for three centuries she has been in the forefront of this form of traffic. The overseas merchants and shipowners of England met this requirement in the same spirit which has characterized their long leadership in seafaring ventures.

This new problem did not immediately result in any modification of naval architecture or of the interior construction of vessels to make them more comfortable for their passengers. Up to the end of the seventeenth century, the tonnage of vessels crossing the Atlantic with passengers increased very little over the known tonnage of the *Mayflower* and of the *Arbella*. Few of them reached or went beyond five hundred tons measurement.

measurement. There was a certain type of vessel which came to be selected as desirable ships for the passenger trade. These were engaged in the wine trade to the Mediterranean ports, which, by reason of their occupation, were specially constructed for that purpose and were known as 'sweet ships,' as they were unusually well caulked and always dry. The *Mayflower* of 1620 was of this class, and it is probable that most of the vessels of the Winthrop Fleet of 1630, in which passengers were mainly carried, were selected from this class of traders.

When and how the cost of transportation was fixed is unknown. The voyage of the Pilgrims offers no basis of computation as they went under a seven-year contract, but it is understood that ten pounds was the sum paid by them for the voyage and they furnished, as far as possible, their own subsistence. This became a new problem in maritime reckoning, as the length of the voyage was always uncertain, sometimes ranging from five to twelve weeks, depending on the weather, winds, and the time of year. The Pilgrims were twelve weeks in crossing in the late fall, while the *Arbella* made the same journey in about eight weeks in the early summer. The price fixed by the Massachusetts Bay Company seems to have been adopted by all subsequent ships. This was decided to be 'at the rate of 5 li. a person' [1] and was meant as applicable only to adults, and for children the following schedule of relative fares was provided: 'Sucking children not to bee reckoned; such as under 4 yeares of age, 3 for one [fare]; under 8, 2 for one; under 12, 3 for 2.'[2]

In addition to the fares for passengers, the cost of shipping household goods increased the financial problem for the emigrant. It was necessary to carry these things across the ocean, as there was no way to obtain them in the early years of

[1] M.C.R., 1, 65.    [2] *Ibid.*, 66.

of an unsettled country. The rate for this service was fixed at
'4 li. a tonn for goods.'[1] For the average family of eight
persons with a ton of freight the cost would be about thirty
pounds, or nearly a thousand dollars in our present money. In
what manner the household goods reached their destination
may be inferred from the unfamiliarity of those English yeo-
men and artisans with the perils of the deep. Very few of
them had ever left the shores of Albion and they were igno-
rant of the inadequacy of these small craft in the trough of the
mountainous Atlantic waves piled high in her savage moods.
A contemporary writer speaks of the giant seas 'hurling their
unfixed goods from place to place' from lack of proper stow-
age.[2] The present generation has scant conception and practically no actual knowledge of the inconveniences which their
ancestors experienced in making the voyage from England to
the American continent. The most that is understood and
appreciated is the diminutive size of the vessels and the long
and hazardous passage required under the best conditions to
reach the 'stern and rockbound coast' of New England.

If the reader can visualize a vessel of two hundred tons
carrying a hundred passengers with a crew of about fifty
*Accommoda-* officers and seamen, with their necessary freight
*tions for* and supplies, he can form an idea of the limita-
*passengers* tions imposed on the Pilgrims in their three
months' voyage from Plymouth, England, to our Plymouth.
The *Mary and John*, which brought the Dorchester emigrants
in 1630, was of about four hundred tons burthen and carried
one hundred and forty passengers. The *Griffin* of three
hundred tons brought about two hundred passengers in eight
weeks from The Downs. Vessels as small as seventy tons engaged in this passenger traffic, and, in addition to the ordinary
discomforts

[1] M.C.R., 1, 65.    [2] Johnson: *Wonder-Working Providence.*

discomforts of such manifest inadequacy of space for comfortable living, most of these vessels carried cattle, which did not add to the pleasure of the voyage even in the calmest weather.

As far as known no one has left a contemporary description of the conditions of Atlantic travel at that time, and the best that can be done to reconstruct them is by utilizing fragmentary references of emigrants to produce a synthetic picture of an average voyage. Turning a wine ship into a passenger vessel with accommodations for one hundred and fifty or two hundred souls becomes a problem of several dimensions. The officers' quarters on the poop deck and the sailors' bunks in the forecastle were always limited in space, and the only possible place for passengers was the space between the towering stern structure and the forecastle or between decks. Below this was the hold, which was used for the cargo, the ordnance, and the stowing of the longboats. In this part of the ship, as we learn from Winthrop's story of the *Arbella*, cabins had been constructed, probably rough compartments of boards for women and children, while hammocks for the men were swung from every available point of vantage.

There is little doubt that the flagship of the Winthrop Fleet of 1630, which brought several persons of the nobility and gentry, was fitted with special cabins for their accommodation. The class distinctions of that time would not permit Sir Richard Saltonstall, the Lady Arbella Johnson, and her brother, Charles Fiennes, Esquire, or John Winthrop, Esquire, and others of like social quality, to rough it in common with the yeoman class of emigrants who came with them. Either the cabins in the stern were turned over to them and the officers found room elsewhere, which is probable, or special compartments were constructed for them, as this ship was owned by a syndicate of members of the Massachusetts Bay

Bay Colony. On this subject Winthrop gives us no definite information, except to mention that 'some Cabbins, which were in the waye of our ordenance,' were taken down when the decks were cleared for action against some suspected 'Dunkirks.' [1]

In the early days of New England emigration, passengers of social standing were few, and there were infrequent applicants for special accommodations. It may be supposed that Sir Henry Vane, son of the Comptroller of the King's Household, and the Lord Leigh, son and heir of the Earl of Marlborough, demanded and received cabin space in the ship which brought them to Boston. Doubtless wealthy emigrants of the better classes, like John Haynes and Roger Harlakenden, followed the example of their noble patrons in engaging better accommodations for their trans-Atlantic voyage. In a lawsuit in which Nathaniel Patten, formerly of Crewkerne, Somerset, was the complainant against Henry Wolcott *et al.*, joint undertakers of the ship *Hopewell* of London, the following charge appears in the account against the defendants:

Itm for a cabbin bought in the ship because I had not convenience in the ship according to agreement for myselfe & family.

For this he entered the sum of £1:10:0 as the cost of this special privilege, and we may accept this as the proximate charge for cabin space on these merchant ships.[2]

It may be left to speculation how the sanitary needs of the passengers were provided for in ordinary weather with smooth seas. The imagination is beggared to know how the requirements of nature were met in prolonged storms in these small boats when men, women, and children were kept under the hatches for safety. This may be mentioned as an inevitable accompaniment of emigration in its beginning.

In

[1] *Journal*, I, 4.     [2] Lechford: *Note Book*, 180.

In the first half of the seventeenth century there had not been developed a system of public advertising and the method by which shipping available for intending    *Arranging* emigrants must have been broadcast by oral    *for the voyage* means. Bristol was the first maritime port which undertook the exploitation of the American continent, and the Channel ports came next — Falmouth, Plymouth, Dartmouth, and Southampton. The Popham Colony of 1606/7 sailed from Falmouth in Cornwall and the *Mayflower* from Southampton in 1620, while the Dorchester Colony of 1630 went from Plymouth. London did not become associated with this traffic until the East Anglians started the Great Emigration under Winthrop. The metropolis, situated on the Thames, near the eastern coast of England, required a sail of about a hundred miles due east to The Downs before the ships could head west to their destination, and was thus at a distinct geographical disadvantage. As a result, vessels from London usually made the Isle of Wight their final point of departure, where they could obtain fresh water and other perishable supplies. Nevertheless, with this handicap London became after 1630 the chief port of embarkation for emigrants, with Ipswich, Great Yarmouth, and Sandwich competing for this patronage.

One may assume that information of ships ready to undertake the Atlantic voyage was in some way made available by carriers and town criers in various sections, and to those who had decided to emigrate it meant a journey to London, Bristol, or Southampton to negotiate for their passage to New England.[1] It must be understood in considering the beginnings of this traffic that it began with ships built as freight carriers with no thought of service as passenger vessels. Englishmen leaving their 'tight little isle' for foreign travel had

[1] *Chancery Affidavits*, xi, 82.

had to meet no inconveniences in crossing the Channel to France, or even to Holland, as the voyage rarely exceeded a few hours to Calais or Boulogne and never more than a day under favorable winds to the Texel. The question of comfort did not enter into the problem. Longer passages to the ports of Spain, Portugal, and the Mediterranean were rarely undertaken except by factors and supercargoes, who could occupy rooms in the high stern superstructure shown in vessels of the period. It can be said with truth that until 1606 no large body of Englishmen had ever left their native land as emigrants to live as colonists on our New England coast. The *Mayflower* of 1620 with its hundred souls was the largest group of emigrants of English birth destined for New England. From these initial adventurers began the attempt of owners of merchant ships to supply the demand for passage to the New World. The experiment had no traditions. It began with the raw material, at the foundations. The master of the commercial freighter had to take into account the needs of his human cargo on a long and perilous voyage instead of casks of Port, Madeira, and Xeres with a cooper to aid in their safe transportation to London Town.

In the lists of passengers and ships that follow in Part II of this volume, there will be found the names of about thirty-*General sources of emigration* eight hundred emigrants, while Drake and Hotten have printed lists but slightly in excess of two thousand (2049). The larger number which appears in this compilation is not of so much importance as the question of their English origins and antecedents. The names of the emigrants who settled the first towns of this Commonwealth can be recovered through a study of the oldest local records, but we should still be lacking the desired knowledge as to who they were and whence they came. To supply this important

important information, as far as possible, has been the object
of the author. To know whence the emigrant started on his
long ocean journey, to identify his companions and neighbors,
and perhaps the leading spirits of his group, is to find help in
the solution of the motive which led him to this fateful decision. We shall never satisfactorily answer the question of the
reasons that actuated this great emigration until we have developed the personal factors behind it. The origins of the
Pilgrims and their English homes have already been the subject of a special study by the author and need not be considered here.[1] They were a limited group of religious zealots and
separatists who had abandoned their homes in England in
1610 to obtain freedom of worship in Holland, and found it
there. In 1620 they again deserted this sanctuary for a specific motive, to preserve their national identity for themselves
and their posterity. They had no other motive, as they were
still welcome in Leyden, and their flight adds nothing to the
discussion of the motives of the adventurous Englishmen who
formed the Great Emigration a decade later.

The several settlements of the early emigrants in this Commonwealth have been more intensively studied than any
other part of the original coastwise population, but no detailed study of the English origins of the pioneer groups has
been undertaken. The local historians have generally drawn
the line of their investigation at the water's edge. The scattered searches of family genealogists in England have located
the equally scattered homes of their ancestors, but these have
only pointed the way by scratching the surface. Few of the
emigrants brought with them any recorded references to their
English homes, and in only a negligible percentage of them
has there survived any dependable tradition of their family
connections.

[1] Charles Edward Banks: *The English Ancestry and Homes of the Pilgrim Fathers.*
(New York, 1929. Published by the Grafton Press.)

connections. In Bradford's 'History of Plymouth Plantation,' where he gives a detailed list of the passengers of the *Mayflower*, there is not one reference to the family origin or home parish of any one of the Pilgrims. Winthrop's 'Journal' has a few casual references to the residences of emigrants, but nowhere does he make an allusion to the definite area whence were drawn the hundreds who came with him in 1630 in the great fleet to plant this Commonwealth. The inference is inevitable that they were not interested in preserving this information, which we now have to seek out at the cost of so much labor and money for the coming generations.

The earliest contemporary statement relating to the numbers who came to Massachusetts was published by Capt. Edward Johnson at the end of Chapter XIV of his "Wonder-Working Providence." He wrote:

For fifteen yeares space to the year 1643... the number of ships that transported passengers in this space of time as is supposed is 298. Men, women and children passing over this wide ocean, as near as at present can be gathered, is also supposed to be 21,200 or thereabouts.

This seems to be sufficiently detailed to give it the color of careful investigation by the writer, and it has been, undoubtedly, the basis for the usual claim that the number of settlers of this territory before 1650 was less than twenty-five thousand, of whom about six thousand were original male progenitors of families, the rest being women, children, and servants.

The problem envisaged in this section of our study of the emigrants is to apply certain ascertained factors in determining the local sources of origin of these six thousand potential males, progenitors of families who came to the Massachusetts Bay Colony before 1650, when the Civil War and domestic conditions in England terminated emigration hither in shiploads.

loads. From that time forward the migration assumed an individual character until the beginning of the next century, when it again developed into wholesale proportions. The statements which follow covering the topographical features of the emigrations of 1620–50 are based on investigations of the origin of 2646 emigrants who arrived in Massachusetts, and include those whose home and family connections are positively known, or about whom enough has been ascertained to establish a satisfactory clue to their origin.

By arranging the results of these researches into the comital divisions of England, then and now having the same lines of demarcation, we shall obtain a macroscopic view of the general emigration situation as it existed for our forefathers. The forty counties of England furnished an extremely diverse contribution, numerically considered, to the settlement of the New England Colonies, varying from twenty-five per cent to zero, and a reference to the accompanying maps will show that the greatest number of emigrants are to be found in the counties bordering on the North Sea and the English Channel with London as the center of the movement. It will be noted that the extreme northern counties of England made no contribution, worth classifying in statistics, to this epochal period in our history. Of these 2646 emigrants the City of London supplied 172, as much as half a dozen of the smaller counties. The next largest city — Bristol — gave us only 28 emigrants. The causes of this wide variation in numbers involve many factors, religious, economic, and political, somewhat intricate for accurate analysis, but this phase of it will be taken up in the following section.

These figures do not answer the personal-interest question which naturally will arise at this time when the Tercentenary of the settlement of the great Massachusetts Bay Colony will stimulate the descendants to know something more of the origin

igin of their ancestors than that they simply emigrated hither; nor does it do more than tabulate the county origins of over twenty-six hundred particular individuals. It would require double this number of emigrants to reach a final conclusion as to the relative county contribution to the statistics of emigration. The most it can show is the prevailing areas. Roughly analyzed, the region known as East Anglia (Norfolk, Suffolk, and Essex) gave 670 emigrants, or 21.5 per cent. London, Middlesex, Sussex, and Kent gave 530 emigrants, or 20 per cent, and the West Country (Dorset, Devon, Somerset, and Cornwall) gave 424 or 16 per cent, making a total of 57 per cent derived from the counties bordering on the North Sea and the English Channel from The Wash round to the Bristol Channel. The remaining considerable sources of county emigration can be credited to the so-called 'Home Counties' (Bedford, Berks, Bucks, Herts, and Surrey) surrounding London which gave 295 emigrants or 11 per cent, and the 'Midlands' (Leicester, Notts, Northants, Worcester, Warwick, and Derby) gave 250 emigrants, or 9 per cent. Four fifths of all the English emigrants to New England resided southward of a line drawn from the Bristol Channel to The Wash.

*List of Counties in England in the order of the heaviest emigration*

| | | | |
|---|---:|---|---:|
| Suffolk | 266 | York | 70 |
| Essex | 244 | Gloucester | 68 |
| Kent | 188 | Hampshire | 67 |
| London | 171 | Northants | 67 |
| Devon | 161 | Lincoln | 63 |
| Norfolk | 160 | Warwick | 58 |
| Somerset | 134 | Bedford | 49 |
| Dorset | 119 | Surrey | 47 |
| Wiltshire | 97 | Leicester | 42 |
| Herts | 96 | Lancashire | 39 |
| Bucks | 75 | Derby | 33 |
| Middlesex | 73 | Sussex | 31 |
| | | | Cambridge |

| | | | |
|---|---|---|---|
| Cambridge | 29 | Cheshire | 12 |
| Nottingham | 28 | Cornwall | 10 |
| Berks | 28 | Rutland | 9 |
| Oxford | 27 | Huntingdon | 8 |
| Worcester | 22 | Hereford | 7 |
| Northumberland | 17 | Durham | 2 |
| Stafford | 14 | Cumberland | 1 |
| Shropshire | 14 | Westmoreland | 0 |

*List of Counties in England in alphabetical order, showing number of emigrants from each county*

| | | | |
|---|---|---|---|
| Bedford | 49 | Lincoln | 63 |
| Berkshire | 28 | London | 171 |
| Buckingham | 75 | Middlesex | 73 |
| Cambridge | 29 | Norfolk | 160 |
| Cheshire | 12 | Northampton | 67 |
| Cornwall | 10 | Northumberland | 17 |
| Cumberland | 1 | Nottingham | 28 |
| Derby | 33 | Oxford | 27 |
| Devon | 161 | Rutland | 9 |
| Dorset | 119 | Shropshire | 14 |
| Durham | 2 | Somerset | 134 |
| Essex | 244 | Stafford | 14 |
| Gloucester | 68 | Suffolk | 266 |
| Hampshire | 67 | Surrey | 47 |
| Hereford | 7 | Sussex | 31 |
| Hertford | 96 | Warwick | 58 |
| Huntingdon | 8 | Westmoreland | 0 |
| Kent | 188 | Wiltshire | 97 |
| Lancashire | 39 | Worcester | 22 |
| Leicester | 42 | York | 70 |

The deductions to be drawn from these tables are two in number: first, that East Anglia and the West Country furnished nearly half the emigration to New England, but the destination of these two groups was quite different. The East Anglian group settled almost exclusively in Massachusetts in the beginning and trekked into Connecticut later. The West Country group generally selected the Provinces of Maine and New Hampshire

*Differences in emigrants from East and West of England*

Hampshire as their future home, doubtless influenced by the paramount interest of Sir Ferdinando Gorges in this region, who was himself a West-Countryman. The objects of the two groups were entirely different. The East Anglians came, as they alleged, to find an outlet for their repressed religious liberty. They were the 'scofflaws' of their day, often flouting contumaciously the statutes of the Kingdom. From them we doubtless inherit our indifference to precedent, disregard for authority, and the tendency to individualism. The West-Countrymen came to carry on trade in the fisheries — 'an honest calling,' quoth King James, 'for it was the trade of the Apostles.' The East Anglian came with his Bible in hand and made it the chief guide of his life. The West-Countryman came to continue the normal life of 'Merrie England' in his new home, giving religion its natural place in his life. This has given the casual historian an excuse to confer an odor of sanctity on Massachusetts and Connecticut and a blanket of wickedness on Maine and New Hampshire. The right of the West-Countryman to the territory of New England was almost by eminent domain. It was the 'sea-dogs' of Devon, Somerset, and Bristol who roused this continent from its centuries of slumber. They made the original voyages hither, laid the foundations for the first settlements, and made its possibilities known to the English world. They did not come here to convert the heathen, reform their own church, or interfere with the method and drapery of worship of others. To this pioneer work East Anglia contributed nothing. They were like the well-known birds who preëmpt the nests prepared by others, and coming in swarms soon overran the country and absorbed all the territory wrenched from the savages by the daring compatriots of Ralegh, Drake, Popham, Gilbert, Weymouth, and Pring.

A further differentiation existed between these two large groups.

groups. The East Anglians emigrated to plant a Biblical Commonwealth according to their newly developed ideas of theology. The West-Countrymen were largely influenced by the opportunity to acquire land, which was promised to emigrants in lots of one hundred acres each — almost a king's ransom in their estimation — of which he could be owner in fee simple. They were land hungry after centuries of vassalage to lords of the manors, leading a hopeless tenant's life without prospect of acquiring independence of their grinding economic conditions. The West-Countryman remained, generally speaking, loyal to his Church. Winthrop sent missionaries into Maine as early as 1640 to convert these "heathen" sea-dogs to his new theology. They came back with an empty game bag. 'There is no hope of gathering a church, for they continue in their superstitious ways,' wrote one of the disappointed proselytizers. Translating this religious jargon: 'the gathering of a church' was a phrase used to express the organization of a Puritan congregation. To the West-Countryman his Church did not need any gathering, as it was already established, and his 'superstitious ways,' in the Puritan connotation, were adhesion to the ritual and vestments of the Established Church. From them we may be said to inherit our respect for law and authority, valuation of precedence, and whatever of conservatism we may be said to possess as a people.

Some curious and interesting local incidents connected with the Great Emigration have been observed. The largest exodus from one locality naturally belongs to London, from which 171 are known to have come, drawn from nearly every parish in the Metropolis; and yet from the small parish of Hingham in Norfolk, with a population of a few hundred, thirty-five families

*Influence of Puritan clergy in emigration*

families emigrated to found the present town of Hingham in this State. It must have nearly depopulated this English town. It is difficult to account for this wholesale hegira from one little place unless the movement began under the leadership of Edmond Hobart in 1633, who preceded by two years his son, the Reverend Peter Hobart, who became the pastor of the first church in our Hingham. Bristol, the second largest seaport in the Kingdom, has only twenty-two known families to its credit as emigrants to our shores; but it may be noted that Bristol was more intimately connected in the first years of emigration with the development of New England than London and, not being affected by the Puritan movement to any extent, its citizens had no urge to leave a contented community. It is known that many of the recalcitrant and suspended clergy turned their eyes to the newly settled Colony of the Massachusetts Bay and looked upon it as a new arena where they could exercise their flair for theological jousting. Numbers of them came alone and others brought with them sympathizers with their rebellious leanings. Most of these clergymen were graduates of the University of Cambridge, which was then known as a nursery of Puritan doctrines. Instances of the local influence of clergymen suspected of Separatist doctrines, or of those who had already felt the heavy hand of Episcopal restraint, may be cited. The Reverend John Wilson and the Reverend George Phillips, who came with Winthrop, were indeed the first ministers to settle in the Bay Colony, but they had acquired no notoriety in ecclesiastical circles as sectaries and they were simply a part of, and not leaders of, the company that came with Winthrop. By far the greatest intellectual and clerical leader who influenced emigration hither was the Reverend Thomas Hooker, a commanding figure in New England history, who was preaching and teaching in and around Chelmsford, Essex,
having

having as coadjutors before 1630 Hugh Peter and John Eliot. His influence was almost county-wide, and he had been early marked by Laud, then Bishop of London (with jurisdiction over Essex), for unfrocking. His assistant, Eliot, of Nazing, came over in the *Lyon* in 1631, arriving in November, as the leader of a number of adherents from that parish who settled in Roxbury. Hooker had already assembled a group of followers residing in Braintree, Essex, and adjacent parishes, ready to leave for the Bay at the first opportunity. This Braintree contingent arrived in the early summer of 1632 and Winthrop called them 'Mr. Hooker's company.' They were the pioneers of Cambridge, later to remove to Hartford to lay the foundations of the Connecticut Colony. The pursuivants of his Diocesan prevented Hooker from joining them and he fled to Holland, coming over the next year in disguise.[1]

The second great character in local influence in England was the Reverend John Cotton, then vicar of the magnificent Church of St. Botolph in Boston, Lincolnshire. He was responsible for the early and important group of emigrants from his flock in Boston as well as from many surrounding parishes. For one devoted follower, Mrs. Anne Hutchinson, who set the Massachusetts Colony by the ears, Cotton is chiefly responsible and she came near converting him to her cause. The Reverend John Lothrop, who had been vicar at Edgerton, Kent, and later in London conducting Separatist services surreptitiously, was undoubtedly the inspiration for the emigration of a large contingent from the Weald of Kent who settled in Scituate. The Reverend Stephen Bachiler, an aged clergyman who had been silenced at Wherwell in Hampshire, emigrated to New England in 1632 and was followed by a considerable number of his former parishioners and supporters from near-by parishes. Rowley, a small parish in Yorkshire in

[1] Winthrop: *Journal*, 1, 105–06.

in the Vale of Bradford, sent thirteen families, most of whom settled in our Rowley, and these can be attributed to the influence of the Reverend Ezekiel Rogers, shepherd of the flock which followed him in his migration. Another famous clergyman, who was practically in hiding at Heddon in Northumberland, brought another group from this part of England and they became his parishioners in his new charge at Cambridge. The progenitor of the famous Mather family, the Reverend Richard, then preaching near Liverpool, brought a group of Lancashire men to settle with him in Dorchester. From the borders of Wales and Gloucestershire the Reverend Richard Blinman came hither in 1640 to settle at Marshfield with a small body of his followers. A dozen families from the little parish of Bishops Stortford, Hertfordshire, is a conspicuous example of the influence of another famous clergyman directing the emigration to New England of his sympathizers. These are typical examples of the spiritual magnets which drew along with them, to begin a new religious life in the wilderness, a considerable portion of their English parishioners.

Another phase in the psychology of emigration is found in what might be called group emigration. It is not probable that they were in any way influenced by religious motives. In scores of small parishes, not known to be in any way connected with prominent clerical emigrants, it is found that there will be from five to ten persons coming from a single hamlet. These groups constituted the great majority of the migration to Massachusetts and they were undoubtedly motivated by economic reasons. They belonged to the copyhold class which for generations had been paying rents to manorial lords and being amerced by fines for trivial violations of the customs of the manor by the stewards. They were coming over to be free men, and scarcely a moiety of them

were

were ready to place themselves in bondage to the clerical oligarchy which was then beginning to fasten itself upon the body politic.

The underlying motives which determined their decision to emigrate were undoubtedly economic in the last analysis. It is impossible to accept seriously the idea that *Land hunger* the large majority of them were willing to aban- *not religion,* *the cause of* don everything they owned merely to be rid of *emigration* the formalism of the church ritual which they *of majority* were supposed to detest. If so, they did not hasten to join the Church here to become 'freemen' in the new Colony nor did they bother much about the restrictions placed on them here by the clerical oligarchy that grew up to challenge their former masters in the English Church in the vigor of their prosecutions for 'heresy.' The average emigrant was generally indifferent to the kind of theological hair-splitting which enabled the learned clergy here to decide that Anne Hutchinson was guilty of eighty errors of doctrine and that one so bulging with untruths would surely rock the foundations of the Colony. Winthrop himself admitted that he emigrated for financial reasons. He had no religious troubles at home that he ever mentioned. That the Puritan leaders came to enjoy unrestricted privileges in church affiliations is probably true but they were a minority in control, both civil and clerical.

A more acute and pressing cause was behind it all. It has been shown clearly by special investigations of a student of acknowledged historical ability, detached from local obsessions, that economic and agrarian distress was acutest in that part of England whence came the greatest numbers during the period of the Great Emigration.[1] This was a widespread situation superimposed on the dead hand of the manorial system

[1] Adams: *Founding of New England*, pp. 121–124.

system which for generations had been bleeding the patient tenantry white. The copy-holders of 1630 were exactly where their ancestors of 1330 left off — hopeless and helpless. The sweat of their brows gave them no return beyond mere existence. To say that the victims of such a system of serfdom to lords of manors could be influenced to abandon a life of profitless drudgery for religious reasons only, would be to convict our ancestors of ignoring their obvious future welfare and that of their children as freeholders. The opportunity to own land in fee simple was offered to them and was more important than the alleged desire for religious liberty. It is difficult to prove 'motives' but two public utterances of emigrants from different parts of England, settled in different colonies here, justifies the opinion held by the author of this volume that social slavery and degradation of the land system at home was the main cause of their hegira.

The first was made in 1621 by William Hilton, a native of Cheshire, who emigrated in the *Fortune* to join the Pilgrims at Plymouth, although not one of the Separatist body, in a letter to his kinsman back home. He wrote

We are all freeholders, the rent day doth not trouble us, and all those good blessings we have.

(Smith: *New England Trials*, Arber Ed., 261.)

The other statement was made about 1633 by George Cleeves, a native of Somersetshire, the founder of Portland, Maine, who said

He would be tenant to never a man in New England.

(*Me. Hist. Soc. Documentary Series*, III, 265.)

These are words from the hearts of men emancipated from the demands of the steward of the manor, busily collecting rents and fines for his lordship. These identical sentiments expressed by men of more than ordinary ability show what
**was**

was in their minds.  As far as they can these two witnesses answer those who think that twenty thousand people came over here for a chance to hear men preach without a surplice!

It should be understood that emigration to parts beyond seas was not an unrestricted right of Englishmen.  Permission to leave England had to be obtained in each indi- *Licenses to* vidual case from the Privy Council and this in- *pass beyond* cluded persons of all classes — nobility, gentry, *the seas* and merchant — who desired this privilege for any reason whatsoever.  The records of the Privy Council are full of these grants, and when travel in Europe was alleged as the occasion for the request the grantee was prohibited from visiting Rome lest he come under the influence of the Catholic Church!  When the North American continent was first opened for colonization under the auspices of the Trading Companies of North and South Virginia, persons desiring to emigrate thither were required to take the Oath of Supremacy and Conformity.  This provision, of course, did not apply to persons 'transported' to Virginia as convicts.  The difficulties which the Pilgrims had in obtaining permission to emigrate as a body of Separatists to Virginia are well known, and it was not until 1620 that King James was induced to look the other way when the *Mayflower* took them on its famous voyage to New England where they were suffered to remain during their good behavior.

Examples of these 'Licenses to pass beyond the seas' are here given:

Martha Butler, 21, wife of Samuel Butler, dwelling in Yarmouth & maid, Judith Wharton, 23, to Amsterdam.  July 6th 1624.

Fines Morrison to visit his Ante at the Queen of Bohemias.  28 July 1633.

Mary Atkinson, to her husband at Rotterdam & for Eliza Browne

Browne & Anne Madder, being poor, to seeke reliefe amongst their freindes. 17 August 1633.

It is probable that persons unable to get permission to emigrate to New England would procure license to visit Holland on some pretext, and thence manage to obtain passage across the Atlantic; or to meet English ships in the Channel by previous arrangement. This was the method adopted by Hooker and Peter in their flight to Boston.

It can be assumed with probability that these licenses to pass beyond seas were the forerunners of our modern passports.

The impressive toll of death which followed the voyages of the *Mayflower* and the Winthrop Fleet, claiming half the *The perils of* passenger list of the Pilgrims in the first winter *disease in* and about a third of the emigrants who settled *ocean travel* the Bay Colony, brings clearly to the reader of the early settlement of New England one of the worst features of ocean travel in that day. The rovers of the Seven Seas who put out from English ports in the sixteenth century had learned by bitter experience that long, deep-water voyages, such as were undertaken by Drake, Ralegh, and Gilbert in their pioneer essays to circumnavigate the globe, or to reach Cathay by the elusive 'Northwest Passage,' became a question of proper food, and it gradually came to their knowledge that man could not survive indefinitely on dried or salted meats. The scientific explanation of it was beyond their comprehension, but these venturesome seamen had arrived at some crude empiricism on the subject of sustaining health during long absences from fresh food on the 'vasty deep.' But they were few, and the knowledge they had acquired was not available or of any direct interest to those who later led the Great Emigration to our shores.

The

The Pilgrims were the first to feel the heavy hand of scorbutic starvation, and when, after nearly ten weeks at sea, their vessel dropped anchor inside the tip of Cape Cod, it is safe to say that there were not many seaworthy men left to navigate the disease-ridden craft. Bradford called it the 'general sickness' for want of definite information on the subject, but in reality they were all suffering from scurvy, the crew as well as passengers, and for weeks many of them were unable to leave the ship. Only the hardiest were able to stand up under the strain of a diet insufficient in quality, not in quantity. Only one thing enabled them to keep going — the casks and hogsheads of English beer which John Alden, the cooper, hired for the purpose, had kept from injury during those long weeks. The crew and passengers had reached the point where an equitable division of this nourishing beverage would not be shared. Added to the perils of the deep which they had just survived was the lack of fresh vegetables to be obtained from the land, as they arrived when winter had congealed the earth and not a green thing was left to supply their starved blood with the vitamins of health. Bradford himself was a scorbutic victim as were all the leaders, and Captain Jones could not leave for the return voyage until late in the spring of 1621 because of the continued invalidism of his crew. He 'durst not put to sea till he saw his men begine to recover and the hart of winter over.'

The Winthrop Fleet suffered the same experience only in lesser degree, though they arrived in midsummer.[1] The long voyage of the *Arbella* began to take its victims soon after arrival. The Lady Arbella Johnson was among the first to go — delicately nurtured in her youth in an earl's castle. She was

[1] Masters of the merchant vessels of this fleet, with only experiences of short voyages to European ports or the Mediterranean, had no knowledge of dietetics to guide them across the Atlantic in sanitary safety.

was soon followed by her husband, then by Edward Rossiter, and then Winthrop's family physician, within two months after reaching their promised haven. The physician's death is a striking instance of the helplessness of the profession in that period in the face of outraged Nature. Neither Giles Heale, the ship's surgeon on the *Mayflower*, nor William Gager, who held a similar office on the *Arbella*, could cope with this situation or adequately prepare against its ravages. Of this inevitable scourge the average emigrant from the inland parishes of England was in absolute ignorance. As a result the slopes of Charlestown Neck became a hospital camp during the autumn and winter after the landing of Winthrop. The aged and weakly went first until, as Dudley states, 'there dyed by estamacon about two hundred at least so lowe hath the Lord brought us.' [1] Winthrop tried to write home cheerful letters, but he could not quite overlook this ghastly picture, referring to his own health 'among so many dead corpses through the heat of Summer and the cold of Winter.' [2]

It was not until that famous Atlantic ferryman, Captain William Pierce, of the *Lyon*, made his hurried emergency voyage to England and back in midwinter, bringing lemons, the remedial palliative of scurvy, that its ravages began to abate in the following spring.

With this experience still in mind, Winthrop, in writing to his wife about preparations for her voyage, soon to follow, advised her to bring 'a gallon of Scurvy grasse to drinke a little 5: or 6: mornings together, with some saltpeter dissolved in it and a little grated or sliced nutmege.' [3]

The

---

[1] Letter to the Countess of Lincoln.    [2] Winthrop: *Life and Letters*, II, 58.

[3] 'Scurvy Grass,' a corruption of Scurvy Cress, is a cruciferous plant (*Cochlearia officinalis*) found in northern Europe in cultivation and in wild form in high latitudes in North America. Early used as an anti-scorbutic and later as a salad. 'Buy any scurvy-grass'

The presence of physicians on these two famous early emigrations brings to attention the beginnings of medical service on trans-Atlantic ships. Doubtless there were professional men on most of the larger vessels who were taken on contingent rewards to be paid for by the passengers. This service was an extra charge amounting to 2s. 6d. for each person covering the voyage. The regulations of the Guild of Barber Surgeons of that date (section 47) specified that the 'furniture' of surgeons employed at sea (instruments, medicines, etc.) should be examined before sailing. The duties and qualifications of this officer are thus detailed by Captain John Smith in his *Accidence for Young Seamen* (London, 1626, p. 3):

> The Chirurgeon is exempted from all duty but to attend the sicke and cure the wounded; and good care would be had that he have a certificate from the *Barber-Surgeons* Hall for his sufficiency, and also that his Chest bee well furnished both for *Physicke* and *Chirurgery* and so neare as may be proper for the clime you goe for, which neglect hath been a losse of many a mans life.

These first terrifying records that place the death star against so many names on the passenger lists of Plymouth and Charlestown were rarely repeated in the succeeding years except on unusually long voyages in stress of weather. Each experience increased knowledge of the needs of preventive preparations.

It came to be understood that the lack of fresh vegetables was the main factor in the causation of scurvy and that lemons and lime juice would furnish the necessary lack. The use of ale or beer to allay thirst and as a mild anti-scorbutic was
based

scurvy-grass' may be read in *The Roaring Girl*, III, 2, by Middleton and Dekker. Saltpeter is a nitrate of potassium which supplied a mineral salt necessary to maintain the alkalinity of the blood.

based on sound therapeutic judgment. Water could not be preserved sweet and potable on these long voyages. The *Arbella* carried forty-two tons of beer (about ten thousand gallons) for her voyage, while only fourteen tons of water, one third the quantity, was provided.

The food supplies of emigrant ships consisted largely of beef and pork, dried or preserved according to the art or 'mystery' of keeping the flesh of animals edible, practiced by the Company of Salters.[1] The 'staff of life' was represented by biscuits made of both brown and white flour, with oatmeal for porridge. The only vegetable they could depend on was dried peas to be cooked into thick soup. Mustard seed was used as a condiment to stimulate their jaded appetites after days and weeks of 'salt horse.' It is safe to conclude that the better class of passengers brought special stores of non-perishable delicacies and necessary utensils to prepare them to supplement the regular meals served from the ship's galley.

A study of the various phases of emigration to New England in colonial times has developed a hitherto unsuspected *Transporta-* and generally unknown feature of the problem. *tion of* It is well known that the English authorities, after *children* the first settlement of Virginia, began to transport in considerable numbers adults for servants who had been convicted of various crimes and misdemeanors, and in the course of a few years this policy became more or less of a scandal and a menace to the well-being of that Colony. In like manner, when the settlement of the New England territory began to engage the attention of the lords and gentlemen who formed the Council for New England, this subject early

[1] Winthrop states that the preserved meat they brought was 'powdered' and that it was 'sweet and good.'

early had their attention. The transportation of children to the new settlements in Virginia was first considered by the officials of London in 1617 as a means of relieving the pressure of the tenement-house districts in the East End of London swarming with homeless waifs, orphans, and foundlings. Every parish had its quota of these unfortunate denizens left at the church porches and a constant charge on the Poor Rates. Sir George Bolles, Alderman and Lord Mayor of London in 1617, issued a proclamation in which he gave utterance to the fear 'lest the overflowing multitude of inhabitants should, like too much blood, infect the whole city with plague and poverty.' Transportation of children to the new Colony in Virginia was suggested as a remedy. A meeting of representatives of the hundred parishes in London was held at Saint Paul's to devise a method of dealing with this question and, as a result, each parish was assessed in varying amounts to accomplish this object. In 1618, one hundred children were transported to Virginia, and the Church Wardens' Accounts of many of the parishes show moneys paid in to the Lord Chamberlain of London as their assessments.

In 1619, the Lord Mayor, Sir William Cockayne, followed the example of his predecessor. The Virginia Company asked for one hundred more children and the City coöperated in procuring them. After some difficulty with recalcitrants, the second consignment was sent in response to this request. It will be a surprise to most people in this section of the country to know that three children were thus 'transported' to New England in the *Mayflower* — Richard, Jasper, and Elinor More. They were brought over under the protection of three different passengers, and that they were orphans seems entirely clear, as their parents did not come over later to join them as would have been the case if they were given into the hands of relatives. Richard More, the only survivor of of the three, made a deposition in his old age (1684) that he was living in the house of Mr. Thomas Weston, ironmonger, in London in 1620 and 'was thence transported to New Plymouth in New England.' His use of the word 'transported' is significant, as that was the phrase used to describe the sending of persons to the Colonies.

The Council for New England took this matter up within two years of its organization. On July 5, 1622, the Council took the following action:

Conserning the proposition to bee made unto the Citty for takeing away of poor Children for New-England. It is thought fitt that there should bee Letters gotten from the Lords for the furtherance hereof to the Citty, and that these Children bee of 14 yeares of age apeese or upwards.[1]

Again, on November 16, 1622, the Council took the following additional action in this matter:

Touching a Letter to bee sent from their Lords to the Lord Mayor of London, the Clerke is appointed to attend the Clerke of the Counsell to bee advised for the Superscription and direction thereof.

Propounded whether the Children shall bee Received by the publike or private undertakers. If for the publike then to bee advised how to give Securety for the Cittys Sattisfaction.[2]

Three months later, on February 18, 1622/3, the Council made the following entry in its records:

Sir Hen: Spelman propoundeth that if the Statutes made the... yeare of Queene Eliz: for the binding forth of poore Children Apprentices bee made use of, by this Councell, in every County it will be Easefull to the Country, and beneficiall to this plantacon.[3]

It will thus be seen that it became the policy for the Council for New England, as it had been for the Virginia Company, to use its territory as a means of relieving the congested population

---

[1] *Records*, Council for New England, 13.   [2] *Ibid.*, 24.   [3] *Ibid.*, 37.

population of London and possibly the other great cities of England. How far this policy was promoted by the Council is not accurately known. Such lists of passengers coming in ships to New England, as have been preserved, contain the names of minors who cannot be assigned to any of the families coming at the same time. The conclusion is inevitable that they were transported under a continuance of this practice as indentured servants or under the protection of adults.

The Church Wardens' Accounts of the Parish of Saint Giles in the Field, London, for 1636 show that these parochial collections for 'transporting of children into New England' were still being made,[1] and as late as 1643, Winthrop records the arrival of a score of them, as follows:

One of our ships the *Seabridge*, arrived with twenty children and some other passengers out of England... and those children, with many more to come after, were sent by money given one fast day in London and allowed by the parliament and city for that purpose.[2]

It will thus be seen that, from the arrival of the *Mayflower* in 1620 to this last-named ship, there was an officially organized traffic in the transportation of children to New England under the auspices of the Lord Mayor and the churches of London.

The records of Bristol show the names of more than ten thousand servants transported to foreign plantations on the Atlantic Coast and the West Indies from 1654 to 1685. This list comprises persons of both sexes. The transportation of children evidently became an organized traffic for commercial profit, and in 1645 Parliament passed an ordinance 'for the Apprehending and bringing to condigne punishment, all such persons as shall steale, sell, buy, inveigle, purloyne, convey, or receive any little Children. And for the strict and diligent

---

[1] *S. P. Dom.*, Charles I, vol. 536, No. 711.  [2] *Journal*, II, 96.

diligent search of all Ships and other Vessels on the River or at the Downes.' It is a well-known fact that a number of the passengers of the *Mayflower*, particularly among the London contingent, brought over minors classed as 'servants' or 'boys' of no known kinship to their masters, and it may be supposed that they were picked up in London with the consent of the authorities. English captains in the early days of the settlement of New England kidnapped Irish boys *en route* to our coast and sold them to the Puritan planters in virtual slavery under the euphemism of apprenticeships,[1] and the story of the Scotch prisoners sold for service in the iron works by Cromwell in 1651 is one of the picturesque phases of this traffic in human lives.[2] In that era apprenticeships served as a polite term for involuntary servitude, and emigrants coming to New England under that designation, in most cases, had no choice in the matter. The laws governing apprenticeships left little freedom of action against the master's will, and the 'submerged tenth' were its principal victims.

During the early years of the reign of Charles, a number of additional restrictions were placed upon the intending emigrants to this region which was being rapidly developed. The first of these was consequent upon the monopoly claimed by the Council for New England of exclusive rights to the fishing privileges on this coast, but this did not affect emigration to any extent. The second restriction related to the export of food supplies for the increasing number of settlements on the seaboard, and in 1634 a number of vessels were held in the Thames on this account. In addition to this there was a general objection to allowing

*Restrictions on emigrants in 1634*

[1] *Essex Court Records*, VIII, 186.
[2] *Proceedings*, Massachusetts Historical Society, LXI, 4-29.

allowing people to leave England for any purpose. The Reverend Henry Dade, Commissary of Suffolk to Archbishop Laud, reported in 1634 to His Grace of Canterbury that

two ships are to sail from Ipswich with men and provision for their abiding in New England in each of which ships are appointed to go about six score passengers whom he supposes are either indebted persons or persons discontented with the government of the Church of England. He hears that as many more are expected not long after to go as altogether will amount to six hundred persons. If suffered to go in such swarms it will be a decrease of the King's people here, an increase of the adversaries to the Episcopal state and will also be an overthrow of trade.

He further adds that after they have reached New England 'they cannot be avocated by reason of the largeness of that continent.'[1]

This appeal to the Archbishop to restrict emigration of the discontented had its effect, and the Privy Council in February, 1634, ordered the detention of eight vessels 'now lying in the River of Thames untill further order.' A week later, after consideration, the masters of the detained ships were called before the Council and ordered to give bond in one hundred pounds for the performance of the following articles:

1. That all & every Person aboard their Ships now bound for New England as aforesaid that shall blaspheme or profane the Holy name of God be severely punish't.

2. That they cause the Prayers contained in the Book of Common Prayers established in the Church of England to be said at the usual hours for Morning & Evening Prayers & that they cause all persons aboard their said Ships to be present at the same.

3. That they do not receive aboard or transport any person that hath not Certificate from the Officers of the Port where he is to imbarque that he hath taken both the Oathes of Alleigeance & Supremacy.

It

[1] P.R.O., *Dom. State Papers*, 1633/4, p. 450.

It was further provided that the masters on their return to England should be relieved of their bonds. From that time henceforth all emigrants to New England were required to take these oaths and be certified by a clergyman of the Established Church or a Justice of the Peace of their conformity to the State Church. This gave rise to wholesale certification of a ship's list of passengers by one clergyman or a Justice of the Peace. This circumstance has provided an element of confusion in attempting to locate the origins of passengers from the residence of the clergyman who provided this blanket certification. Complaisant vicars would furnish these certifications for persons who must have been strangers to them, and the real purpose of the law was thus rendered ineffectual.

But a third restriction was imposed by the authorities interested in the collection of revenue, somewhat in the manner existing at the present time in connection with the payment of our income taxes by persons desiring to leave the United States. The subsidies granted to King Charles by Parliament and his own imposition, without authority of Parliament, of the hated ship subsidy were made the occasion of refusing permission to leave England to those persons taxed in the subsidies. The officials charged with this duty were required to certify that each emigrant was 'no subsidy man.' Like all prohibitory laws deemed to be against the interests of the people, it was successfully evaded. Numbers of subsidiaries reached New England by one device or another; but by far the greatest number of emigrants were of the yeoman tenantry class and had no difficulty in answering all the requirements of the law in respect to emigration to the Colonies.

A fruitful source of evasion of these laws was furnished by the recalcitrant clergy and their more obstreperous supporters

ers among the laity. These clerical remonstrants against the canons of worship according to the forms of the Church of England became entangled in the meshes of the Ecclesiastical Courts, and being put on trial for contumacy were either put on suspension, fined, or imprisoned according to the degree of their offenses. Numbers of them fled secretly to the Continent or went in hiding among friends in London. Thus, Cotton, Dalton, Hooker, Peter, and Shepard began their roundabout journey to their Utopia in New England. The story of the Reverend Thomas Shepard, as told by himself, will give a vivid idea of the extremities to which they were put in evading the pursuivants of the Archbishop, and getting in safety to New England. After reciting his various employments in charge of parishes from each of which he was inhibited by Laud, he finally went into the extreme North of England, where he obtained an appointment at Heddon, Northumberland, and served there for several years. Then he decided to cast in his lot with his Separatist brethren in New England. For some time he was in hiding under the protection of Roger Harlakenden in Essex, and from thence started from Ipswich in 1634 for the Atlantic voyage. The ship ran into a terrific storm in the North Sea, and, after many hours of helplessness, during which the main mast was chopped down to save her from foundering, they drifted into Yarmouth almost a wreck. Following this he went to London, and there found sanctuary in a friend's home, where he remained concealed for another year. He then embarked in the *Defence* with his friend Harlakenden under the name of John Shepard, husbandman.[1] The rest of his story is related in his own words:

In our voyage upon the sea the Lord was very tender of me and kept me from sea-sickness. The ship we came in was very rotten and

[1] 3 M.H.S., VIII, 268-76.

and unfit for such a voyage, and therefore the first storm we had we had a very great leak, which did much appall and affect us. Yet the Lord discovered it unto us when we were thinking of returning back again; and much comforted our hearts. We had many storms in one of which my dear wife took such a cold, and got such weakness as that she fell into a consumption of which she afterwards died. And also the Lord preserved her, with the child in her arms, from imminent and apparent death. For by the shaking of the ship in a violent storm her head was pitched against an iron bolt, and the Lord miraculously preserved the child and recovered my wife. This was a great affliction to me, and was a cause of many sad thoughts in the ship, how to behave myself when I came to New England. And so the Lord after many sad storms and wearisome days, and many longings to see the shore brought us to the sight of it upon October 2 Anno 1635. My dear wife's great desire being now fulfilled, which was to leave me in safety from the hands of mine enemies, and among God's people, and also the child under God's ordinances.

Winthrop thus describes the devices employed by John Cotton and Thomas Hooker:

They gat out of England with much difficulty, all places being belaid to have taken Mr. Cotton who had been long sought for to have been brought into the High Commission; but the master being bound to touch at the Wight, the pursuivants attended there, and, in the meantime, the said ministers were taken in at the Downs.

In like manner Subsidy Records show that Roger Goodspeed, of Buckinghamshire, Andrew Hallett, of Somerset, and William Odell, of Bedfordshire, reached New England without payment of taxes levied for the ship subsidy. Another type of underground emigration is certified by the oath of a deponent in a chancery suit in the following affidavit (names omitted) under date of April 14, 1638:[1]

About ffebr was 12 moneth the plt pcured him to goe wth him to this Citty of London where they both stayed 3 or 4 dayes to treate

[1] *Chancery Affidavits*, vol. 11, Easter, 82.

treate wth certaine merchants about his the sd Complts goeinge & passinge into New England, the Complt haveinge a sonne there and many debt & troubles here falling upon him; after wch tyme it was comonly reported that the Complt that Springe would goe for New England. And about Easter then followinge he began to obscure & withdrawe himselfe for feare of arrests (as was conceaved). And did by night convey divers of his goods to take wth him; And about May last was shipped at Gravesend & passed into or neere the Downes to goe for New England. But was arrested & brought backe againe to Gravesend (as he believeth) where making a speedy Composision with some of his creditors by means of one Adgare & other his friends he wth one of his sonnes was againe shipped to goe for New England and hath bine ever since genrally reported to be gon thither and aswell amongst his Neighbors in the sd parish as genrally in the country thereabouts reputed to be nowe in New England.

In April, 1637, a proclamation was issued 'to restrain the disorderly transporting of His Majesty's subjects to the Colonies without leave.' It commanded that 'no license should be given them, without a certificate that they have taken the oaths of Supremacy and Allegiance, and had conformed to the discipline of the Church of England.' *Further embargo on emigration in 1637-38*

In May, 1638, a fresh proclamation was published 'commanding owners and masters of vessels that they do not fit out any with passengers and provisions for New England, without license from the Commissioners of Plantations.'[1]

By this time the merchants of New England who had been seriously affected by these new prohibitions, and the friends of intending emigrants who desired to come to New England, were aroused to protest against this arbitrary action of the English authorities. They drew up a statement of their rights

as

---

[1] Chalmers, *Annals*, I, 161; Rushworth's *Collections*, II, 409; Rymer's *Fœdera*, xx, 143, 223.

as Englishmen under the Charter of the Massachusetts Bay Colony in the following form:

A particuler of the liberties graunted to the Planters of New England, their Factors and Agentes by his Ma'tes Lettres Patentes Dated 4 Marcij Ao 4o Car. (1628/9).

1. Libertie to Transport as manie of his Mat'es leige people as are willing to goe to New England except such persons as should be restrained by special name.

2. Libertie to Transport all shippinge/

3. Libertie to Transport Armor weapons ordinance municions powder shott Corne victualls and all maner of Clothing implementes furniture beastes Cattell horses merchandises and all other things necessarie for the plantacion for use and defence with the people/

4. Libertie to goe Custome free for the same by the space of 7 yeares from the date of the Patent/

5. Libertie to be Custome free for the space of 21 yeares for all goodes and merchandises exported or imported except only paying 5 li. per centum/

6. That the site of the Lettres patentes or duplicat or the Inrolem't shalbe to the Tresurer Chauncellor Barons of the Exchequer and to all Customers Farmors Searchers and other Officers a sufficient discharge and warrant in that behalfe for exportacione or importacion of goods at V li. per Centum/

These abstracts from the provisions of the Charter placed squarely before His Majesty the invasion of their rights granted by him ten years before, and were attached to the following petition:

To the Kings Most Excellent Ma'tie

The humble peticion of the Planters of New England; Most humbly shew: —

That a restrainte hath formerly bine made that noe shipp intendinge for the Plantacions in New England shall have liberty to goe that voyage untill they have Lycence from the Lords of his Ma'ties privie Counsell, which hath bine a meanes to inrich the Agentes that procured such Lycences, but hath impoverished the

Planters

Planters and Merchantes, whoe have paid for the same, and much time hath passed before such Lycences could be obteyned, the voyages of the shipps have by that meanes bine hindred, the passengers estates much weakened and much of their goodes have bine spoyled by the long stay of the shipps after they have bine freighted before they could be cleered/

That a restraint hath bine, to transport to the said plantacions, divers necessaries for food, apparell and municion, without which and some supply, (as yet), from this Kingdome those Planters cannot comfortably subsist, nor be secure from enimies/

That the Searchers after some shipps have bine laden, have caused them to be unladen and unpacked & broken upp their goodes, to the greate charge and damage of the Owners thereof. That greate Customes & taxes have bine laid uppon such goodes and merchandize as have bine transported to those parts, soe that some things could not be carried thither by reason of the greate impost laid on them although not otherwise prohibited wch hath bin a greate discouragem't to the Planters/

Now forasmuch as this Kingdome being supplied from forraign partes with divers necessaries which in itselfe it hath not, may very probably in short time be supplied from New England, which in case of restraint elsewhere. wilbe for the greate security of this Nation, as namely With Cordage, Cables, sailes, canvas pitch and tarre (there being greate store of pitch trees), and likewise good mastes, (there being goodly mast trees bigg enough to fitt the tallest shipp in England), as alsoe with all sortes of timber fitt for Navigation, which is soe decayed in this Nation that within theis seaven last yeares ites advanced to neere double value/

The peticioners humbly pray That the Merchants and planters in the severall places of New England and of this Kingdome may have freedom to transport to the said plantacions all their portable estates which by law are not forbidden with all other necessaries for food apparell tackle and municion and other thinges fittinge for the plantacion. And that the said Merchants and planters may have priviledge to freight shipps to the said plantacions without any lycence tax or penalty whatsoever, And that all goodes and merchandize for the supportacion and incouragement of the said planters may bee free of all Customes and impostes exportable and importable to & from the same. And that the graunt of the

peticioners

peticioners humble desires may receave a speedy dispatch in regard
the season for the Newfoundland voyage is now approaching, which
opportunity being lost, the charge of transportacion to the said
plantacions wilbe almost double/

    And your peticioners shall daily pray &c/

By this time Charles was getting deeper and deeper in the
struggle for his 'Divine right' to rule without the aid of
Parliament, and his ship subsidy was arousing the resent-
ment of all classes affected by its provisions. He had no time
to consider the 'rights' of his subjects in distant America and
this petition went into a pigeon-hole, from whence it never
emerged. The die was soon cast between him and his subjects and Civil War had begun. In ten years his head was to
roll off the block and he was branded as a traitor.

The voyage across the Atlantic was charted upon a course
generally adopted by all masters of ships as a matter of

*The long*     necessity and expediency. The point to be
*voyage*       reached on the New England coast was Boston
*oversea*      Harbor, and whether the point of departure was
London or Bristol, the course was laid directly from the
Lizard or the Scilly Isles southwest to the Azores, and thence
on a due west parallel of North Latitude 43° 15′, which would
bring the vessel directly south of Cape Sable, Nova Scotia,
and to the Isles of Shoals. Usually ships would put into
Terceira, or one of the Azores, for water and fresh provisions,
and this was often a rendezvous for ships sailing in company
with others. When the Gulf of Maine was reached and the
navigator came into permanent view of the coast of New
England, the remainder of his course was determined by the
well-known shore line. The earliest explorers made Monhegan their landfall and thence the Three Turks' Heads
(Agamenticus), the Isles of Shoals, and Cape Ann.

                                                    The

The mariners of that period used the crude nautical devices available to them to bring their craft to the destined port. They had only the cross staff to ascertain their latitude; but while the elevation of the sun could be measured with practical accuracy by this instrument and the degrees of latitude figured out, there was no way to determine longitude at sea. The required paraphernalia for this calculation were not perfected until the latter half of the next century. To overcome this difficulty the east or west positions at a given time were expressed in terms of dead reckoning by estimating the marine leagues sailed from day to day from a given point of departure.

It is a puzzle to imagine what things occupied the time of these emigrants for ten weeks on the crowded decks of the small vessels which took them across the three thousand miles that lay between the continents. Even to-day with our many permitted diversions time hangs heavily. Certainly those residents of the rural hamlets left nothing of interest behind them, and so missed nothing in their drab lives when exchanging their pithless parochial existence ashore for the monotonous doldrums of a swaying deck at sea. Ships carrying religious groups, like the *Mayflower* or the *Arbella*, indulged in daily services when their spiritual leaders 'exercised' the Godly in prayer and sermon. We can readily believe that Mistress Anne Hutchinson furnished enough excitement aboard the *Griffin* when she engaged the Reverend John Lothrop and the Reverend Zachariah Symmes in theological bouts, but these were exceptional ships, as the vast majority of emigrants came without ministerial leaders to entertain them. If the voyage were stormy, they were obliged to go below decks and kill time in the darkness. Doubtless they went to bed at sundown, as there was no way to light the decks. They rose at the break of day to begin
another

another like round of nothing in particular. In smooth weather fishing might be enjoyed when the Grand Banks were reached, and the sight of an occasional whale or a school of porpoises furnished many a thrill to their wondering eyes. If traveling with consorts, visiting parties might be arranged when sea conditions permitted. Instances of such kinds occurred several times during the passage of the Winthrop Fleet across the Atlantic.

As far as known there is no record of the loss of an emigrant ship bound for New England during the years of the Great Emigration. One was wrecked at Pemaquid on the Maine coast in 1635, but no lives were lost. On the other hand, at least two vessels carrying voyagers to England in the same period were never heard from. They were, of course, subject to capture by French and Spanish pirates and some were so taken on their return. Altogether this is a remarkable record considering the small size of these ships and the usual dangers of ocean navigation even for modern ships of ten, twenty, and fifty times their tonnage. When one sees the huge liners of to-day limping into port, their decks piled and rigging clogged with ice, he cannot but marvel that these cockleshells could make voyages in all weathers and survive. It took courage to start across the ocean in December in a hundred-ton boat, but that is what Roger Williams did in the *Lyon* in 1630, landing in Boston in February, 1631, with his young wife and a dozen other equally brave men and women.

Arrived at his destination after weeks of tossing on the restless ocean, the emigrant either followed a prescribed course planned in advance or sat down to consider where he was and to make a choice of a habitation. Perhaps his first thoughts were of the strangeness of the scene about him, unlike anything he was accustomed to in his old parish home. He may have compared the plain wooden houses and their mud

mud chimneys with the picturesque stone cottages and their familiar brick chimneys in his native village. Instead of a gray, ivy-covered church with its tower or steeple, he saw a plain barnlike structure which the people called a 'meeting-house.' He could see a change in the countenances of the people. Every one walked with his head erect and every face had a hopeful look. There was no tipping of caps to lords and gentlemen. He remembered his former estate as a tenant paying homage and quit rents as his ancestors had done, and he realized that he had left all that behind.

If he had come with a group to settle in a town already organized, where former neighbors or friends had already sat down, his programme was simple. If not, he usually found welcome at an inn at Boston or Charlestown, where he could obtain plenty of advice about the advantages of settlements already started or learn of projects for beginning new ones on the ever-widening western fringe of outlying villages. He might be coaxed to join the newer colony lately started in the Connecticut Valley. There was no limit to his choice of a home in the wilderness, and emigrants made two or three moves before coming to a final halt. Land was free to him for the asking under easy conditions of permanency, and it is not strange that with all this boundless opportunity open to him, he still looked with longing eyes on every new settlement where he could enlarge his acreage. Here we leave him, a free man in a free country where no lord of the manor took his toll, and where he became a sovereign in the body politic and his voice was heard and respected.

# PART II

Lists of Passengers and the Ships which Brought Them

# PART II

*Lists of Passengers and the Ships which Brought Them*

## 1620

MAYFLOWER of London, two hundred tons, Christopher Jones, Master. Left Southampton August 5, and arrived at Cape Cod December 11, with one hundred and one passengers. The ship was detained at Dartmouth and Plymouth, England, about two weeks for repairs to her consort, the *Speedwell*. The entire company settled at Plymouth.[1]

| | |
|---|---|
| JOHN CARVER | of Doncaster, Yorkshire |
| Mrs. Katherine Carver | |
| Desire Minter | |
| John Howland | servant; of London |
| Roger Wilder | servant |
| William Latham | servant |
| Jasper More | servant |
| . . . . . . . . . . . . | maidservant |
| | |
| WILLIAM BREWSTER | of Scrooby, Nottinghamshire |
| Mrs. Mary Brewster | |
| Love Brewster | |
| Wrestling Brewster | |
| Richard More | servant |
| . . . . . . More | servant |
| | |
| EDWARD WINSLOW | of Droitwich, Worcestershire |
| Mrs. Elizabeth Winslow | |
| George Soule | servant; of Eckington, Worcestershire |
| Elias Story | servant; of London |
| Ellen More | servant |
| | |
| WILLIAM BRADFORD | of Austerfield, Yorkshire |
| Mrs. Dorothy Bradford | |

ISAAC ALLERTON

[1] Bradford: *History of Plimmoth Plantation*; Banks: *English Ancestry and Homes of the Pilgrims.*

| | |
|---|---|
| ISAAC ALLERTON | of London; merchant |
| Mrs. Mary Allerton | |
| Bartholomew Allerton | |
| Remember Allerton | |
| Mary Allerton | |
| John Hooke | servant |
| | |
| SAMUEL FULLER | of Redenhall, county Norfolk |
| William Button | servant |
| | |
| JOHN CRACKSTON | |
| John Crackston, Jr. | |
| | |
| MYLES STANDISH | |
| Mrs. Rose Standish | |
| | |
| CHRISTOPHER MARTIN | of Great Burstead, Essex |
| Mrs. Mary Martin | |
| Solomon Prower | stepson |
| John Langmore | servant |
| | |
| WILLIAM MULLINS | of Dorking, county Surrey; merchant |
| Mrs. Alice Mullins | |
| Joseph Mullins | |
| Priscilla Mullins | |
| Robert Carter | servant |
| | |
| WILLIAM WHITE | |
| Mrs. Susanna White | |
| Resolved White | |
| Peregrine White | |
| William Holbeck | servant |
| Edward Thompson | servant |
| | |
| STEPHEN HOPKINS | of Wotton-under-Edge, Gloucestershire |
| Mrs. Elizabeth Hopkins | |
| Giles Hopkins | |
| Constance Hopkins | |
| Damaris Hopkins | |
| Oceanus Hopkins | |
| Edward Dotey | servant; of London |
| Edward Lister | servant; of London |

RICHARD WARREN

| | |
|---|---|
| RICHARD WARREN | of London; merchant |
| JOHN BILLINGTON | of London |
| Mrs. Ellen Billington | |
| John Billington, Jr. | |
| Francis Billington | |
| EDWARD TILLEY | of London |
| Mrs. Anne Tilley | |
| Henry Sampson | kinsman |
| Humility Cooper | kinswoman |
| JOHN TILLEY | of Saint Andrews Undershaft, London |
| Mrs. Elizabeth Tilley | |
| Elizabeth Tilley | |
| FRANCIS COOKE | |
| John Cooke | |
| THOMAS ROGERS | |
| Joseph Rogers | |
| THOMAS TINKER | |
| Mrs. . . . . . . Tinker | |
| . . . . . . Tinker | |
| JOHN RIGDALE | of London |
| Mrs. Alice Rigdale | |
| JAMES CHILTON | of Canterbury, Kent; tailor |
| Mrs. . . . . . . Chilton | |
| Mary Chilton | |
| EDWARD FULLER | of Redenhall, county Norfolk |
| Mrs. . . . . . . Fuller | |
| Samuel Fuller | |
| JOHN TURNER | |
| . . . . . . Turner | |
| . . . . . . Turner | |
| FRANCIS EATON | of Bristol; carpenter |
| Mrs. Sarah Eaton | |
| Samuel Eaton | |

MOSES FLETCHER

| | |
|---|---|
| MOSES FLETCHER | of Sandwich, Kent |
| JOHN GOODMAN | |
| THOMAS WILLIAMS | of Yarmouth, county Norfolk |
| DIGORY PRIEST | of London |
| EDMUND MARGESSON | |
| PETER BROWNE | probably of Great Burstead, Essex |
| RICHARD BRITTERIDGE | |
| RICHARD CLARKE | |
| RICHARD GARDINER | of Harwich, county Essex |
| THOMAS ENGLISH | |
| GILBERT WINSLOW | brother of Edward Winslow |
| JOHN ALDEN | of Harwich, county Essex; cooper |
| JOHN ALDERTON | |

1621

FORTUNE of London, Thomas Barton, Master. She left London about August and arrived at Cape Cod November 9, 'with thirty-five passengers,' but only thirty-two are known by name. They all came from London or its suburbs. The entire company settled at Plymouth.[1]

| | |
|---|---|
| JOHN ADAMS | |
| WILLIAM BASSETT | of Bethnal Green, Middlesex; iron-worker |
| WILLIAM BEALE | |
| JONATHAN BREWSTER | son of Elder Brewster |
| | CLEMENT BRIGGS |

[1] Banks: *English Ancestry and Homes of the Pilgrims.*

| | |
|---|---|
| CLEMENT BRIGGS | of Southwark, county Surrey; fell-monger |
| EDWARD BOMPASSE | |
| JOHN CANNON (or Carman) | |
| WILLIAM CONNOR | |
| ( ROBERT CUSHMAN<br>ʁ Thomas Cushman | of Rolvenden, Kent; wool-carder |
| STEPHEN DEANE | probably from Southwark; miller |
| PHILLIPE DE LA NOYE | of Leyden, Holland |
| THOMAS FLAVELL | of London |
| . . . . . . FORD | probably from Southwark; leather-dresser |
| Mrs. Martha Ford<br>William Ford<br>. . . . . . Ford | |
| WILLIAM HILTON | of Northwich, county Chester; vintner (?) |
| ROBERT HICKS | of Southwark, county Surrey; fell-monger |
| BENEDICT MORGAN | of Saint James, Clerkenwell, London; mariner |
| THOMAS MORTON | of Austerfield, Yorkshire |
| AUGUSTINE NICOLAS | probably from Leyden |
| WILLIAM PALMER<br>. . . . . . Carvanyell | of Stepney, London; nailer |
| WILLIAM PITT | of Saint Peter, London; armorer |
| THOMAS PRENCE | of All Saints, Barking, London |
| MOSES SIMONSON | of Leyden |
| HUGH STACIE | |

JAMES STEWARD

JAMES STEWARD

WILLIAM TENCH          probably of London

JOHN WINSLOW           brother of Edward Winslow

WILLIAM WRIGHT

### 1622

SPARROW, . . . . . . Rogers, Master, one hundred tons. Arrived at Damariscove, Maine, 'with 60 lustie men,' sent out by Thomas Weston. They came to Massachusetts Bay.[1]

SWAN. A small vessel bringing seven passengers sent out by Thomas Weston. Arrived at Damariscove, Maine, in June. They came to Massachusetts Bay.[2]

PHINEAS PRATT

( . . . . . . ) a small vessel, name unknown, sent by Weston, arrived at Damariscove in July.

### 1623

ANNE, William Peirce, Master. She arrived at Plymouth about July 10, and 'brought 60 persons for the Generall.'[3] The entire company settled at Plymouth.[4]

ANTHONY ANNABLE

[1] Winslow: *Goode Newes.*          [2] Pratt: *Narrative.*
[3] Bradford: *History of Plimmoth Plantation,* I, 314.
[4] Banks: *English Ancestry and Homes of the Pilgrims.*

| | |
|---|---|
| ANTHONY ANNABLE | of All Saints, Cambridge, county Cambridge |
| Mrs. Jane Annable<br>...... Annable<br>...... Annable | |
| EDWARD BANGS<br>Mrs. Lydia Bangs<br>Jonathan Bangs<br>John Bangs | of Panfield, Essex; shipwright |
| ROBERT BARTLETT | |
| THOMAS CLARK | |
| CHRISTOPHER CONANT | of Saint Lawrence, Jewry, London; grocer |
| ANTHONY DIX | |
| JOHN FAUNCE | probably from Purleigh, Essex |
| EDMOND FLOOD | |
| GODBERT GODBERTSON<br>Mrs. Sarah Godbertson<br>Mary Priest<br>Sarah Priest | of Leyden; hat-maker |
| TIMOTHY HATHERLEY | of Saint Olaves, Southwark, county Surrey; feltmaker |
| WILLIAM HEARD | |
| EDWARD HOLMAN | probably from Clapham, county Surrey |
| MANASSEH KEMPTON | of Colchester, Essex |
| ROBERT LONG | |
| EXPERIENCE MITCHELL | of Duke's Place, London |
| THOMAS MORTON, JR. | probably son of Thomas Morton of the *Fortune* |
| Mrs. Ellen Newton | |
| | JOHN OLDHAM |

JOHN OLDHAM
  Mrs. . . . . . . Oldham
  Lucretia Oldham
  Christian Penn

JOSHUA PRATT

JAMES RAND                   probably of St. George, Southwark,
                               county Surrey

ROBERT RATCLIFF

NICHOLAS SNOW                 of Hoxton, county Middlesex
  Mrs. Alice Southworth       of Duke's Place, London

FRANCIS SPRAGUE
  Anna Sprague
  Mercy Sprague

THOMAS TILDEN                 probably of Stepney, London
  Mrs. . . . . . . Tilden
  . . . . . . Tilden

STEPHEN TRACY                 of Yarmouth, Norfolk
  Mrs. Tryphosa Tracy
  . . . . . . Tracy

RALPH WALLEN
  Mrs. Joyce Wallen

  Mrs. Hester Cooke           wife of Francis
  Mrs. Elizabeth Flavell      wife of Thomas
  Mrs. Bridget Fuller         wife of Samuel
  Mrs. . . . . . . Hilton     wife of William
  William Hilton, Jr.
  Mary Hilton
  Mrs. Margaret Hicks         wife of Robert
  Mrs. Frances Palmer         wife of William
  Mrs. Elizabeth Warren       wife of Richard of the *Mayflower*
  Mary Warren
  Elizabeth Warren
  Anne Warren
  Sarah Warren

                                          Abigail Warren

Abigail Warren
Mary Becket
Patience Brewster
Fear Brewster
Mrs. Barbara Standish   wife of Myles
Thomas Southworth   son of Mrs. Alice Southworth
William Palmer, Jr.   son of William of the *Fortune*

LITTLE JAMES, Emanuel Altham, Captain, and John Bridges, Master. She was a new vessel of forty-four tons, built by the Plymouth Adventurers to remain at the Colony. She was three months in crossing.[1] All these passengers settled at Plymouth.

WILLIAM BRIDGES   probably of London

EDWARD BURCHER   of Saint Saviour's, Southwark
  Mrs. ...... Burcher

JOHN JENNEY   of Norwich, county Norfolk; cooper
  Mrs. Sarah Jenney   of Monk Soham, county Suffolk
  Samuel Jenney
  Abigail Jenney
  Sarah Jenney

GEORGE MORTON   of Harworth, county Notts; merchant
  Mrs. Juliana Morton

(......) a vessel belonging to Thomas Weston arrived in March, probably at Damariscove.[2]

Roger Conant
Mrs. Roger Conant, wife

PROPHET DANIEL.

[1] Banks: *English Ancestry and Homes of the Pilgrim Fathers*, 169–73.
[2] Bradford: *History of Plimmoth Plantation* (Ford ed.), I, 418.

PROPHET DANIEL. A vessel of this name was at Poole, Dorset, in February, 1623, 'on a voyage to New England.' [1]


YORKE BONAVENTURE, Captain Christopher Levett, Master. She brought a party of colonists to Casco Bay, Maine.


JONATHAN, of Plymouth. It is said that the destination of this ship was Boston Harbor.[2] She sailed from Plymouth, England.

DAVID THOMPSON          of Plymouth, Devonshire, England, apothecary

Mrs. Amias Thompson
John Thompson


KATHERINE, Joseph Stratton, Master, one hundred and eighty tons, sent out by Sir Ferdinando Gorges with 'sundrie passengers' including 'six gentlemen and divers men to do his labour and other men with their families.' [3] Arrived at Weymouth.

ROBERT GORGES          son of Sir Ferdinando Gorges, Governor of New England

*Rev.* WILLIAM MORRELL

*Rev.* WILLIAM BLACKSTONE of Horncastle, county Lincoln

SAMUEL MAVERICK          of Northleigh, county Cornwall and Plymouth

EDWARD GIBBONS

[1] *New York Genealogical and Biographical Records*, 47, p. 109.
[2] Bolton: *Real Founders of New England*, 163.     [3] *Ibid.*, 67.

EDWARD GIBBONS

WILLIAM JEFFREYS — of Chittingley, county Sussex, gentle-man

JOHN BURSLEY

EDWARD JOHNSON — Settled at York, Maine, 1631


1624

CHARITY, of London, one hundred tons, Tobias White, Master; arrived at Plymouth in April. Among her passengers were the following:

Edward Winslow — (returning from England)

*Rev.* JOHN LYFORD — of Loughall, Armagh, Ireland — Plymouth

Mrs. Sarah Lyford
Obadiah Lyford
Mordecai Lyford
Martha Lyford
Anne Lyford
Ruth Lyford


UNITY, of London, Captain ...... Wollaston, Master. She arrived about May with thirty-five persons, who settled at Mount Wollaston, Braintree, among whom were the following:

Thomas Morton — of Clifford's Inn, London, Attor-ney-at-Law. — 'Merrie Mount.'

Lieut. Ficher
Humphrey Rasdell — of London, merchant

ZOUCH PHENIX.

ZOUCH PHENIX. She was consort of the *Unity*, or arrived with her in the spring of this year. It is believed she sailed from Weymouth, and brought the following passengers, who settled at Cape Anne.[1]

THOMAS GARDNER
    Mrs. ...... Gardner
    George Gardner
    Richard Gardner
    Joseph Gardner

JOHN BALCH
    Mrs. Agnes Balch
    Benjamin Balch
    John Balch

THOMAS GRAY

WALTER KNIGHT

WILLIAM TRASK

JOHN TILLEY

PETER PALFREY

JOHN WOODBURY

## 1625

JACOB, probably under the command of William Peirce, as Master, arrived at Plymouth early this year with cattle. Edward Winslow returned in her from England, but no other passengers are known.[2]

Other vessels arrived at Plymouth this year, but it is not known that they brought passengers.

1628

[1] Banks MSS.        [2] Bradford, I, 411.

1628

ABIGAIL, Henry Gaudens, Master, sailed from Weymouth, Dorset, June 20, and arrived at Salem September 6, with the new government for 'London's Plantation,' under the Governorship of Captain John Endicott.[1]

| | | |
|---|---|---|
| JOHN ENDICOTT<br>Mrs. Anna Endicott | | Salem [2] |
| CHARLES GOTT<br>Mrs. Joyce Gott | of Cambridge, England | Salem |
| RICHARD BRACKENBURY | Folke or Holnest, Dorset | Salem |
| WILLIAM BRACKENBURY | Folke or Holnest, Dorset | Salem |
| HUGH LASKIN<br>Mrs. ...... Laskin<br>Edith Laskin | Childhay, Dorset | Salem |
| LAWRENCE LEACH | perhaps from Ash, Martock,<br>Somerset | Salem |
| ROGER MOREY | Drimpton, Dorset | Salem |
| JOHN ELFORD | Chetnold, Dorset | Salem |
| THOMAS PUCKET | Upcerne, Dorset | Salem |

MARMADUKE, John Gibbs, Master, arrived this year at Plymouth.[3]

WHITE ANGEL,

---

[1] Essex Institute, LXVI, 322–23.

[2] The reader will note on this and the following pages that after the name of the emigrant there will appear his age, when known, his occupation, his English residence, if it has been ascertained, and the town in New England where he first settled.

[3] Bradford, II, 33.

WHITE ANGEL, Christopher Burkett, Master, arrived at Plymouth.[1]

ISAAC ALLERTON

*Rev.* JOHN ROGERS

PLEASURE, William Peters, Master, arrived this year at Plymouth.[2]

### 1629

TALBOT, of London, Thomas Beecher, Master, carrying nineteen pieces of ordnance. Sailed about May 11 from the Isle of Wight, and arrived at Salem July 29, with about one hundred planters.[3] 'We have allso sent some servants in the ship called the Talbot.'[4] Also some 'servants' of Saltonstall and Johnson. She started from Gravesend.

| | | |
|---|---|---|
| *Rev.* FRANCIS HIGGINSON | of Leicester, England | Salem |
| Mrs. Anne Higginson | | |
| John Higginson | | |
| Francis Higginson | | |
| Timothy Higginson | | |
| Theophilus Higginson | | |
| Samuel Higginson | | |
| Anne Higginson | | |
| Mary Higginson | | |
| Charles Higginson | | |
| Neophytus Higginson | | |
| | | JOHN BLACK |

---

[1] Bradford, II, 33.     [2] *Ibid.*
[3] Higginson: *Journal.*     [4] Sherley to Bradford, II, 64.

| | | |
|---|---|---|
| JOHN BLACK | | Charlestown |
| *Rev.* RALPH SMITH | of Denton, Lancashire | Salem |

LYON'S WHELP, John Gibbs, Master. Sailed from Gravesend April 25, 1629, 'With above forty planters out of the Countyes of Dorset and Somerset,'[1] and arrived at Salem in the middle of July. She brought '6 fishermen from Dorchester.'[2]

| | | | |
|---|---|---|---|
| RALPH SPRAGUE | 30 | of Upway, county Dorset | Charlestown |
| Mrs. Joanna Sprague | | of Fordington, county Dorset | |
| John Sprague | 4 | | |
| Jonathan Sprague | 3 | | |
| Richard Sprague | 1 | | |
| WILLIAM SPRAGUE | 19 | brother of Ralph | Charlestown |
| RICHARD SPRAGUE | 25 | brother of Ralph | Charlestown |
| WILLIAM DODGE | | of Middle Chinnoch, county Somerset | Salem |
| HUGH TILLIE | | | Salem |
| WILLIAM EADS | | | Salem |
| FRANCIS WEBB | | | Salem |
| WILLIAM ROYAL | | | Salem |
| THOMAS BRAND | | | |
| THOMAS MINOR | 22 | of Chew Magna, county Somerset | Charlestown |

LYON,

[1] Higginson: *Journal.*
[2] *Massachusetts Colonial Records*, I, 395; *Sprague Genealogy*, 1923, pp. 43–48.

LYON, William Peirce, Master; sailed from Bristol in May and arrived at Plymouth in August. She had landed some goods and passengers 'at Salem and the Bay.' [1] The following passengers probably came in her:

| | | |
|---|---|---|
| ISAAC ALLERTON | (returning from England) | Plymouth |
| THOMAS MORTON | (returning from England) | Plymouth |
| JEFFREY MASSEY | of Knutsford, county Chester cordwainer | Salem |
| HENRY HERRICK | | Salem |
| THOMAS JAMES | | Salem |
| WILLIAM JAMES | | Salem |

GEORGE BONAVENTURE, Thomas Cox, Master, of three hundred tons, with twenty pieces of ordnance, sailed from Gravesend May 4, and arrived at Salem in July. 'She brought fifty-two planters.' [2]

| | |
|---|---|
| *Rev.* SAMUEL SKELTON | Salem |
| Mrs. Susanna Skelton | |
| Samuel Skelton, Jr. | |
| Susanna Skelton | |
| Mary Skelton | |
| SAMUEL SHARPE | Salem |
| Mrs. Alice Sharpe | |
| THOMAS GRAVES | Charlestown |
| Mrs. ...... Graves | |
| ...... Graves | |
| ...... Graves | |
| | ...... Graves |

[1] Bradford, II, 67.    [2] Higginson: *Journal.*

...... Graves
...... Graves
...... Graves
(a boy)
(a maid)

FOUR SISTERS, of London, Roger Harman, Master. Sailed from Gravesend April 5, 'with passengers,' number not stated.[1]

...... Sailed from Gravesend in March for Salem. 'Altogether these six ships brought 350 passengers.'[2] In these six ships the following named passengers probably came to Salem and places around Boston Harbor, but it is not possible to assign them to individual vessels:

| | | |
|---|---|---|
| JOHN BROWNE | of London, lawyer | Salem |
| SAMUEL BROWNE | of London, merchant | Salem |
| *Lt. Col.* WALTER NORTON | of Sharpenhoe, county Bedford and London | Charlestown |
| WILLIAM JENNISON | of Colchester, county Essex | Charlestown |
| ALEXANDER WIGNALL | | Charlestown |
| DR. LAMBERT WILSON | | Salem |
| ISAAC RICKMAN | | |
| JOHN HOLGRAVE | | Salem |
| GEORGE NORTON | | Salem |

EDWARD TOMLINS

[1] Higginson: *Journal.*    [2] Smith: *Advertisement for Planters.*

| | | |
|---|---|---|
| EDWARD TOMLINS | of London | Lynn |
| JOHN NORTON | | |
| RICHARD WATERMAN | | Salem |
| HENRY HOUGHTON | | Salem |
| ROBERT MOULTON | | Charlestown |
| WILLIAM NODDLE | | Boston Harbor |
| *Rev.* FRANCIS BRIGHT | of Rayleigh, county Essex | Charlestown |
| JOHN MEECH | | Charlestown |
| SIMON HOYT | | Charlestown |
| WALTER PALMER | | Charlestown |
| NICHOLAS STOWERS | | Charlestown |
| JOHN STICKLINE | | Charlestown |

MAYFLOWER, William Peirce, Master, left Gravesend in March with thirty-five passengers, mostly from Leyden, Holland, destined for Plymouth. She arrived May 15.[1]

| | | |
|---|---|---|
| RICHARD MASTERSON | of Ashford and Sandwich, Kent and Leyden | Plymouth |
| Mrs. Mary Masterson | | |
| Nathaniel Masterson | | |
| Sarah Masterson | | |
| THOMAS BLOSSOM | of Cambridge, England and Leyden, Holland | Plymouth |
| Mrs. Anne Blossom | | |
| Thomas Blossom, Jr. | | |
| Elizabeth Blossom | | |
| Mrs. Bridget Robinson | widow of Rev. John of Leyden | Plymouth |
| Isaac Robinson | | |
| | | Mercy Robinson |

[1] Bradford, II, 65.

Mercy Robinson
Fear Robinson

| THOMAS WILLETT | of Leyden | Plymouth |
|---|---|---|
| RICHARD CLAYDON | of Sutton, county Bedford | Salem |
| BARNABAS CLAYDON | of Sutton, county Bedford | Salem |
| RICHARD HAWARD | of Sutton, county Bedford | Salem |
| RICHARD INGERSOLL | of Sandy, county Bedford | Salem |

    Mrs. Anne Ingersoll
    George Ingersoll
    Joanna Ingersoll
    John Ingersoll
    Sarah Ingersoll
    Alice Ingersoll

## 1630
### THE WINTHROP FLEET

Eleven vessels brought 'the Great Emigration' of this year, viz:

### ARBELLA the flagship

| | |
|---|---|
| AMBROSE | WILLIAM AND FRANCIS |
| TALBOT | HOPEWELL |
| JEWEL | WHALE |
| CHARLES | SUCCESS |
| MAYFLOWER | TRIAL |

The first five ships sailed April 8 from Yarmouth, Isle of Wight, and arrived at Salem June 13 and following days. The other half of the fleet sailed in May and arrived in July at various dates. Altogether they brought about seven hundred passengers of whom the following are presumed to have been on these ships.[1]

DANIEL ABBOTT

[1] Banks: *The Winthrop Fleet of 1630.*

| | | |
|---|---|---|
| DANIEL ABBOTT | | Cambridge |
| ROBERT ABELL | of Hemington, Leicestershire | Boston |
| WILLIAM AGAR | probably of Nazing, Essex | Watertown |
| GEORGE ALCOCK | probably of Leicestershire | Roxbury |
| Mrs. ...... Alcock | | |
| FRANCIS ALEWORTH | | |
| THOMAS ANDREW | | Watertown |
| SAMUEL ARCHER | | Salem |
| WILLIAM ASPINWALL | of Manchester, Lancashire | Boston |
| Mrs. Elizabeth Aspinwall | | |
| Edward Aspinwall | | |
| JOHN AUDLEY | | Boston |
| JOHN BAKER | | Charlestown |
| Mrs. Charity Baker | | |
| WILLIAM BALSTON | | Boston |
| Mrs. Elizabeth Balston | | |
| WILLIAM BARSHAM | | Watertown |
| THOMAS BARTLETT | | Watertown |
| GREGORY BAXTER | perhaps of Sporle, Norfolk | Roxbury |
| WILLIAM BEAMSLEY | | Boston |
| Mrs. Anne Beamsley | | |
| THOMAS BEECHER | of Stepney, Middlesex | Charlestown |
| Mrs. Christian Beecher | | |
| EDWARD BELCHER | of Guilsborough, Northamptonshire | Boston |
| Mrs. Christian Belcher | | |
| Edward Belcher, Jr. | | |

EDWARD BENDALL

| | | |
|---|---|---|
| EDWARD BENDALL | of Southwark, county Surrey | Boston |
| Mrs. Anne Bendall | | |
| JOHN BENHAM | | Dorchester |
| JOHN BIGGES | of Groton, county Suffolk | Boston |
| Mrs. Mary Bigges | | |
| JOHN BLACK | | Charlestown |
| JOHN BOGGUST | probably of Boxted, Essex | |
| JOHN BOSWELL | of London | Boston |
| ZACCHEUS BOSWORTH | of Stowe, IX Churches, county Northants | Boston |
| GARRET BOURNE | | Boston |
| NATHANIEL BOWMAN | | Watertown |
| Mrs. Anna Bowman | | |
| SIMON BRADSTREET | of Horbling, county Lincoln | Cambridge |
| Mrs. Anne Bradstreet | | |
| BENJAMIN BRAND | probably of Edwardston, county Suffolk | Boston |
| AUGUSTINE BRATCHER | | Charlestown |
| ...... BREASE | probably of Edwardston, county Suffolk | |
| WILLIAM BRENTON | of Hammersmith, county Middlesex | Boston |
| Isabel Brett | | |
| HENRY BRIGHT | of Bury Saint Edmunds, county Suffolk | Watertown |
| ABRAHAM BROWNE | of Hawkdon, Suffolk | Watertown |
| Mrs. Lydia Browne | | |
| JAMES BROWNE | | Boston |
| | RICHARD BROWNE | |

| | | |
|---|---|---|
| RICHARD BROWNE<br>Mrs. Elizabeth Browne<br>George Browne<br>Richard Browne, Jr. | of Hawkdon, Suffolk | Watertown |
| WILLIAM BUCKLAND | of Essex | Boston, Hingham,<br>and Rehoboth |
| RICHARD BUGBY<br><br>Mrs. Judith Bugby | perhaps Saint John Hack-<br>ney, Middlesex | Roxbury |
| RICHARD BULGAR<br>Mrs. ...... Bulgar | | Boston |
| WILLIAM BURNELL | | Boston |
| JEHU BURR<br><br>Mrs. ...... Burr<br>Jehu Burr | probably of Essex | Roxbury and Fair-<br>field, Connecticut |
| ROBERT BURROUGHS | | |
| JOHN CABLE | probably of Essex | Dorchester and<br>Fairfield |
| THOMAS CAKEBREAD<br><br>Mrs. Sarah Cakebread | of Hatfield Broadoak,<br>Essex | Dedham |
| CHARLES CHADWICK<br>Mrs. Elizabeth Chadwick<br><br>Anne Chambers | | Watertown |
| WILLIAM CHASE<br><br>Margery Chauner | probably of county Essex | Roxbury |
| WILLIAM CHEESEBROUGH<br><br>Mrs. Anne Cheesebrough<br>Sarah Cheesebrough<br><br>Peter Cheesebrough | of Boston, Lin-<br>colnshire | Boston, Rehoboth |

Peter Cheesebrough
Samuel Cheesebrough
Nathaniel Cheesebrough

| | | |
|---|---|---|
| EPHRAIM CHILD | of Bury Saint Edmunds, Suffolk | Watertown |
| Mrs. Elizabeth Child | | |
| RICHARD CHURCH | perhaps of Polstead, Suffolk | Boston |
| JOHN CLARKE | of county Suffolk | Boston |
| WILLIAM CLARKE | of London | Watertown |
| Mrs. Elizabeth Clarke | | |
| RICHARD CLOUGH | | Charlestown |
| . . . . . . COBBETT | | |
| WILLIAM CODDINGTON | of Boston, Lincolnshire | Boston and Newport |
| Mrs. Mary Coddington | | |
| WILLIAM COLBRON | of Brentwood, Essex | Boston |
| Mrs. Margery Colbron | | |
| ANTHONY COLBY | | Boston and Salisbury |
| Mrs. Susanna Colby | | |
| WILLIAM FROTHINGHAM | of Holderness, Yorkshire | Charlestown |
| Mrs. Anne Frothingham | | |
| JOHN GAGE | probably of Polstead, Suffolk | Boston |
| Mrs. Amy Gage | | |
| WILLIAM GAGER | of Suffolk, surgeon | Charlestown |
| HUGH GARRETT | | Charlestown |
| RICHARD GARRETT | probably of Chelmsford, Essex | Boston |
| Mrs. . . . . . . Garrett | | |
| Hannah Garrett | | |
| . . . . . . Garrett | | |

CHRISTOPHER GIBSON

| | | |
|---|---|---|
| CHRISTOPHER GIBSON | of Wendover, county Bucks | Dorchester |
| Mrs. Mary Gibson | | |
| Elizabeth Gibson | of Saint Andrew the Great, Cambridge | Salem |
| RALPH GLOVER | of London | Boston |
| JOHN GLOVER | of Rainhill, Lancashire | Dorchester |
| Mrs. Anne Glover | | |
| THOMAS GOLDTHWAITE | | Roxbury |
| Mrs. Elizabeth Goldthwaite | | |
| HENRY GOSNALL | probably of Bury Saint Edmunds, Suffolk | Boston |
| Mrs. Mary Gosnall | | |
| JOHN GOSSE (GOFFE) | | Watertown |
| Mrs. Sarah Gosse | | |
| JOHN GOULWORTH | | |
| RICHARD GRIDLEY | of Groton, Suffolk | Boston |
| Mrs. Grace Gridley | | |
| Joseph Gridley | | |
| Abraham Gridley | | |
| Bridget Giver | of Saffron Walden, Essex | Boston |
| GARRETT HADDON | | Cambridge, Salisbury |
| Mrs. Margaret Haddon | | |
| ROBERT HALE | | Charlestown |
| Mrs. Joan Hale | | |
| JOHN HALL | of Whitechapel, London | Charlestown |
| Mrs. Joan Hall | | |
| Mrs. Phillippa Hammond | | |
| ROBERT HARDING | probably of Boreham, Essex | Boston |
| THOMAS HARRIS | | |

| | | |
|---|---|---|
| THOMAS HARRIS<br>Mrs. Elizabeth Harris | | Charlestown |
| JOHN COLE | of Groton, Suffolk | Boston |
| RICE COLE<br>Mrs. Arrold Cole | | Charlestown |
| ROBERT COLE | of Navistock, Essex | Roxbury |
| SAMUEL COLE<br>Mrs. Anne Cole | of Mersey, Essex | Boston |
| EDWARD CONVERSE | probably of Shenfield,<br>Essex | Charlestown |
| Mrs. Sarah Converse<br>Phineas Converse<br>John Converse<br>Josiah Converse<br>James Converse | | |
| Margaret Cooke | | |
| WILLIAM COWLISHAW<br>Mrs. Anne Cowlishaw | of Nottingham | Boston |
| JOHN CRABB | | |
| GRIFFIN CRAFTS<br>Mrs. Alice Crafts<br>Hannah Crafts | | Roxbury |
| JOHN CRANWELL | of Woodbridge, Suffolk | Boston |
| BENJAMIN CRIBB | | |
| JAMES CRUGOTT | | |
| WILLIAM DADY | probably of Wanstead,<br>Essex | Charlestown |
| Mrs. Dorothy Dady | | |
| EDWARD DEEKES<br>Mrs. Jane Deekes | | Charlestown |
| | | JOHN DEVEREUX |

| | | |
|---|---|---|
| JOHN DEVEREUX | probably of Stoke by Nayland, Suffolk | |
| ROBERT DIFFY | | Watertown |
| JOHN DILLINGHAM | of Bitteswell, Leicestershire | Boston |
| Mrs. Sarah Dillingham | | |
| Sarah Dillingham | | |
| WILLIAM DIXON | | Boston and York, Maine |
| JOHN DOGGETT | Watertown and Martha's Vineyard | |
| Mrs. ...... Doggett | | |
| John Doggett | | |
| Thomas Doggett | | |
| JAMES DOWNING | | |
| THOMAS DUDLEY | of Yardley, Northamptonshire | Cambridge |
| Mrs. Dorothy Dudley | | |
| Samuel Dudley | | |
| Anne Dudley | | |
| Patience Dudley | | |
| Sarah Dudley | | |
| Mercy Dudley | | |
| Thomas Dudley | | |
| ...... DUTTON | | |
| JOHN EDMONDS | | Boston |
| Mrs. Mary Edmonds | | |
| BIGOD EGGLESTON | of Settrington, Yorkshire | Dorchester, Windsor |
| ARTHUR ELLIS | | |
| JOHN ELSTON | | Salem |
| THOMAS FAYERWEATHER | | Boston |
| ROBERT FEAKE | of London, goldsmith | Watertown |
| CHARLES FIENNES | | |

ABRAHAM FINCH

| | | |
|---|---|---|
| ABRAHAM FINCH<br>Abraham Finch, Jr.<br>Daniel Finch<br>John Finch | of Yorkshire (?) | Watertown |
| JOHN FIRMAN | of Nayland, Suffolk | Watertown |
| GILES FIRMIN<br>Mrs. Martha Firmin | of Nayland, Suffolk | |
| EDWARD FITZRANDOLPH | of Sutton in Ashfield,<br>Notts | Scituate |
| THOMAS FOX | | Cambridge |
| RICHARD FOXWELL<br><br>Mrs. . . . . . . Foxwell<br>John Foxwell | probably of Lon-<br>don, tailor | Boston, Barnstable |
| SAMUEL FREEMAN<br><br>Mrs. Apphia Freeman<br>Henry Freeman | of St. Anne, Blackfriars,<br>London | Watertown |
| THOMAS FRENCH<br><br>Mrs. Susan French<br>Thomas French, Jr.<br>Alice French<br>Dorcas French<br>Susan French<br>Anne French<br>John French<br>Mary French | of Assington,<br>Suffolk | Boston and Ipswich |
| HENRY HARWOOD<br><br>Mrs. Elizabeth Harwood | probably of Shenfield,<br>Essex | Boston |
| . . . . . . HAWKE | | |
| JOHN HAWKINS | | |
| | | WILLIAM HAWTHORNE |

| | | |
|---|---|---|
| WILLIAM HAWTHORNE | of Binfield, Berks | Dorchester and Salem |
| FRANCIS HESSELDEN | | |
| Margaret Hoames | | |
| (ATHERTON) HOFFE | | |
| EDWARD HOPWOOD | | |
| JOHN HORNE | | Salem |
| SAMUEL HOSIER | of Colchester, Essex | Watertown |
| THOMAS HOWLETT | of county Suffolk | Boston |
| WILLIAM HUDSON | probably of Chatham, Kent | Boston |
| Mrs. Susan Hudson | | |
| Francis Hudson | | |
| William Hudson | | |
| WILLIAM HULBIRT | | Boston and Northampton |
| RICHARD HUTCHINS | | |
| GEORGE HUTCHINSON | of London | Charlestown |
| Mrs. Margaret Hutchinson | | |
| THOMAS HUTCHINSON | of London | Charlestown |
| MATTHIAS IJONS | probably of Roxwell, Essex | Boston |
| Mrs. Anne Ijons | | |
| EDMUND JAMES | of Earls Barton, Northants | Watertown |
| Mrs. Reana James | | |
| THOMAS JAMES | of Earls Barton, Northants | Salem |
| Mrs. Elizabeth James | | |
| WILLIAM JAMES | of Earls Barton, Northants | Salem |
| Mrs. Elizabeth James | | |
| JOHN JARVIS | | Boston |
| DAVY JOHNSON | | Dorchester |
| FRANCIS JOHNSON | | |

| | | |
|---|---|---|
| FRANCIS JOHNSON<br>Mrs. Joan Johnson | of London | Salem |
| ISAAC JOHNSON<br>Lady Arbella Johnson | of Clipsham, Rutland | Boston |
| JOHN JOHNSON<br>Mrs. Margaret Johnson | | Roxbury |
| RICHARD JOHNSON<br>Mrs. Alice Johnson | | Charlestown |
| Bethia Jones | | Boston |
| EDWARD JONES | of Chester, mercer | Charlestown |
| LEWIS KIDBY<br>Mrs. ...... Kidby<br>...... Kidby<br>Edward Kidby | of Groton, Suffolk | Boston |
| HENRY KINGSBURY<br>Mrs. Margaret Kingsbury<br>Henry Kingsbury, Jr. | of Groton, Suffolk | Boston |
| THOMAS KINGSBURY | | |
| NICHOLAS KNAPP<br><br>Mrs. Elinor Knapp | probably of Bures<br>Saint Mary, Suffolk | Watertown |
| WILLIAM KNAPP<br><br>Mrs. ...... Knapp<br>John Knapp<br>Anne Knapp<br>Judith Knapp<br>Mary Knapp<br>James Knapp<br>John Knapp<br>William Knapp, Jr. | probably of Bures<br>Saint Mary, Suffolk | Watertown |
| GEORGE KNOWER<br>THOMAS KNOWER | of London | Charlestown |

| | | |
|---|---|---|
| THOMAS KNOWER | of London, clothier | Charlestown |
| EDWARD LAMB | | Watertown |
| THOMAS LAMB | | Roxbury |
|    Mrs. Elizabeth Lamb | | |
|    Thomas Lamb, Jr. | | |
|    John Lamb | | |
|    Samuel Lamb | | |
| ROGER LAMB | | |
| HENRY LAWSON | | |
| WILLIAM LEARNED | probably of Bermond-sey, Surrey | Charlestown |
|    Mrs. Judith Learned | | |
| WILLIAM LEATHERLAND | | Boston |
| JOHN LEGGE | | Lynn |
| EDMOND LOCKWOOD | of Combs, Suffolk | Cambridge |
|    Mrs. Elizabeth Lockwood | | |
|    ...... Lockwood | | |
| ROBERT LOCKWOOD | of Combs, Suffolk | Watertown |
| RICHARD LYNTON | probably from London | Watertown |
|    Mrs. ...... Lynton | | |
|    Anna Lynton | | |
|    Lydia Lynton | | |
| HENRY LYNN | | Boston |
|    Mrs. Sarah Lynn | | |
| JOHN MASTERS | | Watertown |
|    Mrs. Jane Masters | | |
|    Sarah Masters | | |
|    Lydia Masters | | |
|    Elizabeth Masters | | |
|    Nathaniel Masters | | |
|    Abraham Masters | | |
| THOMAS MATSON | of London, gunsmith | Boston |
|    Mrs. Amy Matson | | |

THOMAS MAYHEW

| | | |
|---|---|---|
| THOMAS MAYHEW | of Tisbury, Wilts | Watertown, Martha's Vineyard |

Mrs. . . . . . . Mayhew
Thomas Mayhew, Jr.

| | |
|---|---|
| (ALEXANDER) MILLER | probably the servant of Israel Stoughton [1] |

RICHARD MILLET

| | | |
|---|---|---|
| JOHN MILLS | probably of Lavenham, Suffolk | Boston |

Mrs. Susan Mills
Joy Mills
Mary Mills
John Mills
Susanna Mills
Recompense Mills

| | | |
|---|---|---|
| ROGER MOREY | of Dorsetshire | Salem |
| RALPH MORLEY | of London | Charlestown |

Mrs. Katherine Morley

| | | |
|---|---|---|
| RICHARD MORRIS | probably of London | Boston |

Mrs. Leonora Morris

| | | |
|---|---|---|
| THOMAS MORRIS | probably of Nottingham | Boston |

Mrs. Sarah Morris

Mary Morton

| | | |
|---|---|---|
| THOMAS MOULTON | | Charlestown |

Mrs. Jane Moulton

| | | |
|---|---|---|
| RALPH MOUSALL | probably of London | Charlestown |

Mrs. Alice Mousall

| | | |
|---|---|---|
| THOMAS MUNT | probably of Colchester, Essex | Boston |

Mrs. Dorothy Munt

| | | |
|---|---|---|
| GREGORY NASH | | Charlestown |

Mrs. . . . . . . Nash

Anne Needham

. . . . . . NICOLLS

[1] *Massachusetts Colonial Records*, I, 100.

...... NICOLLS

INCREASE NOWELL          of London              Charlestown
    Mrs. Parnell Nowell

JOHN ODLIN               (*see* Audley)

JOHN PAGE                of Dedham, Essex       Watertown
    Mrs. Phoebe Page
    John Page, Jr.
    Daniel Page

THOMAS PAINTER                          Boston and Hingham
    Mrs. Katherine Painter

ABRAHAM PALMER           of Canterbury, Kent    Charlestown
    Mrs. Grace Palmer

EDWARD PALSFORD

RICHARD PALSGRAVE        probably of London     Charlestown
    Mrs. Anne Palsgrave
    John Palsgrave
    Anna Palsgrave
    Mary Palsgrave
    Sarah Palsgrave

ROBERT PARKE             probably of Bures, county
                            Suffolk

    Mrs. Martha Parke
    Thomas Parke
    ...... Parke
    ...... Parke
    ...... Parke

ROBERT PARKER                                   Boston

*Capt.* DANIEL PATRICK                          Watertown
    Mrs. ...... Patrick

WILLIAM PELHAM                                  Boston

JAMES PEMBERTON                                 Charlestown
    Mrs. Alice Pemberton

                                         JOHN PEMBERTON

| | | |
|---|---|---|
| JOHN PEMBERTON<br>Mrs. Elizabeth Pemberton | | Boston |
| JAMES PENN<br>Mrs. Katherine Penn | | Boston |
| WILLIAM PENN | of Birmingham,<br>Warwick | Charlestown |
| JAMES PENNIMAN<br>Mrs. Lydia Penniman | of Widford, county Essex | Boston |
| ISAAC PERRY | | Boston |
| Anne Pettit | | Salem |
| *Rev.* GEORGE PHILLIPS<br>Mrs. ...... Phillips<br>Samuel Phillips<br>Abigail Phillips<br>Elizabeth Phillips | of Raynham, Norfolk | Watertown |
| JOHN PHILLIPS<br>Mrs. Joan Phillips | | Dorchester |
| JOHN PHILLIPS | | Plymouth |
| JOHN PICKERING<br>Mrs. Esther Pickering<br>George Pickering<br>John Pickering<br>Joan Pickering | probably of Suffolk | Cambridge |
| JOHN PICKWORTH | | |
| JOHN PIERCE<br>Mrs. Parnell Pierce<br>Experience Pierce<br>Mercy Pierce<br>Samuel Pierce | | Dorchester |
| JOSIAH PLAISTOW | of Ramsden Crays, Essex | Boston |
| *Mrs.* ANNE POLLARD | came from Saffron Walden,<br>Essex, as a girl | |
| | | JOHN POND |

| | | |
|---|---|---|
| JOHN POND | of Groton, Suffolk | Boston |
| ROBERT POND<br>Mrs. Mary Pond | of Groton, Suffolk | Dorchester |
| JOHN PORTER<br>Mrs. Margaret Porter<br>...... Porter<br>...... Porter<br>...... Porter<br>...... Porter | perhaps of Bromfield, Essex | Roxbury |
| ABRAHAM PRATT<br>Mrs. Jane Pratt | of London, surgeon | Roxbury |
| WILLIAM PYNCHON<br>Mrs. Agnes Pynchon<br>John Pynchon<br>Anne Pynchon<br>Mary Pynchon<br>Margaret Pynchon | of Writtle, Essex | Dorchester |
| EDWARD RAINSFORD<br>Mrs. ...... Rainsford | | Dorchester |
| PHILIP RATCLIFFE | probably of London | Salem |
| THOMAS RAWLINS<br>Mrs. Mary Rawlins<br>Thomas Rawlins<br>Nathaniel Rawlins<br>John Rawlins<br>Joan Rawlins<br>Mary Rawlins | | Roxbury |
| THOMAS READE<br>Mrs. Priscilla Reade | of Wickford, Essex | Salem |
| JOSEPH READING | | Boston |
| MILES READING | | Boston |
| ...... REEDER | | |
| | | JOHN REVELL |

JOHN REVELL

ROBERT REYNOLDS probably of Boxford, Suffolk Boston
 Mrs. Mary Reynolds
 Nathaniel Reynolds
 Ruth Reynolds
 Tabitha Reynolds
 Sarah Reynolds

EZEKIEL RICHARDSON of Westmill, county Charlestown
        Herts
 Mrs. Susanna Richardson

ROBERT ROYCE perhaps of Exning, Suffolk Boston
 Mrs. Elizabeth Royce

JOHN RUGGLES probably of Glemsford, Boston
      Suffolk
 Mrs. Frances Ruggles
 ...... Ruggles

JEFFREY RUGGLES of Sudbury, Suffolk
 Mrs. Margaret Ruggles

JOHN SALES of Lavenham, Suffolk Charlestown
 Mrs. ...... Sales
 Phoebe Sales

*Sir* RICHARD SALTONSTALL of London Watertown
 Richard Saltonstall, Jr.
 Samuel Saltonstall
 Robert Saltonstall
 Rosamond Saltonstall
 Grace Saltonstall

ROBERT SAMPSON

JOHN SANFORD perhaps of High Ongar, Essex Boston

*Rev.* GILES SAXTON of Yorkshire Charlestown

ROBERT SCOTT Boston

JOHN SEAMAN Watertown

           ROBERT SEELY

| | | |
|---|---|---|
| ROBERT SEELY | | Watertown |
| ...... SARGEANT | | |
| ROBERT SHARPE | of Roxwell, Essex | Boston |
| THOMAS SHARPE | of London, leather-seller | Boston |
| Mrs. ...... Sharpe | | |
| ...... Sharpe | | |
| Thomas Sharpe | | |
| ...... SHUT | | |
| ...... SIMPSON | | |
| ...... SMEAD | of Coggeshall, Essex | |
| Mrs. Judith Smead | | |
| William Smead | | |
| ...... SMITH | of Buxhall, Suffolk | |
| Mrs. ...... Smith | | |
| ...... Smith | | |
| ...... Smith | | |
| FRANCIS SMYTH | perhaps of Dunmow, Essex | Roxbury |
| Mrs. ...... Smyth | | |
| ISAAC STEARNS | of Stoke Nayland, Suffolk | Watertown |
| Mrs. Mary Stearns | | |
| John Stearns | | |
| Abigail Stearns | | |
| Elizabeth Stearns | | |
| Hannah Stearns | | |
| ELIAS STILEMAN | of Saint Andrew Undershaft, London | Salem |
| Mrs. Judith Stileman | | |
| Elias Stileman, Jr. | | |
| ISRAEL STOUGHTON | of Coggeshall, Essex | Dorchester |
| Mrs. Elizabeth Stoughton | | |
| THOMAS STOUGHTON | of Coggeshall, Essex | Dorchester |
| Mrs. ...... Stoughton | | |
| | | WILLIAM SUMNER |

| | | |
|---|---|---|
| WILLIAM SUMNER<br>Mrs. Mary Sumner<br>William Sumner, Jr. | of Bicester, Oxford | Dorchester |
| PHILIP SWADDON | | Watertown |
| Anna Swanson | | |
| WILLIAM TALMADGE<br>Mrs. . . . . . . | of Newton Stacey, Hants | Boston |
| GREGORY TAYLOR<br>Mrs. Achsah Taylor | | Watertown |
| JOHN TAYLOR<br>Mrs. . . . . . . Taylor<br>. . . . . . Taylor | of Haverhill, Suffolk | Boston |
| WILLIAM TIMEWELL | | |
| EDWARD TOMLINS | of London | Lynn |
| NATHANIEL TURNER | probably of London | Saugus |
| ROBERT TURNER | probably of Southwark,<br>Surrey | Boston |
| ARTHUR TYNDAL | of Great Maplestead, Essex | Boston |
| *Capt.* JOHN UNDERHILL<br>Mrs. Helen Underhill | of Holland | Boston |
| WILLIAM VASSALL<br>Mrs. Anne Vassall<br>Judith Vassall<br>Francis Vassall<br>John Vassall<br>Anne Vassall | of Prittlewell, Essex | Charlestown |
| THOMAS WADE | | |
| ROBERT WALKER<br>Mrs. Sarah Walker | of Manchester, Lancashire | Boston |
| . . . . . . WALL<br>Mrs. . . . . . . Wall | | |
| | | THOMAS WARD |

| | | |
|---|---|---|
| THOMAS WARD | probably of Bedingham, Norfolk | Dedham |
| JOHN WARREN Mrs. Margaret Warren | of Nayland, Suffolk | Watertown |
| WILLIAM WATERBURY Mrs. Alice Waterbury | of Sudbury, Suffolk | Boston |
| JOHN WATERS Mrs. Frances Waters Mary Waters ...... Waters ...... Waters | of Nayland, Suffolk | Charlestown |
| ...... WEAVER | | |
| RICHARD WEBB Mrs. Elizabeth Webb | of Nayland, Suffolk | Cambridge |
| JONAS WEED | | Watertown |
| JOIST WEILLUST | of Holland | Boston |
| ROBERT WELDON Mrs. Elizabeth Weldon | | Charlestown |
| FRANCIS WESTON Mrs. Margaret Weston Lucy Weston | | Salem |
| SAMUEL WILBORE Mrs. Anne Wilbore | | Boston |
| *Mrs.* PRUDENCE WILKINSON Sarah Wilkinson John Wilkinson Elizabeth Wilkinson | | Charlestown |
| THOMAS WILLIAMS | | Charlestown |
| THOMAS WILLIAMS *als* HARRIS Robert Williams | | |
| ...... WILSBY | | |
| | | *Rev.* JOHN WILSON |

| | | |
|---|---|---|
| *Rev.* JOHN WILSON | of Sudbury, Suffolk | Boston |
| DAVID WILTON | | Dorchester |
| Elizabeth Wing | | |
| JOHN WINTHROP | of Groton, Suffolk | Boston |
| Henry Winthrop | | |
| Stephen Winthrop | | |
| Samuel Winthrop | | |
| WILLIAM WOODS | | Boston |
| JOHN WOOLRICH | probably of London | Charlestown |
| Mrs. Sarah Woolrich | | |
| . . . . . . WORMWOOD | | |
| RICHARD WRIGHT | of Stepney, Middlesex | Boston |
| Mrs. Margaret Wright | | |
| Elinor Wright | | |
| ROBERT WRIGHT | of London | Boston |

LYON. This ship was famous in the history of the early emigration to Massachusetts, and her Master was equally noted for his skillful seamanship and his sympathy with the policy of the Puritan leaders. In 1630, 1631, and 1632 she made four voyages hither in quick succession under his command with the regularity and safety of a ferry, and on one of them saved the new settlement from starvation and death by her timely arrival with provisions and anti-scorbutics. The official connection of the *Lyon* with the Winthrop Fleet is of the same character as related of the *Mary and John*, as both were doubtless approved by the Governor and Assistants. In his letter of March 28, 1630, to his wife, written from the *Arbella*, off the Isle of Wight, after noting the sailing of the *Mary and John*, Winthrop wrote: 'and the ship which goes from Bristowe

Bristowe (Bristol) carrieth about eighty persons.' [1] This was the *Lyon* and she probably sailed from that port to accommodate passengers living in the West Counties — Lancashire, Cheshire, Warwick, Gloucestershire, and Somerset. That they were authorized to settle in the limits of the Bay Patent seems assured as there is no evidence to the contrary following their arrival. The date of her departure is not known (probably in March) but her arrival at Salem is reported 'in the latter part of May,' [2] some time before the *Arbella* reached that port. The identity of this ship is not established as there were several of her name in existence at that period. In view of her valuable services to the Colony it is to be hoped that the necessary search may be made to fix her home port, previous history, tonnage, and ownership.

Of Captain William Peirce, her Master, more particulars are known. He had sailed to Plymouth in 1623 as Master of the *Anne* of London, bringing the last lot of passengers to the Pilgrim settlement. He was then a resident of Ratcliffe, parish of Stepney, London, and at that date was about thirty-one years old. He made a voyage to Salem in 1629 as Master of the *Mayflower* (not the Pilgrim ship) and thereafter he was in constant traffic in passengers and merchandise across the Atlantic. He took up his residence in Boston in 1632 and was admitted freeman May 14, 1634.[3] His wife, Bridget, joined the church February 2, 1632/3; perhaps a second wife, as a William Peirce, mariner of Whitechapel, was licensed in 1615 to marry Margaret Gibbs. Whitechapel and Stepney are adjoining parishes. He became a Town and Colony official and was engaged in coastwise shipping thereafter. He compiled an Almanac for New England which was the second issue in 1639 from the Daye press at Cambridge. In 1641 he was killed by the Spaniards while on a voyage to the island of New Providence,

dence, Bahamas Group, whither he was taking passengers for settlement.[1]


MARY AND JOHN, Thomas Chubb, Master. She sailed from Plymouth, England, March 20, with one hundred and forty passengers from the counties of Somerset, Dorset, and Devon under the patronage of the Reverend John White. She arrived at Nantasket May 30, and all the passengers settled at Mattapan which was renamed Dorchester.[2] There is no list of the emigrants, but the following persons are believed to have come in this ship according to evidences from contemporary authorities. All settled at Dorchester, Massachusetts.[3]

THOMAS BASKOM

AARON COOKE

ROGER CLAPP

NICHOLAS DENSLOW
    Mrs. Elizabeth Denslow
    ...... Denslow

GEORGE DYER
    Mrs. ...... Dyer
    Elizabeth Dyer
    Mary Dyer

JOHN DRAKE
    Mrs. Elizabeth Drake
    Job Drake
    John Drake
    Jacob Drake
    ...... Drake

NATHANIEL DUNCAN

[1] Banks: *The Winthrop Fleet of 1630*, p. 106.    [2] Clapp: *Memoirs*.
[3] Banks: *The Winthrop Fleet*, pp. 100–05.

NATHANIEL DUNCAN  of Exeter, Devon
 Mrs. Elizabeth Duncan
 Peter Duncan
 Nathaniel Duncan, Jr.

THOMAS FORD  of Simsbury, Dorset
 Mrs. Elizabeth Ford
 Joanna Ford
 Abigail Ford
 Mary Ford
 Hepsibah Ford

HUMPHREY GALLOP  of Mosterton, Dorset
 Mrs. Anne Gallop

JOHN GALLOP  of Mosterton, Dorset
 Mrs. Christobel Gallop
 John Gallop, Jr.
 Joan Gallop

GILES GIBBES
 Mrs. Katherine Gibbes
 Gregory Gibbes
 Jacob Gibbes
 Samuel Gibbes
 Benjamin Gibbes
 Sarah Gibbes

JONATHAN GILLETT

JOHN GREENWAY
 Mrs. Mary Greenway
 Anne Greenway
 Elizabeth Greenway
 Susanna Greenway
 Katherine Greenway
 Mary Greenway

WILLIAM HANNUM  of Dorchester, Dorset

WILLIAM HILL  of Lyme Regis, Dorset
 Mrs. Sarah Hill

         William Hill, Jr.

William Hill, Jr.
Ignatius Hill
James Hill

JOHN HOLMAN                    of Swyre, Dorset

JOHN HOSKINS
Mrs. ...... Hoskins
John Hoskins, Jr.
Thomas Hoskins

GEORGE HULL                    of Crewkerne, Somerset
Mrs. Thomasine Hull
Josias Hull
Mary Hull
Martha Hull
Elizabeth Hull
Naomi Hull
Cornelius Hull

WILLIAM LOVELL
Mrs. Wyborough Lovell

ROGER LUDLOW                   of Maiden Bradley, Wiltshire
Mrs. ...... Ludlow
Jonathan Ludlow
Joseph Ludlow
Roger Ludlow, Jr.
Anne Ludlow
Mary Ludlow
Sarah Ludlow

*Rev.* JOHN MAVERICK           of Beaworthy, Devon
Mrs. Mary Maverick
Elias Maverick
Moses Maverick
Antipas Maverick
Abigail Maverick
Mary Maverick
Margaret Maverick

JOHN MORE

GEORGE PHELPS

GEORGE PHELPS

WILLIAM PHELPS
  Mrs. Anne Phelps
  William Phelps, Jr.
  Samuel Phelps
  Nathaniel Phelps
  Sarah Phelps

HUMPHREY PINNEY
  Mrs. ...... Pinney

ELTWEED POMEROY          of Beaminster, Dorset
  Mrs. ...... Pomeroy
  ...... Pomeroy

THOMAS RICHARDS          of Pitminster, Somerset
  Mrs. Welthian Richards
  John Richards
  James Richards
  Mary Richards
  Anne Richards
  Alice Richards

WILLIAM ROCKWELL         of Fitzhead, Somerset
  Mrs. Susanna Rockwell
  John Rockwell
  Ruth Rockwell

*Dr.* BRIAN ROSSITER

EDWARD ROSSITER          of Combe Saint Nicholas, Somerset
  Mrs. ...... Rossiter
  Jane Rossiter
  ...... Rossiter

RICHARD SOUTHCOTE        of Mohuns Ottery, Devon

RICHARD SYLVESTER

STEPHEN TERRY            of Dorchester, Dorset
  Mrs. ...... Terry
  ...... Terry

JOHN TILLEY

| | |
|---|---|
| JOHN TILLEY<br>Mrs. ...... Tilley | of Chilthorne, Somerset |
| NICHOLAS UPSALL<br>Mrs. Dorothy Upsall | of Dorchester, Dorset |
| *Rev.* JOHN WARHAM<br>Mrs. ...... Warham<br>Mary Warham<br>Susanna Warham | of Exeter, Devon |
| HENRY WAY<br>Mrs. Elizabeth Way<br>Samuel Way<br>Richard Way<br>Henry Way<br>Susanna Way | of Bridport, Dorset |
| ROGER WILLIAMS<br>Mrs. (Lydia) Williams | probably W. Harptree, Somerset |
| HENRY WOLCOTT<br>Mrs. Elizabeth Wolcott<br>John Wolcott<br>Anna Wolcott<br>Henry Wolcott, Jr.<br>George Wolcott | of Tolland, Somerset |

THOMAS AND WILLIAM, Captain William Bundick, Master, sailed from Gravesend in May and arrived July 1. She was called 'Mr. Huson's ship.'[1]

HANDMAID. This ship left London August 10 and arrived at Plymouth October 29, with sixty passengers.[2]

GIFT,

---

[1] *Life and Letters of John Winthrop*, II, 43; Bradford, II, 114 *n.*
[2] Winthrop: *Journal*, I, 53.

GIFT, Captain...... Brook, Master. Arrived August 20 at Charlestown. 'She had been twelve weeks at sea and lost one passenger.'[1] She was called 'the French ship.'

FRIENDSHIP. This vessel arrived 'aboute the midle of Sommer' in the Bay.[2] The only known passenger was TIMOTHY HATHERLY.

SWIFT, Stephen Reekes, Master, of seventy tons. She sailed from Bristol in April for Saco and Casco Bay in Maine with passengers and freight.[3] It is probable that the following named emigrants came in her:

| | | |
|---|---|---|
| GEORGE CLEEVES | of Shrewsbury, vintner | Casco Bay |
| Mrs. Joan Cleeves | | |
| Elizabeth Cleeves | | |
| | | |
| THOMAS LEWIS | of Shrewsbury, vintner | Saco |
| Mrs. Elizabeth Lewis | | |
| Thomas Lewis | | |
| Mary Lewis | | |
| Judith Lewis | | |
| Elizabeth Lewis | | |

### 1631

LYON, William Peirce, Master, sailed from Bristol December 1, 1630, and arrived February 5, with 'about twenty passengers and two hundred tons of goods.'[4]

Rev. ROGER WILLIAMS.

---

[1] Winthrop: *Journal*, I, 51.   [2] Bradford, II, 99.
[3] P.R.O. High Court of Admiralty Examinations, vol. 49.
[4] Winthrop: *Journal*, I, 57.

| | | |
|---|---|---|
| *Rev.* ROGER WILLIAMS | | Salem |
| Mrs. Mary Williams | | |
| JOHN THROCKMORTON | | Salem |
| Mrs. Rebecca Throckmorton | | |
| John Throckmorton | | |
| Patience Throckmorton | | |
| JOHN PERKINS | of Hilmorton, Warwick | Boston |
| Mrs. Judith Perkins | | |
| John Perkins | | |
| Elizabeth Perkins | | |
| Mary Perkins | | |
| Thomas Perkins | | |
| Jacob Perkins | | |
| EDMOND ONGE | of Lavenham, Suffolk | Watertown |
| Mrs. Frances Onge | | |
| Simon Onge | | |
| Jacob Onge | | |
| WILLIAM PARKE | | Roxbury |

WHITE ANGEL, sailed from Bristol for Saco, Maine, and arrived in July 'with cattle and provisions for the Bay and Plymouth.' [1]

| | |
|---|---|
| ISAAC ALLERTON | (returning from England) |
| ...... SOUTHCOTT | (returning from England) |

FRIENDSHIP. She sailed from Barnstaple in May and arrived July 14 at Boston. [2]

PLOUGH OF WOOLWICH,

[1] Winthrop: *Journal*, I, 65.   [2] Bradford, II, 174.

PLOUGH OF WOOLWICH, sixty tons, Captain......
Graves, Master. She sailed from London and arrived July
6 at Nantasket. She brought the 'Company of Husband-
men,' destined for the Province of Maine, having a patent of
forty square miles about Casco Bay and the Kennebec River.
They were dissatisfied with the country and removed to
Massachusetts.[1] She brought ten passengers.

LYON, William Peirce, Master. She left London about
August 23 and arrived at Nantasket November 2, bringing
'in all about sixty persons.'[2] The following named are known
to have come in her:

| | | |
|---|---|---|
| Mrs. Margaret Winthrop (wife of the Governor) | | Boston |
| Adam Winthrop | | |
| Anne Winthrop | | |
| JOHN WINTHROP, JR. | of Groton, Suffolk | Boston |
| *Rev.* JOHN ELLIOT | of Nazing, Essex | Roxbury |
| PHILIP ELLIOT | of Nazing, Essex | Roxbury |
| RICHARD LYMAN | of High Ongar, Essex | Roxbury |
| Mrs. Sarah Lyman | | |
| Phyllis Lyman | | |
| Richard Lyman, Jr. | | |
| Sarah Lyman | | |
| John Lyman | | |
| Robert Lyman | | |
| SAMUEL WAKEMAN | | Roxbury |
| Mrs. Elizabeth Wakeman | | |

It

[1] V. C. Sanborn, in *Genealogist*, XIX, 270.
[2] Winthrop: *Journal*, I, 70.

It is thought that the following emigrants came in this ship as they appeared in Cambridge shortly after:

| | | |
|---|---|---|
| JOHN STEELE | of Fairstead, county Essex | Cambridge |
| Mrs. Rachel Steele | | |
| Samuel Steele | | |
| John Steele | | |
| Hannah Steele | | |
| GEORGE STEELE | of Fairstead, county Essex | Cambridge |
| Mrs. Margery Steele | | |
| Margery Steele | | |
| Joan Steele | | |
| Mary Steele | | |
| James Steele | | |
| ANDREW WARNER | of county Essex | Cambridge |
| Mrs. ...... Warner | | |
| Mary Warner | | |
| Andrew Warner | | |
| STEPHEN HART | | Cambridge |
| NICHOLAS CLARK | perhaps of Nazing, county Essex | Cambridge |

## 1632

WHALE, Captain...... Graves, Master. She sailed from Southampton April 8 and arrived May 26, with 'about thirty passengers, all in health.'[1]

| | | |
|---|---|---|
| *Rev.* JOHN WILSON | (returning) | Boston |
| JOHN SMITH | | |
| Mrs. Anne Smith | | |
| ...... Smith | | |
| | | ANTHONY JUPE |

[1] Winthrop: *Journal*, 1, 80.

| ANTHONY JUPE | of London | |
| NATHANIEL MERRIMAN | of London | Wallingford, Connecticut |
| RICHARD DUMMER | of Bishopstoke, Southants | Roxbury |
| NATHANIEL HARRIS | | |
| JOHN SMYTH | | |

WILLIAM AND FRANCIS, Captain...... Thomas, Master.
She left London March 9 and arrived June 5, 'with about
sixty passengers.' [1]

| *Rev.* THOMAS WELD | of Terling, county Essex | Roxbury |
| Mrs. Margaret Weld | | |
| John Weld | | |
| Thomas Weld | | |
| Samuel Weld | | |
| Edmund Weld | | |
| *Rev.* STEPHEN BACHILER | of Newton Stacy, county Hants | Saugus |
| Mrs. Helen Bachiler | | |
| John Sanborn | | |
| William Sanborn | | |
| Stephen Sanborn | | |
| THOMAS PAINE | | |
| THOMAS WOODFORD | | Roxbury |
| THOMAS THOMAS | | Springfield |
| EDWARD WINSLOW | (returning from England) | Plymouth |
| JOHN SMALLEY | | Plymouth |
| JOHN WHETSTONE | | Scituate |
| WILLIAM HILL | | |

[1] Winthrop: *Journal*, I, 80–81; *Gen. Reg.*, XII, 274.

| | | |
|---|---|---|
| WILLIAM HILL | of Upminster, county Essex | Roxbury |
| *Rev.* WILLIAM PERKINS | of London | Roxbury |
| WALTER HARRIS | of London | Plymouth |
| JOSEPH MANNERING | | |
| JOHN LEVIN | | |
| THOMAS OLIVER | | Boston |
| Mrs. Anne Oliver | | |
| John Oliver | | |
| James Oliver | | |
| Peter Oliver | | |
| . . . . . . Oliver | | |
| . . . . . . Oliver | | |
| THOMAS HAYWARD | | |
| JOHN HART | | |
| WILLIAM NORTON | | |
| ROBERT GAMLIN | probably from Kent | Roxbury |
| Mary Gamlin | | |
| ROBERT GAMLIN, JR. | | |
| Mrs. Elizabeth Gamlin | | |
| John Mayo | | |
| CHRISTOPHER HUSSEY | of Dorking, county Surrey | Saugus and Hampton, New Hampshire |
| Mrs. Theodate Hussey | | |
| Stephen Hussey | | |
| Mrs. Mary Hussey | mother | |

CHARLES. Sailed from Barnstaple April 10 and arrived June 5 at Boston, 'with about twenty passengers, all safe and

and in health.' [1] The only passenger whose name has been preserved is

| | | |
|---|---|---|
| TIMOTHY HATHERLY | of Barnstaple, county Devon | Plymouth |

The following emigrants probably came in this ship, as they came this year:

| | | |
|---|---|---|
| MATTHEW ALLYN | of Braunton, county Devon | Cambridge |
| Mrs. Margaret Allyn | | |
| Mary Allyn | | |
| John Allyn | | |

JAMES, Captain...... Grant, Master. Sailed from London about the first week in April, and arrived at Boston June 5. She 'brought twelve passengers.' [2]

JOHN BANCROFT
Mrs. Jane Bancroft

HUGH MOSIER                                    Casco Bay, Maine

HENRY SHERBORNE                    Portsmouth, New Hampshire
Sarah Jones

JOHN GREENE                                          Charlestown
Mrs. Perseverance Greene of Amsterdam
John Greene
Jacob Greene
Abigail Greene
Joseph Greene

LYON,

[1] Winthrop: *Journal*, I, 81.      [2] *Ibid.*

LYON, William Peirce, Master, sailed from London June 22 and arrived September 16 at Boston. 'He brought one hundred and twenty three passengers, whereof fifty children, all in health. They had been twelve weeks aboard and eight weeks from Land's End.' [1]

| | | |
|---|---|---|
| WILLIAM WADSWORTH | of Braintree, county Essex | Cambridge |
| Mrs. ...... Wadsworth | | |
| Sarah Wadsworth | | |
| William Wadsworth | | |
| Mary Wadsworth | | |
| John Wadsworth | | |
| | | |
| JOHN TALCOTT | of Braintree, county Essex | Cambridge |
| Mrs. Dorothy Talcott | | |
| John Talcott | | |
| Mary Talcott | | |
| | | |
| JOSEPH ROBERTS | | |
| | | |
| JOHN COGSWELL | of Halstead, county Essex | Roxbury |
| Mrs. Mary Cogswell | | |
| | | |
| ROBERT SHELLEY | | Roxbury |
| Mrs. Anne Shelley | | |
| | | |
| JOHN WATSON | | Roxbury |
| | | |
| WILLIAM HEATH | | Roxbury |
| Mrs. Mary Heath | | |
| Isaac Heath | | |
| Mary Heath | | |
| Anna Heath | | |
| | | |
| RICHARD ALLIS | | |
| | | |
| THOMAS UFFORD | of Newbourne, county Suffolk | Springfield |
| Mrs. Isabel Ufford | | |
| | | John Ufford |

[1] Winthrop: *Journal,* I, 92.

John Ufford
Isabel Ufford

ISAAC MORRILL                of Hatfield Broadoak, Essex   Roxbury
   Mrs. ...... Morrill
   Sarah Morrill
   Katherine Morrill

JOHN WITCHFIELD              of London                     Dorchester
   Mrs. ...... Witchfield

JONATHAN WADE                of Northampton                Charlestown
   Mrs. Susanna Wade

ROBERT BARTLETT

JOHN WHIPPLE                 of Bocking, Essex             Dorchester

JOHN BROWNE                                                Plymouth
   Mrs. Dorothy Browne
   Mary Browne
   John Browne
   James Browne
   William Browne

JOHN CHURCHMAN

THOMAS WILLETT               of Yarmouth, Norfolk          Plymouth

JOHN TOTMAN                                                Roxbury

NATHANIEL RICHARDS                                         Cambridge
   Mrs. ...... Richards

WILLIAM CURTIS               of Nazing, county             Roxbury
                    Essex

   Mrs. Sarah Curtis
   Thomas Curtis
   Mary Curtis
   John Curtis
   Philip Curtis

NICHOLAS CLARK                                             Cambridge
                                      DANIEL BREWER

| | | |
|---|---|---|
| DANIEL BREWER | | Roxbury |
| Mrs. Joanna Brewer | | |
| Daniel Brewer | | |
| Anne Brewer | | |
| Joanna Brewer | | |
| JOHN BREWER | of county Sussex | Cambridge |
| JOHN BENJAMIN | of Heathfield Sussex | |
| Mrs. Abigail Benjamin | | |
| WILLIAM JAMES | | |
| EDWARD CARRINGTON | | Charlestown |
| WILLIAM GOODWIN | of Bocking, county Essex | Cambridge |
| Mrs. ...... Goodwin | | |
| Elizabeth Goodwin | | |
| OZIAS GOODWIN | of Bocking, county Essex | Cambridge |
| Mrs. ...... Goodwin | | |
| William Goodwin | | |
| JOHN WHITE | | Cambridge |
| Mrs. Mary White | | |
| Nathaniel White | | |
| Mary White | | |
| JAMES OLMSTEAD | of Fairstead, county Essex | Cambridge |
| Mrs. Joyce Olmstead | | |
| Nehemiah Olmstead | | |
| Nicholas Olmstead | | |
| Richard Olmstead | | |
| John Olmstead | | |
| Rebecca Olmstead | | |
| SETH GRANT | | |
| WILLIAM LEWIS | | Cambridge |
| Mrs. Felix Lewis | | |
| William Lewis | | |
| EDWARD ELMORE | perhaps from London | Cambridge |
| | Mrs. ...... Elmore | |

Mrs. ...... Elmore
Richard Elmore
Edward Elmore

EDWARD HOLMAN            of Clapham, county Surrey    Plymouth

CHARLES  GLOVER                                        Salem


## 1633

WILLIAM, William Trevor, Master, 'arrived at Plymouth with some passengers and goods for the Massachusetts Bay.' [1]

TIMOTHY  HATHERLY        (returning)                Scituate


......, John Corbin, Master. Arrived at Piscataqua 'with passengers.' [2]


WILLIAM AND JANE, William Burdock, Master. She came from London in April and arrived in Boston 'in six weeks and brought thirty passengers.' [3]


ELIZABETH BONAVENTURE, John Graves, Master, left Yarmouth, Norfolk, the first week in May and arrived at Boston on June 15, 'with ninety five passengers.' [4] The
following

[1] Winthrop: *Journal*, 1, 99; *Documentary History of New York*, 1, 73, 93.
[2] 3 M.H.S. Coll., IX, 262.
[3] Winthrop: *Journal*, 1, 100.        [4] *Ibid.*, 1, 102.

following emigrants from Hingham, Norfolk, who arrived this year probably came in this ship:

| | | |
|---|---|---|
| EDMOND HOBART | of Hingham, county Norfolk | Charlestown |
| Mrs. Margaret Hobart | | |
| Nazareth Hobart | | |
| Edmond Hobart | | |
| Thomas Hobart | | |
| Joshua Hobart | | |
| Rebecca Hobart | | |
| Sarah Hobart | | |
| | | |
| HENRY GIBBS | of Hingham, county Norfolk | Charlestown |
| | | |
| RALPH SMITH | of Hingham, county Norfolk | Charlestown |
| | | |
| NICHOLAS JACOB | of Hingham, county Norfolk | Watertown |
| Mrs. Mary Jacob | | |
| John Jacob | | |
| Mary Jacob | | |
| | | |
| THOMAS CHUBBOCK | of Hardingham, county Norfolk | Charlestown |
| Mrs. Alice Chubbock | | |
| Sarah Chubbock | | |
| Rebecca Chubbock | | |
| | | |
| Mrs. Elishua Crowe | | Charlestown |
| | | |
| SIMON HUNTINGTON | of Norwich, county Norfolk | Roxbury |
| Mrs. Margaret Huntington | | |
| Christopher Huntington | | |
| Anne Huntington | | |
| Simon Huntington | | |
| Thomas Huntington | | |

......, arrived

......, arrived at Boston July 24, after a voyage of twelve weeks from Weymouth, England, 'with about eighty passengers who sate down at Dorchester.' [1] The only passenger positively known is:

| | | |
|---|---|---|
| GEORGE WAY | of Dorchester, Dorset | Dorchester |

The following named persons probably came in this ship, as they were granted lots in Dorchester immediately after its arrival:

| | | |
|---|---|---|
| JOHN COGAN | of Saint Petrock, Exeter, Devon | Dorchester |
| Mrs. Abigail Cogan<br>Abigail Cogan | | |
| JOHN HILL | of Lyme Regis, Dorset | Dorchester |
| ELIAS PARKMAN | of Sidmouth, Devon | Dorchester |
| JOHN ROCKETT | of Dorsetshire | Dorchester |
| RICHARD ROCKETT | of Dorsetshire | Dorchester |
| PHILIP RANDALL<br>Mrs. Joan Randall<br>Philip Randall<br>Philura Randall | of Allington, Dorset | Windsor |
| AQUILA PURCHASE<br>Mrs. Anne Purchase<br>Oliver Purchase<br>Sarah Purchase | of Dorchester, Dorset | Dorchester |
| WILLIAM HORSFORD | | |

WELCOME. She probably sailed from Plymouth, Devon, in January

[1] Winthrop: *Journal*, 1, 103; comp. Banks MSS.

January of this year and arrived at Richmond Island, Maine, with the Trelawny colony to begin a settlement there.

JOHN WINTER
   Mrs. ...... Winter
   Sarah Winter


MARY AND JANE, ...... Rose, Master. 'She came from London in seven weeks and brought one hundred and ninety six passengers.'[1] A number came from Kent.

WILLIAM CODDINGTON
   Mrs. Mary Coddington


GRIFFIN. This ship of 300 tons arrived September 4, 'Having been eight weeks from the Downs. She brought about two hundred passengers.'[2]

| | | |
|---|---|---|
| *Rev.* JOHN COTTON | of Boston, Lincolnshire | Boston |
|    Mrs. Sarah Cotton | | |
| *Rev.* THOMAS HOOKER | of Tilton, county Leicester | Cambridge |
|    Mrs. Susanna Hooker | | |
|    John Hooker | | |
|    Samuel Hooker | | |
|    Sarah Hooker | | |
|    Joanna Hooker | | |
|    Mary Hooker | | |
| WILLIAM PEIRCE | | |
| ATHERTON HOUGH | of Boston, Lincolnshire | Boston |
|    Mrs. Elizabeth Hough | | |
|    Samuel Hough | | |
| | | JOHN HAYNES |

[1] Winthrop: *Journal*, I, 100.    [2] *Ibid.*, I, 105–06.

| | | |
|---|---|---|
| JOHN HAYNES | of Copford Hall, Essex | Cambridge |
| THEOPHILUS CUSHING | of Hingham, county Norfolk | |
| *Rev.* SAMUEL STONE <br> Mrs....... Stone <br> Rebecca Stone <br> Mary Stone <br> Sarah Stone | of Hertford, county Herts | Cambridge |
| JOSEPH MYGATT <br><br> Mrs. Anne Mygatt <br> (John Colt) | of Roxwell, county <br> Essex (?) | Watertown |
| THOMAS LEVERETT <br> Mrs. Anne Leverett <br> John Leverett <br> Jane Leverett <br> Anne Leverett | of Boston, Lincolnshire | Boston |
| EDMUND QUINCY <br><br> Mrs. Judith Quincy <br> Edmund Quincy | of Wigsthorpe, county <br> Northants | Boston |

BIRD, ...... Yates, Master, arrived at Boston September 4, having been 'twelve weeks at sea, being at her first coming out driven Northerly to fifty three.' [1]

JAMES, ...... Grant, Master, arrived at Salem October 10, 'having been but eight weeks between Gravesend and Salem. She brought about thirty for Virginia and about twenty for this place.' [2]

*Rev.* WILLIAM LEVERIDGE

[1] Winthrop: *Journal*, I, 107.  [2] *Ibid.*, I, 111.

| | | |
|---|---|---|
| *Rev.* WILLIAM LEVERIDGE | of Drawlington, county Warwick | Dover, New Hampshire |
| THOMAS WIGGIN | (returning to New England) | Dover, New Hampshire |

Mrs. Katherine Wiggin
Thomas Wiggin, Jr.
Mary Wiggin


. . . . . . ., . . . . . . two ships, names unknown, 'making ready' at Barnstaple, Devon, in April, were reported in the late fall as ready 'to bring passengers & catell for to plant in the bay.'[1]


JONAS of London, John Crowther, Master, of three hundred and forty tons. She was chartered March 4 for a voyage to 'Charlestowne or Boston Towne,' but it is not known when she arrived or whether she brought passengers.


## 1634

HERCULES, John Kiddey, Master. She left London March 24, and Southampton, April 18, with twelve passengers.[2]

| | | |
|---|---|---|
| JOHN ANTHONY | of Hampstead, Middlesex | Portsmouth, Rhode Island |

NATHANIEL DAVIS

ROBERT EARLY

WILLIAM ELLIOT

WILLIAM FIFIELD

[1] 3 M.H.S. Coll., IX, 262.
[2] Winthrop: *Journal*, I, 127; Records of the Privy Council.

| | | |
|---|---|---|
| WILLIAM FIFIELD | | Hampton, New Hampshire |
| THOMAS FOSTER | of Ipswich, county Suffolk | Boston |
| WILLIAM FOSTER | of Ipswich, county Suffolk | Ipswich |
| MATTHEW HEWLETT | | |
| GEORGE KING | | |
| WILLIAM LATCOME | | |
| HENRY PHELPS | | Salem |
| THOMAS RIDER | | Weymouth |

CLEMENT AND JOB
REFORMATION
TRUE LOVE
ELIZABETH BONAVENTURE
SEA FLOWER
PLANTER
NEPTUNE

These ships 'bound for New England & now lying in the River of Thames,' were held by order of the Privy Council on February 22, 'untill further order.' On February 28 they were released under bond of £100 to conform to certain 'articles.' It is probable that most of them came into Boston during the week of May 12–17 'with store of passengers and cattle.' [1] Winthrop said they had enjoyed a 'short passage.' Of the 'store' of passengers less than a score is known.

| | | |
|---|---|---|
| SAMUEL GREENHILL | of Staplehurst, county Kent | Hartford |
| Mrs. ...... Greenhill | | |
| Rebecca Greenhill | | |
| | | SIMON WILLARD |

[1] Winthrop: *Journal*, I, 125.

| | | |
|---|---|---|
| SIMON WILLARD | of Horsmonden, county Kent | Cambridge |
| Mrs. Mary Willard | | |
| Mary Willard | | |
| TIMOTHY STANLEY | of Ashford, county Kent | Cambridge |
| Mrs. Elizabeth Stanley | | |
| Timothy Stanley | | |
| THOMAS STANLEY | of Ashford, county Kent | Cambridge |
| JOHN STANLEY | of Ashford, county Kent | Cambridge |
| Mrs. ...... Stanley | | |
| John Stanley | | |
| ...... Stanley | | |
| Ruth Stanley | | |
| WILLIAM PANTRY | of Staplehurst, county Kent | Cambridge |
| Mrs. Hannah Pantry | | |
| John Pantry | | |

......, a ship, name unknown, arrived at Pemaquid, Maine, the latter part of April, 'which brought thirty passengers for this place.'[1]

'In June of this year there arrived here fourteen great ships and one at Salem.'[2] These included some of those detained by the Privy Council as previously noted. In one of these ships came:

| | | |
|---|---|---|
| JOHN HUMPHREY, *Esq.* 37 | of Chaldon, Dorset, gent. | Salem |
| Lady Susan Humphrey | | |
| Sarah Humphrey | | |
| | | John Humphrey |

[1] Winthrop: *Journal*, I, 123.     [2] *Ibid.*, I, 127.

John Humphrey
Dorcas Humphrey
Ann Humphrey


MARY AND JOHN, Robert Sayres, Master, sailed from Southampton March 24, 1633/4, but the time of her arrival is not recorded.[1]

WILLIAM TRACEY

JOHN MARSH

JOHN LUFF

HENRY TRASK

| | | |
|---|---|---|
| WILLIAM MOODY | | Ipswich |
| Mrs. Sarah Moody | | |
| Joshua Moody | | |
| ROBERT SEAVER | | Roxbury |
| THOMAS AVERY | | Salem |
| HENRY TRAVERS | | Newbury |
| THOMAS SWEET | | |
| *Rev.* JOHN WOODBRIDGE | of Stanton, county Wilts | Ipswich |
| THOMAS WEST | | |
| THOMAS SAVERY | of Highworth, county Wilts | Plymouth |
| WILLIAM SAVERY | of Highworth, county Wilts | Plymouth |
| CHRISTOPHER OSGOOD | of Marlborough, county Wilts | Ipswich |
| Mrs. Margery Osgood | | |
| | | JOSEPH MILES |

[1] Drake: *Founders of New England*, 70–71.

| | | |
|---|---|---|
| JOSEPH MILES | | Salem |
| WILLIAM NEWBY | | |
| ROBERT NEWMAN | | |
| THOMAS NEWMAN | | Ipswich |
| Mrs. ...... Newman | | |
| John Newman | | |
| WILLIAM CLARKE | | |
| NICHOLAS EASTON | | Ipswich |
| Mrs. ...... Easton | | |
| RICHARD KENT | | Ipswich |
| Mrs. Jane Kent | | |
| Mary Kent | | |
| Richard Kent | | |
| WILLIAM BALLARD | | Salem |
| ABRAHAM MUSSEY | | |
| JOHN MUSSEY | | |
| WILLIAM FRANKLIN | | Newbury |
| MATTHEW GILLETT | | Salem |
| THOMAS COLE | | Salem |
| Mrs. Anna Cole | | |
| *Rev.* THOMAS PARKER | | Newbury |
| JOHN SPENCER | | Ipswich |
| WILLIAM SPENCER | | |
| HENRY SHORT | | Ipswich |
| WILLIAM HIBBENS | of Boston, county Lincoln | Boston |
| Mrs. Anne Hibbens | | |
| HENRY LUNT | | Newbury |
| JOSEPH POPE | | Salem |
| | | PHILIP FOWLER |

| | | |
|---|---|---|
| PHILIP FOWLER | of Marlborough, county Wilts | Ipswich |

Mrs. Mary Fowler
Mary Fowler
Samuel Fowler
Hester Fowler
Joseph Fowler
Thomas Fowler

| | |
|---|---|
| RICHARD JACOB | Ipswich |
| DANIEL LADD | Salisbury |
| ROBERT KINGMAN | Ipswich |
| JOHN BARTLETT | |
| ROBERT COKER | Newbury |
| STEPHEN JORDAN | Salisbury |
| JOHN GODFREY | |

| | | |
|---|---|---|
| *Rev.* JAMES NOYES | of Cholderton, county Wilts | Newbury |

Mrs. Sarah Noyes
Nicholas Noyes

| | |
|---|---|
| RICHARD BROWNE | Ipswich |

Mrs. Edith Browne
George Browne

| | |
|---|---|
| RICHARD LITTLEHALE | Newbury |
| RICHARD REYNOLDS | |
| WILLIAM WHITE | |

| | | |
|---|---|---|
| JOHN WHEELER | of Salisbury, county Wilts | Salisbury |

Mrs. Anne Wheeler
David Wheeler
Anne Wheeler
Roger Wheeler

Elizabeth Wheeler

Elizabeth Wheeler
Mercy Wheeler
ADRIAN VINCENT

GRIFFIN. This ship arrived at Boston September (18), with about one hundred passengers and cattle for the plantations.[1]

| | | |
|---|---|---|
| *Rev.* JOHN LOTHROP | from London | Scituate |
| Mrs. ...... Lothrop | | |
| Thomas Lothrop | | |
| Samuel Lothrop | | |
| Joseph Lothrop | | |
| John Lothrop | | |
| Benjamin Lothrop | | |
| Jane Lothrop | | |
| Barbara Lothrop | | |
| WILLIAM HUTCHINSON | of Alford, county Lincoln | Boston |
| Mrs. Anne Hutchinson | | |
| Edward Hutchinson | | |
| Faith Hutchinson | | |
| Bridget Hutchinson | | |
| William Hutchinson | | |
| Samuel Hutchinson | | |
| Anne Hutchinson | | |
| Mary Hutchinson | | |
| Susanna Hutchinson | | |
| *Rev.* ZACHARIAH SYMMES | of Canterbury, county Kent | Charlestown |
| Mrs. Sarah Symmes | | |
| William Symmes | | |
| Mary Symmes | | |
| Elizabeth Symmes | | |
| Huldah Symmes | | |
| Hannah Symmes | | |
| Rebecca Symmes | | |

WILLIAM BARTHOLOMEW

[1] Winthrop: *Journal*, I, 134.

| | | |
|---|---|---|
| WILLIAM BARTHOLOMEW<br>Mrs. Mary Bartholomew | | Ipswich |
| NATHANIEL HEATON<br>Mrs. Elizabeth Heaton<br>Samuel Heaton<br>Jabez Heaton<br>Leah Heaton<br>Mary Heaton | of Alford, county Lincoln | Boston |
| THOMAS LYNDE<br><br>Mrs. Margaret Lynde<br>Thomas Lynde<br>Henry Lynde | of Dunstable, county<br>Bedford | Charlestown |
| WILLIAM HAINES | of Dunstable, county<br>Bedford | Salem |
| RICHARD HAINES | of Dunstable, county<br>Bedford | Salem |

HERCULES of Sandwich, John Witherley, Master, sailed in the spring of this year, and is probably the *Hercules* 'of Dover' mentioned by Winthrop as being here in the summer.'[1]

| | | |
|---|---|---|
| NATHANIEL TILDEN<br>Mrs. Lydia Tilden<br>Joseph Tilden<br>Mary Tilden<br>Sarah Tilden<br>Judith Tilden<br>Lydia Tilden<br>Stephen Tilden<br>Thomas Tilden<br>Thomas Lapham<br>George Sutton | of Tenterden | Scituate |

Edward Ford

[1] *Journal*, I, 127; comp. Gen. Reg. LXXV, 217 and LXXIX, 107.

Edward Ford
Edward Jenkins
James Bennett
Sarah Couchman
Mary Perien

JONAS AUSTIN                   of Tenterden            Cambridge
  Mrs. Constance Austin
  Jonas Austin
  Mary Austin
  Lydia Robinson

ROBERT BROOKE                  of Maidstone, mercer     Marblehead
  Mrs. Anne Brooke
  Thomas Brooke
  John Brooke
  Samuel Brooke
  Elizabeth Brooke
  Dorothy Brooke
  Abraham Gallant
  James Gallant

THOMAS HEYWOOD                 of Aylesford, tailor      Cambridge
  Mrs. Susan Heyward
  Thomas Heyward
  John Heyward
  Elizabeth Heyward
  Susan Heyward
  Martha Heyward

WILLIAM WITHERELL              of Maidstone, school-    Charlestown
                                 master
  Mrs. Mary Witherell
  Samuel Witherell
  Daniel Witherell
  Thomas Witherell
  Anne Richards

FAINTNOT WINES                 of Ashford, hemp-        Charlestown
                                 dresser

THOMAS BONNEY                  of Sandwich, shoemaker   Charlestown
                                                        HENRY EWELL

| | | |
|---|---|---|
| HENRY EWELL | of Sandwich, shoemaker | Scituate |
| WILLIAM HATCH<br>Mrs. Jane Hatch<br>Walter Hatch<br>John Hatch<br>William Hatch<br>Anne Hatch<br>Jane Hatch<br>William Holmes<br>Joseph Ketcherell<br>Robert Jennings<br>Simon Sutton<br>Lydia Wells | of Sandwich, merchant | Sandwich |
| SAMUEL HINCKLEY<br>Mrs. Sarah Hinckley<br>Elizabeth Hincle, a kinswoman | of Tenterden | Scituate |
| ISAAC COLE<br>Mrs. Joan Cole<br>Isaac Cole<br>Jane Cole<br>Rose Tritton | of Sandwich, carpenter<br><br><br><br>of Ashford | Charlestown |
| THOMAS CHAMPION | of Ashford | |
| THOMAS BESBEECH<br>Mary Besbeech<br>Alice Besbeech<br>Elizabeth Iggleden<br>Jane Iggleden<br>Sarah Iggleden<br>John Iggleden<br>Thomas Nealwy<br>Joseph Pacheing (Patchen)<br>Agnes Love | of Sandwich | Cambridge |
| JOHN LEWIS<br>Mrs. Sarah Lewis | of Tenterden | Scituate |
| PARNELL HARRIS | of Bow, London | |
| | | JAMES SAYERS |

| | | |
|---|---|---|
| JAMES SAYERS | of Northbourne, tailor | |
| COMFORT STARR<br>Thomas Starr<br>Comfort Starr<br>Mary Starr<br>'Truth-shall-prevail Starr<br>Samuel Dunkin<br>John Turvey | of Ashford, chirurgeon | Cambridge |
| JOSIAH ROOTES | of Great Chart, county<br>Kent | Salem |
| EMMA MASON | of Eastwell, widow | Salem |
| Mrs. Margaret Jones | of Sandwich (wife of Thomas<br>of Cambridge) | |
| JOHN BEST | of St. George's Canter-<br>bury, tailor | Salem |
| THOMAS BRIGDEN<br>Mrs. Thomasine Brigden<br>Thomas Brigden<br>Mary Brigden | of Faversham, hus-<br>bandman | Charlestown |

ELIZABETH, of Ipswich, William Andrews, Master. She sailed from Ipswich 'bound for New England the last of April, 1634,' and arrived in July at Boston.[1]

| | | |
|---|---|---|
| EDMOND LEWIS | 33 | Watertown |
| Mrs. Mary Lewis | 32 | |
| John Lewis | 3 | |
| Thomas Lewis | ¾ | |
| RICHARD WOODWARD | 45 miller | Watertown |
| Mrs. Rose Wood-<br>ward | 50 | |
| | | George Woodward |

[1] Public Record Office MSS.

| | | | |
|---|---|---|---|
| George Woodward | 13 | | |
| John Woodward | 13 | | |
| JOHN SPRING | 45 | | Watertown |
| Mrs. Elinor Spring | 46 | | |
| Mary Spring | 11 | | |
| Henry Spring | 6 | | |
| John Spring | 4 | | |
| William Spring | ¾ | | |
| THURSTON RAYNER | 40 | of Elmsett, county Suffolk | Watertown |
| Mrs. Elizabeth Rayner | 36 | | |
| Thurston Rayner | 13 | | |
| Joseph Rayner | 11 | | |
| Edward Rayner | 10 | | |
| Elizabeth Rayner | 9 | | |
| Sarah Rayner | 7 | | |
| Lydia Rayner | 1 | | |
| RICHARD KIMBALL | 39 | of Rattlesden, county Suffolk | Watertown |
| Mrs. Ursula Kimball | ( ) | | |
| Henry Kimball | 15 | | |
| Elizabeth Kimball | 13 | | |
| Richard Kimball | 11 | | |
| Mary Kimball | 9 | | |
| Martha Kimball | 5 | | |
| John Kimball | 3 | | |
| Thomas Kimball | 1 | | |
| HENRY KIMBALL | 44 | of Rattlesden, county Suffolk | Watertown |
| Mrs. Susan Kimball | 35 | | |
| Elizabeth Kimball | 4 | | |
| Susan Kimball | 1½ | | |
| THOMAS SCOTT | 40 | of Rattlesden, county Suffolk | Cambridge |
| Mrs. Elizabeth Scott | | | |

Mrs. Elizabeth Scott 40
Elizabeth Scott 9
Abigail Scott 7
Thomas Scott 6

Mrs. Martha Scott 60

| | | | |
|---|---|---|---|
| ISAAC MIXER | 31 | of Capel Saint Mary, county Suffolk | Watertown |
| Mrs. Sarah Mixer | 33 | | |
| Isaac Mixer | 4 | | |
| GEORGE MUNNINGS | 37 | of Rattlesden, county Suffolk | Watertown |
| Mrs. Elizabeth Munnings | 41 | | |
| Elizabeth Munnings | 12 | | |
| Abigail Munnings | 7 | | |
| JOHN BARNARD | 30 | of Dedham, county Essex (?) | Watertown |
| Mrs. Phebe Barnard | 27 | | |
| John Barnard | 2 | | |
| Samuel Barnard | 1 | | |
| Thomas King | 15 | | |
| THOMAS KILBOURNE | 24 | of Wood Ditton, county Cambridge | Wethersfield |
| Mrs. Elizabeth Kilbourne | 20 | | |
| JOHN CROSS | 50 | | Ipswich |
| Mrs. Anne Cross | 38 | | |
| HUMPHREY BRADSTREET | 40 | of Capel Saint Mary, county Suffolk | Ipswich |
| Mrs. Elizabeth Bradstreet | 30 | | |
| Anna Bradstreet | 9 | | |
| John Bradstreet | 3 | | |
| | | | Martha Bradstreet |

| | | | |
|---|---|---|---|
| Martha Bradstreet | 2 | | |
| Mary Bradstreet | 1 | | |
| WILLIAM BLOOMFIELD | 30 | | Cambridge |
| Mrs. Sarah Bloom- | | | |
| field | 25 | | |
| Sarah Bloomfield | 1 | | |
| SAMUEL SMITH | 32 | | Wethersfield |
| Mrs. Elizabeth Smith | 32 | | |
| Samuel Smith | 9 | | |
| Elizabeth Smith | 7 | | |
| Mary Smith | 4 | | |
| Philip Smith | 1 | | |
| ROBERT DAY | 30 | | Ipswich |
| Mrs. Mary Day | 28 | | |
| THOMAS HASTINGS | 29 | | Watertown |
| Mrs. Susan | | | |
| Hastings | 34 | | |
| MARTIN UNDERWOOD | 38 | of Elmham, county Suffolk | Watertown |
| Mrs. Martha Under- | | | |
| wood | 31 | | |
| ROBERT GOODALE | 30 | of Dennington, county Suffolk (?) | Salem |
| Mrs. Katherine | | | |
| Goodale | 28 | | |
| Mary Goodale | 4 | | |
| Abraham Goodale | 2 | | |
| Isaac Goodale | ½ | | |
| HENRY GOLDSTONE | 43 | | Watertown |
| Mrs. Anne Gold- | | | |
| stone | 45 | | |
| Anne Goldstone | 18 | | |
| Mary Goldstone | 15 | | |
| WILLIAM CUTTING | 26 | | |
| Richard Cutting | 11 | | |
| | | | ROBERT SHERIN |

| | | | |
|---|---|---|---|
| ROBERT SHERIN | 32 | | |
| HENRY GLOVER | 24 | | Dedham |
| JOHN PALMER | 24 | | |
| DANIEL PIERCE | 23 | | Newbury |
| JOHN CLARKE | 22 | | |
| JOHN FIRMIN | 40 | | Watertown |
| John Laverick | 15 | | |
| Sarah Reynolds | 20 | | |
| Susan Munson | 25 | | |
| Rebecca Isaac | 36 | | |
| Anne Dorifall | 24 | | |
| John Sherman | 20 | | |
| JOSEPH MOSSE | 24 | | |

FRANCIS of Ipswich, John Cutting, Master, 'bound for New England the last of Aprill, 1634.' She sailed from Ipswich.[1]

| | | | |
|---|---|---|---|
| JOHN BEETTS | 40 | of Claydon, county Oxford | Cambridge |
| WILLIAM HAILTON | 23 | | |
| NICHOLAS JENNINGS | 22 | | |
| WILLIAM WESTWOOD | 28 | | Cambridge |
| Mrs. Bridget Westwood | 32 | | |
| Cleare Draper | 30 | | |
| John Lea | 13 | | |
| ROBERT ROSE | 40 | of Elmswell, county Suffolk | Wethersfield |
| Mrs. Margery Rose | 40 | | |
| John Rose | 15 | | |
| | | | Robert Rose |

[1] Public Record Office MSS.

| | | | |
|---|---|---|---|
| Robert Rose | 15 | | |
| Elizabeth Rose | 13 | | |
| Mary Rose | 11 | | |
| Samuel Rose | 9 | | |
| Sarah Rose | 7 | | |
| Daniel Rose | 3 | | |
| Dorcas Rose | 2 | | |
| JOHN BARNARD | 36 | of Burnham, county Essex (?) | Cambridge |
| Mrs. Mary Barnard | 38 | | |
| Henry Hayward | 7 | | |
| WILLIAM FREEBORN | 40 | | Boston |
| Mrs. Mary Freeborn | 33 | | |
| Mary Freeborn | 7 | | |
| Sarah Freeborn | 2 | | |
| John Albury | 14 | | Portsmouth, Rhode Island |
| ANTHONY WHITE | 27 | | Watertown |
| EDWARD BUGBY | 40 | | Roxbury |
| Mrs. Rebecca Bugby | 32 | | |
| Sarah Bugby | 4 | | |
| ABRAHAM NEWELL | 50 | | Roxbury |
| Mrs. Frances Newell | 40 | | |
| Faith Newell | 14 | | |
| Grace Newell | 13 | | |
| Abraham Newell | 8 | | |
| John Newell | 6 | | |
| Isaac Newell | 2 | | |
| RICHARD HOLDEN | 25 | of Lindsey, county Suffolk | Watertown |
| JUSTINIAN HOLDEN | 23 | of Lindsey, county Suffolk | Watertown |
| ROBERT WING | 60 | of Lawford, county Suffolk | Boston |
| Mrs. Judith Wing | 43 | | |
| JOHN GREENE | 27 | | |
| Dorcas Greene | 15 | | |
| | | | ROBERT PEASE |

| | | | |
|---|---|---|---|
| ROBERT PEASE | 27 | of Great Baddow, county Essex | Salem |
| Robert Pease | 3 | | |
| JOHN PEASE | 27 | of Great Baddow, county Eooex | Salem |
| HUGH MASON | 28 | of Maldon, county Essex | Watertown |
| Mrs. Hester Mason | 22 | | |
| ROWLAND STEBBINS | 40 | of Bocking, county Essex | Springfield |
| Mrs. Sarah Stebbins | 43 | | |
| Thomas Stebbins | 14 | | |
| Sarah Stebbins | 11 | | |
| Elizabeth Stebbins | 6 | | |
| John Stebbins | 8 | | |
| Mary Winch | 15 | | |
| Mrs. Mary Blosse | 40 | of Brandeston, county Suffolk | Watertown |
| Richard Blosse | 11 | | |
| THOMAS SHERWOOD | 48 | | Fairfield |
| Mrs. Alice Sherwood | 47 | | |
| Anna Sherwood | 14 | | |
| Rose Sherwood | 11 | | |
| Thomas Sherwood | 10 | | |
| Rebecca Sherwood | 9 | | |
| JOHN MAPES | 21 | | Southold, Long Island (?) |
| Thomas King | 19 | | |
| ROBERT COE | 38 | of Boxford, county Suffolk | Watertown |
| Mrs. Anna Coe | 43 | | |
| John Coe | 8 | | |
| Robert Coe | 7 | | |
| Benjamin Coe | 5 | | |
| THOMAS BOYDEN | 21 | | Scituate |
| RICHARD WATTLIN | 28 | | |
| | | | JOHN LIVERMORE |

| JOHN LIVERMORE | 28 of Little Thurlow, county Suffolk | Watertown |
| RICHARD PEPYS | 27 of Ashen, county Essex | Boston |
| Mrs. Mary Pepys | 30 of Belchamp Water, county Essex | |
| Mary Pepys | 3½ | |
| Stephen Beckett | 11 | |
| Judith Garnett | 26 | |
| Mrs. Elizabeth Hammond | 47 of Lavenham, county Suffolk | Watertown |
| Elizabeth Hammond | 15 | |
| Sarah Hammond | 10 | |
| John Hammond | 7 | |
| THURSTON CLARKE | 44 of Ipswich, Suffolk | Plymouth |
| Faith Clarke | 15 | |

HOPEWELL of London, Thomas Babb, Master, arrived about November 1.[1]

REGARD of Barnstaple, two hundred tons, arrived November 13 at Boston, 'with twenty passengers and about fifty cattle.' [2]

| JOHN MANSFIELD | of Exeter, Devon | |
| RICHARD FRYE | of Holy Trinity, Exeter | Dorchester |
| GEORGE STRANGE | of Littleham, county Devon | Dorchester |
| Mrs. Wilmot Strange | | |
| George Strange | | |
| Philip Strange | | |
| Emma Strange | | |
| Grace Strange | | |

REBECCA,

REBECCA. This vessel arrived in Boston (date unknown) and left December 18.[1]

...... Another vessel, name unknown, arrived at Boston with about one hundred passengers and cattle for the plantations.[2]

## 1635

...... This unknown vessel left the port of Weymouth in Dorsetshire in March of this year with about twenty families and servants under the leadership of the Reverend Joseph Hull, gathered largely from the parishes of Batcombe and Broadway in Somersetshire. The ship arrived May 5, and practically all of the passengers went to the plantation at Wessaguscus by permission of the General Court which officially changed the name of the settlement to Weymouth in July.[3]

| | | | |
|---|---|---|---|
| (*Rev.*) JOSEPH HULL | 40 | clergyman of Northleigh, Devon | Weymouth, York Maine |
| Mrs. Agnes Hull | 25 | | |
| Joan Hull | 15 | | |
| Joseph Hull | 13 | | |
| Tristram Hull | 11 | | |
| Temperance Hull | 9 | | |
| Elizabeth Hull | 7 | | |
| Griselda Hull | 5 | | |
| Dorothy Hull | 3 | | |
| Judith French | 20 | servant | |
| John Wood | 28 | servant | |

MUSACHIELL BARNARD

[1] Winthrop: *Journal*, I, 142.    [2] *Ibid.*, I, 134.
[3] Mass. Col. Rec., I, 157 and Public Record Office MSS.

| | | | |
|---|---|---|---|
| MUSACHIELL BARNARD | 24 | of Batcombe, clothier | Weymouth |
| Mrs. Mary Barnard | 28 | | |
| John Barnard | 3 | | |
| Nathaniel Barnard | 1 | | |
| Richard Parsons | 30 | servant | |
| | | | |
| FRANCIS BABER | 36 | chandler | Scituate |
| | | | |
| ...... JESSOP | 22 | joiner | |
| | | | |
| WALTER JESSOP | 21 | weaver | |
| | | | |
| TIMOTHY TABOR | 35 | of Batcombe, tailor | |
| Mrs. Jane Tabor | 35 | | |
| Jane Tabor | 10 | | |
| Anne Tabor | 8 | | |
| Sarah Tabor | 5 | | |
| William Fever | 20 | servant | |
| | | | |
| JOHN WHITMARSH | 39 | | |
| Mrs. Alice Whit- | | | |
| marsh | 35 | | |
| John Whitmarsh, Jr. | 11 | | |
| Jane Whitmarsh | 7 | | |
| Joseph Whitmarsh | 5 | | |
| Richard Whitmarsh | 2 | | |
| | | | |
| WILLIAM READ | 28 | of Batcombe, tailor | Weymouth |
| Mrs. Susan Read | 29 | | |
| Hannah Read | 3 | | |
| Susan Read | 1 | | |
| Richard Adams | 29 | servant | |
| Mary Adams | 26 | | |
| Mary Adams | 1 | | |
| | | | |
| ZACHARY BICKNELL | 45 | Barrington, Somerset | Weymouth |
| Mrs. Agnes Bicknell | 27 | | |
| John Bicknell | 11 | | |
| John Kitchen | 23 | servant | |
| | | | |
| GEORGE ALLEN | 24 | [?] perhaps Saltford, Somerset | Weymouth |
| | | Mrs. Katherine Allen | |

| | | | |
|---|---|---|---|
| Mrs. Katherine | | | |
| Allen | 30 | | |
| George Allen | 16 | | |
| William Allen | 8 | | |
| Matthew Allen | 6 | | |
| Edward Poole | 26 | servant | |
| | | | |
| HENRY KINGMAN | 40 | perhaps Frome, Somerset | Weymouth |
| Mrs. Joan Kingman | 39 | | |
| Edward Kingman | 16 | | |
| Jane Kingman | 11 | | |
| Anne Kingman | 9 | | |
| Thomas Kingman | 7 | | |
| John Kingman | 2 | | |
| John Ford | 30 | servant | |
| | | | |
| WILLIAM KING | 30 | | Salem |
| Mrs. Dorothy King | 34 | | |
| Mary King | 12 | | |
| Katherine King | 10 | | |
| William King, Jr. | 8 | | |
| Anna King | 6 | | |
| | | | |
| THOMAS HOLBROOKE | 34 | of Broadway, Somerset | Weymouth |
| Mrs. Jane Hol- | | | |
| brooke | 34 | | |
| John Holbrooke | 11 | | |
| Thomas Hol- | | | |
| brooke, Jr. | 10 | | |
| Anne Holbrooke | 5 | | |
| Elizabeth Holbrooke | 1 | | |
| | | | |
| THOMAS DIBBLE | 22 | husbandman | |
| Frances Dibble | 24 | sister | |
| | | | |
| ROBERT LOVELL | 40 | husbandman | Weymouth |
| Mrs. Elizabeth Lov- | | | |
| ell | 35 | | |
| Zacharias Lovell | 15 | | |
| Anne Lovell | 13 | | |
| John Lovell | 8 | | |
| | | | Ellen Lovell |

| | | | |
|---|---|---|---|
| Ellen Lovell | 1 | twin | |
| James Lovell | 1 | twin | |
| Joseph Kitchen | 16 | servant | |
| Alice Kinham | 22 | | |
| | | | |
| ANGEL HOLLARD | 21 | Netherbury, Dorset | Weymouth |
| Mrs. Katherine Hol- | | | |
| lard | 22 | | |
| George Laud | 22 | servant | |
| Sarah Laud, his | | | |
| kinswoman | 18 | | |
| | | | |
| RICHARD JONES | | of Dinder, Somerset | Dorchester |
| | | | |
| RICHARD MARTYN | 44 | of Batcombe, husbandman | |
| Mrs. Joan Martyn | 44 | | |
| | | | |
| HUMPHREY SHEPHERD | 32 | husbandman | |
| | | | |
| JOHN UPHAM | 35 | husbandman | Weymouth |
| Mrs. Elizabeth Up- | | | |
| ham | 32 | | |
| Nathaniel Upham | 5 | | |
| Elizabeth Upham | 3 | | |
| John Upham | 1 | | |
| Sarah Upham | 26 | | |
| William Grane | 14 | | |
| | | | |
| RICHARD WADE | 60 | of Simsbury, cooper | Dorchester |
| Mrs. Elizabeth | | | |
| Wade | 56 | | |
| Dinah Wade | 22 | | |
| Henry Lush | 17 | servant | |
| Andrew Hallett | 28 | servant | |
| John Hoble | 13 | servant | |
| Robert Huste | 40 | husbandman | |
| John Woodcock | 2() | | |
| Richard Porter | 3() | husbandman | |

CHRISTIAN

CHRISTIAN of London, John White, Master. She sailed from London in March and arrived at Boston in June. Her passengers were 'certified' by the minister of Saint Mildred, Breadstreet, London.[1]

| | | |
|---|---|---|
| THOMAS BASSETT | 37 | Windsor, Connecticut |
| HENRY STILES | 40 of Millbrook, county Bedford | Windsor, Connecticut |
| FRANCIS STILES | 35 of Millbrook, county Bedford | Windsor, Connecticut |
| Mrs. Rachel Stiles | 28 | |
| JOHN STILES | 33 of Millbrook, county Bedford | Windsor, Connecticut |
| Mrs. Joan Stiles | 35 | |
| Henry Stiles | 3 | |
| John Stiles | ¾ | |
| Jane Morden | 30 | |
| Thomas Barber | 21 | |
| JOHN DYER | 28 | Boston (?) |
| JOHN HARRIS | 28 | |
| JAMES HARWOOD | 30 | |
| John Reeves | 19 | Salem |
| THOMAS FOULFOOT | 22 | |
| JAMES BUSKETT | 28 | |
| Thomas Cooper | 18 | Windsor, Connecticut |
| Edward Preston | 13 | New Haven |
| JOHN CRIBB | 30 | |
| George Chappell | 20 | |
| ROBERT ROBINSON | 41 | |
| EDWARD PATTESON | 33 | New Haven |
| FRANCIS MARSHALL | 30 | Boston |
| | | RICHARD HEYLEI |

[1] Public Record Office MSS., and Drake: *Founders*, 14.

| RICHARD HEYLEI | 22 | |
| Thomas Halford | 20 | |
| THOMAS HAWKES-WORTH | 33 | Salisbury |

DESIRE, Edward Boswell, Master. She sailed in June with the following named passengers 'pr Cert. from ij Justices of Peace and minister of all Saintes Northampton.' The date of her arrival is not known.[1]

| WILLIAM HOEMAN | 40 husbandman | |
| Mrs. Winifred Hoeman | 35 | |
| Hannah Hoeman | 8 | |
| Jeremy Hoeman | 6 | |
| Mary Hoeman | 4 | |
| Sarah Hoeman | 2 | |
| Abraham Hoeman | ¼ | |
| Alice Ashby | 20 maidservant | |
| JOHN BROWNE | 27 tailor; certified by minister of Baddow, Essex | Ipswich |
| Thomas Hart | 24 servant | |
| Mary Denny | 24 servant | |
| Anne Leake | 19 servant | |

LOVE, Joseph Young, Master. Probably sailed in July or August with the following named passengers but the date of arrival is not known.[2]

| WILLIAM CHERRALL | 26 baker |
| Mrs. Ursula Cherrall | |

FRANCIS HARMAN

[1] Public Record Office MSS., and Drake: *Founders*, 31-33.     [2] *Ibid.*, 40.

| | |
|---|---|
| FRANCIS HARMAN | 43 |
| John Harman | 12 |
| Sarah Harman | 10 |
| Walter Parker | 18 |

| | | |
|---|---|---|
| WILLIAM BROWNE | 26 | fisherman |
| Mrs. Mary Browne | 26 | |

GREAT HOPE of Ipswich, arrived about the middle of August and presumably brought passengers, but there is no record of them. She was caught in the same storm that wrecked the *Angel Gabriel*, and nearly did so to the *James*. She was a large ship of four hundred tons and was driven onto 'Mr. Hoff's Point and brought back again presently by a N. W. wind, and ran ashore at Charlestown.'[1]

SUSAN AND ELLEN, Edward Payne, Master. She sailed in May, but the date of her arrival is not of record. No certificates of residence accompanied this list.[2]

| | | | |
|---|---|---|---|
| JOHN PROCTOR | 42 | draper | Ipswich |
| Mrs. Martha Proctor | 28 | | |
| John Proctor | 3 | | |
| Mary Proctor | 1 | | |
| Alice Street | 28 | | |
| WALTER THORNTON | 36 | husbandman | |
| Mrs. Joanna Thornton | 34 | | |
| JOHN NORTH | 20 | | Ipswich |
| | | | Mrs. Mary Pynder |

[1] Winthrop: *Journal*, 1, 155.
[2] Public Record Office MSS., and Drake: *Founders*, 23, 25, 29.

| | | | |
|---|---|---|---|
| Mrs. Mary Pynder | 53 | | |
| Francis Pynder | 20 | | |
| Mary Pynder | 17 | | |
| Joanna Pynder | 14 | | |
| Anna Pynder | 12 | | |
| Katherine Pynder | 10 | | |
| John Pynder | 8 | | |
| RICHARD SKOLFIELD | 22 | | Ipswich |
| EDWARD WEEDEN | 22 | | Lynn |
| George Wilby | 16 | | |
| Richard Hawkins | 15 | | |
| THOMAS PARKER | 30 | | Lynn |
| Simon Bird | 20 | | |
| JOHN MANSFIELD | 34 | | Boston |
| CLEMENT COLE | 30 | | Boston |
| John Jones | 20 | | |
| William Burrows | 19 | | |
| Philip Atwood | 13 | | |
| William Snow | 18 | | |
| EDWARD LUMMUS | 24 | *see* Loomis | Ipswich |
| RICHARD SALTONSTALL | 23 | husbandman | Watertown |
| Muriel Saltonstall | 22 | | |
| Muriel Saltonstall | ¾ | | |
| THOMAS WELLES | 30 | | Ipswich |
| PETER COOPER | 28 | | Rowley |
| WILLIAM LAMBERT | 26 | | |
| JEREMY BELCHER | 22 | | Ipswich |
| SAMUEL PODD | 25 | | Ipswich |
| Mary Clifford | 25 | | |
| Jane Coe | 30 | | |
| Mary Riddlesden | 17 | | |

MATTHEW HITCHCOCK

| | | | |
|---|---|---|---|
| MATTHEW HITCHCOCK | 25 | | Watertown |
| Elizabeth Nichols | 25 | | |
| Tomazine Carpenter | 35 | | |
| Anne Fowle | 25 | | |
| Edmond Gordon | 18 | | |
| THOMAS SYDLIE | 22 | | |
| Margaret Leach | 22 | | |
| Mary Smith | 21 | | |
| Elizabeth Swayne | 16 | | |
| Penelope Pelham | 16 | | |
| Anne Welles | 20 | | |
| Dionis Taylor | 48 | | |
| Hannah Smith | 30 | | |
| William Buttrick | 18 | | |
| JOHN CORRINGTON | 33 | | |
| Mrs. Mary Corring-<br>ton | 33 | | |
| RALPH HUDSON | 42 | draper of Kingston-on-<br>Hull, Yorks | Cambridge |
| Mrs. Mary Hudson | 42 | | |
| Hannah Hudson | 14 | | |
| John Hudson | 12 | | |
| Elizabeth Hudson | 5 | | |
| THOMAS BRIGHAM | 32 | of Yorkshire | Cambridge |
| Benjamin Thwing | 16 | | |
| Anne Gilson | 34 | | |
| Judith Kirk | 18 | | |
| JOHN MORE | 41 | | |
| HENRY KNOWLES | 25 | | |
| GEORGE RICHARDSON | 30 | | Watertown |
| EDWARD TOMLINS | 30 | | Lynn |
| Benjamin Tomlins | 18 | | |
| | | | Barbara Ford |

| | | | |
|---|---|---|---|
| Barbara Ford | 16 | | |
| Joan Broomer | 13 | | |
| RICHARD BROOKE | 24 | | Lynn |
| Thomas Brooke | 18 | | |
| SIMON CROSBY | 26 | husbandman of Spalding-in-the-Moor, Yorks | Cambridge |
| Mrs. Anne Crosby | 25 | | |
| Thomas Crosby | 2 months | | |
| RICHARD ROWTON | 36 | husbandman | Salem |
| Mrs. Anne Rowton | 36 | | |
| Edmond Rowton | 6 | | |
| PERCIVAL GREENE | 32 | husbandman | Cambridge |
| Mrs. Ellen Greene | 32 | | |
| Margaret Dix | 18 | | |
| JOHN TRANE | 25 | | Watertown |
| JOHN ATHERSON | 24 | | |
| Anne Blason | 27 | | |
| (*Rev.*) PETER BULK-ELEY | 50 | of Odell, county Bedford | Concord |
| Mrs. Grace Bulkeley | 30 | | |
| John Bulkeley | 15 | | |
| Benjamin Bulkeley | 11 | | |
| Daniel Bulkeley | 9 | | |
| Priscilla Jarman | 10 | | |
| Elizabeth Taylor | 10 | | |
| Anne Lieford | 13 | | |

JAMES of Bristol, sailed June 4, arrived August 17, '... having one hundred passengers, honest people of Yorkshire, being put into the Isles of Shoals, lost three anchors: and setting sail, no canvas nor ropes would hold, but she was driven within a cable's length of the rocks at Pascataquack, when suddenly

suddenly the wind, coming to N. W., put them back to the Isles of Shoals, and, being there ready to strike upon the rocks, they let out a piece of their mainsail, and weathered the rocks.' [1]

| | | |
|---|---|---|
| *Rev.* RICHARD MATHER | Toxteth, Lancashire | Dorchester |
| Mrs. Katherine Mather | | |
| Samuel Mather | | |
| Timothy Mather | | |
| Nathaniel Mather | | |
| Joseph Mather | | |
| *Rev.* DANIEL MAUDE | | Boston |
| NATHANIEL WALES | | Dorchester |
| BARNABAS FAWER | | Dorchester |
| Mrs. Dinah Fawer | | |
| THOMAS ARMITAGE | | Ipswich |
| JOSEPH ARMITAGE | | Lynn |
| GODFREY ARMITAGE | | Lynn |
| MATTHEW MITCHELL | Halifax, Yorkshire | Charlestown |
| Mrs. Susan Mitchell | | |
| Jonathan Mitchell | | |
| GEORGE KENDRICK | | Scituate |
| Mrs. Jane Kendrick | | |
| JOHN SMITH | | |
| Mrs. Mary Smith | | |
| Mary Smith | | |

JAMES of London, William Cooper, Master, three hundred tons. She sailed from Southampton April 5 and arrived June 3 with passengers and cattle. Winthrop calls her master 'Mr. Graves'

[1] Winthrop: *Journal*, I, 156; Mather: *Journal.*

Graves' and says that he 'had come every year for these seven years.'[1]

| | | |
|---|---|---|
| AUGUSTINE CLEMENT | of Reading, county Berks, painter | Boston |
| Mrs. Elizabeth Clement | | |
| Samuel Clement | | |
| Elizabeth Clement | | |
| Thomas Wheeler | servant | |
| THOMAS BROWNE | of Malford, county Wilts, weaver | Newbury |
| HERCULES WOODMAN | of Malford, county Wilts, mercer | Newbury |
| JOHN EVERED als WEBB | of Marlborough, county Wilts, husbandman | Boston |
| STEPHEN EVERED als WEBB | of Marlborough, county Wilts | Boston |

Giles Butler  
George Cousins  
Thomas Colman     of Marlborough, county Wilts, laborers  
Thomas Goddard  
John Pithouse

| | | |
|---|---|---|
| ANTHONY MORSE | 29 of Marlborough, county Wilts, shoemaker | Newbury |
| Mrs. Mary Morse | | |
| WILLIAM MORSE | of Marlborough, county Wilts, shoemaker | Newbury |
| JOHN PARKER | of Marlborough, carpenter | Brookline |
| Mrs. Jane Parker | | |
| John Parker | | |
| Margaret Parker | | |
| Sarah Parker | | |
| John Hyde | of Marlborough, tailor | |
| Richard Walker | of Marlborough, shoemaker | |
| Maudit Ingles | of Marlborough, fuller | |

THOMAS DAVIS

[1] *Journal*, I, 152.

| THOMAS DAVIS | of Marlborough, sawyer |
| Mrs. Christian Davis | |
| Thomas Carpenter | of Amesbury, county Wilts, carpenter |

WILLIAM PADDY of London, skinner Plymouth

EDMUND HAWES of London, cutler Plymouth

EDMUND BATTER * of Salisbury, county Wilts, maltster
Mrs. Sarah Batter
John Small servant

THOMAS ANTRUM * of Salisbury, county Wilts, weaver
Thomas Browne servant

JOSHUA VEREN * of Salisbury, county Wilts, Salem
    roper

Mrs. Jane Veren
Hilliard Veren
Dorcas Veren

PHILIP VEREN * of Salisbury, county Wilts, Salem
    roper

Mrs. Dorcas Veren
Philip Veren
Nathaniel Veren
Joshua Veren

MICHAEL SHAFFLIN 30 Charlestown

  GEORGE SMYTH tailor

JOHN GREEN surgeon

ZACCHEUS CURTIS of Downton, county Wilts Topsfield

HENRY ROSE of Plaitford, county Wilts, laborer

NICHOLAS BATT of Devizes, county Wilts, Newbury
    linen weaver
Mrs. Lucy Batt
Anne Batt

                              JOHN PIKE

* These passengers are called 'late of New England,' but the reason for this designation is not clear.

| | | |
|---|---|---|
| JOHN PIKE | of Langford, county Wilts | Newbury |
| Mrs. . . . . . . Pike | | |
| John Pike | | |
| Robert Pike | | |
| Dorothy Pike | | |
| Israel Pike | | |
| Anne Pike | | |

THOMAS SCOATES — of Salisbury, county Wilts, laborer

JOHN MUSSELWHITE — of Langford, county Wilts, laborer

SAMPSON SALTER — of Caversham, county Oxford, Newport
fisherman

HENRY KING — of Brenchley, county Kent, laborer

WILLIAM ANDREWS — of Hampsworth county York-   Salem
shire (?)

JOHN KNIGHT — of Romsey, county Hants, tailor

RICHARD KNIGHT — of Romsey, county Hants, tailor

THOMAS SMITH — of Romsey, county Hants,      Ipswich
weaver

NICHOLAS HOLT — 27 of Romsey, county Hants,   Newbury
tanner

ROBERT FIELD — of 'Yealing' (probably Eling),   Boston
county Hants

ANTHONY THATCHER — of Salisbury, county       Yarmouth
Wilts, tailor

Mrs. Mary Thatcher

Peter Higdon — servant

James Browne — 17 of Southampton

Lawrence Seager — 17 of Southampton

HENRY LEVERAGE — of Salisbury, county Wilts, tailor

WILLIAM PARSONS — of Salisbury, county Wilts, tailor

JOHN EMERY — 34 of Romsey, county Hants,   Newbury
carpenter

Mrs. . . . . . . Emery

Mrs. ...... Emery
Anne Emery
Elinor Emery
John Emery

ANTHONY EMERY                    of Romsey, county Hants,  Newbury
                                     carpenter         and Kittery, Me.
Mrs. Frances Emery
James Emery
Rebecca Emery

WILLIAM KEMP                     servant to Anthony Emery   Duxbury


...... On June 7 (Sunday), 'there came in seven other
...... ships, and one to Salem, and four more to the mouth
...... of the bay, with store of passengers and cattle.
...... They all came in within six weeks.'[1] It is probable
...... that these ships were the *James, Elizabeth, Christian,*
...... *Planter, Hopewell, Rebecca, Elizabeth & Anne,* and
...... *Increase,* with five others whose names are not of
...... record. The passenger lists of seven of these ships
...... will follow; and included with them are these per-
...... sons known to have come this year, but it is not
...... possible to assign them to a particular vessel.

*Rev.* PETER HOBART              of Southold, Suffolk        Hingham
Mrs. ...... Hobart
Joshua Hobart
Jeremiah Hobart
Elizabeth Hobart
Josiah Hobart

ANTHONY COOPER                   of Hingham, Norfolk         Hingham
Mrs. ...... Cooper
...... Cooper
                                                     ...... Cooper

[1] Winthrop: *Journal,* I, 152.

...... Cooper
...... Cooper
...... Cooper
Deborah Cooper
Sarah Cooper
...... Cooper
...... Cooper

| | | |
|---|---|---|
| WILLIAM LARGE | of county Norfolk | |
| Mrs. ...... Large | | |
| JOHN SMART | of county Norfolk | Hingham |
| Mrs. ...... Smart | | |
| Richard Smart | | |
| James Smart | | |
| GEORGE LUDKIN | of county Norfolk | Hingham |
| *Mrs.* ...... Ludkin | | |
| Aaron Ludkin | | |
| JOHN FARROW | of Hingham, Norfolk | Hingham |
| Mrs. Frances Farrow | | |
| ...... Farrow | | |

PLANTER of London, Nicholas Trerice, Master. She sailed from London about April 10 and arrived at Boston June 7, following.[1]

The following passengers were certified from Stepney:

| | | | |
|---|---|---|---|
| NICHOLAS DAVIES | 40 | tailor of Wapping | Charlestown |
| Mrs. Sarah Davies | 48 | | |
| Joseph Davies | 13 | | |
| William Locke | 6 | | Woburn |
| JOHN MADDOX | 43 | sawyer | Salem |
| JAMES LANNIN | 26 | glover | |

ROBERT STEVENS

[1] Public Record Office MSS., and Drake: *Founders*, 15–21.

| | | |
|---|---|---|
| ROBERT STEVENS | 22 sawyer | Braintree (?) |
| JOHN MOORE | 24 laborer | |
| JAMES HAYWARD | 22 servant | |
| Judith Phippen | 16 servant | |

The following passengers certified from St. Albans, Herts:

| | | | |
|---|---|---|---|
| JOHN TUTTLE | 39 | mercer of Saint Albans, Herts | Ipswich |
| Mrs. Joan Tuttle | 42 | | |
| John Lawrence | 17 | | |
| William Lawrence | 12 | | |
| Mary Lawrence | 9 | | |
| Abigail Tuttle | 6 | | |
| Simon Tuttle | 4 | | |
| Sarah Tuttle | 2 | | |
| John Tuttle | 1 | | |
| Mrs. Joan Antrobus | 65 | | |
| Mary Wrast | 24 | | |
| Thomas Greene | 15 | | |
| Nathan Haford | 16 | servant | |
| Mary Chittwood | 24 | | |
| THOMAS OLNEY | 35 | shoemaker | Salem |
| Mrs. Marie Olney | 30 | | |
| Thomas Olney, Jr. | 3 | | |
| Epenetus Olney | 1 | | |
| GEORGE GIDDINS | 25 | husbandman of Clapham, county Beds | Ipswich |
| Mrs. Jane Giddins | 20 | | |
| MICHAEL WILLIAM-SON | 30 | servant | |
| THOMAS CARTER | 25 | servant | |
| Elizabeth Morrison | 12 | servant | |
| MARTIN SAUNDERS | 40 | currier of Sudbury, county Suffolk | Braintree |
| Mrs. Rachel Saunders | 40 | | |
| | | | Mary Saunders |

| | | |
|---|---|---|
| Mary Saunders | 15 | |
| Leah Saunders | 10 | |
| Judith Saunders | 8 | |
| Martin Saunders | 4 | |
| Mary Fuller | 15 servant | |
| Richard Smith | 14 servant | |
| Richard Ridley | 16 servant | |
| FRANCIS NEWCOM | 30 husbandman | Braintree |
| Mrs. Rachel New-com | 20 | |
| Rachel Newcom | 2½ | |
| John Newcom | ¾ | |
| ANTHONY STANION | 24 glover | Boston |
| DANIEL HANBURY | 29 | |
| Francis Dexter | 13 | |
| William Dawes | 15 | |
| EDMOND WEAVER | 28 husbandman of Aymestrey, Hereford | |
| Mrs. Margaret Weaver | 30 | |
| JAMES WEAVER | 23 stationer of Aymestrey, Hereford | |
| RICHARD TUTTLE | 32 husbandman of Ringstead, Northants | Boston |
| Mrs. Anne Tuttle | 41 | |
| Anne Tuttle | 12 | |
| John Tuttle | 10 | |
| Rebecca Tuttle | 6 | |
| Isabel Tuttle | 70 (probably mother) | |
| Mary Wolhouston | 30 | |
| WILLIAM TUTTLE | 26 husbandman of Ringstead, Northants | Boston |
| Mrs. Elizabeth Tuttle | 23 | |
| John Tuttle | 3½ | |
| Anne Tuttle | 2¼ | |
| Thomas Tuttle | ¼ | |
| | | Cicely Clark |

| | | |
|---|---|---|
| Cicely Clark | 16 | |
| Mary Bill | 11 | |
| Philip Atwood | 12 | |
| Bartholomew Faldoe | 16 | |
| Elizabeth Swayne | 20 | |
| Margaret Leach | 15 | |
| Hannah Smith | 18 | |
| Anne Wells | 15 | |

| | | | |
|---|---|---|---|
| FRANCIS BUSHNELL | 26 | carpenter from Berkshire | Salem |
| Mrs. Mary Bushnell | 26 | | |
| Martha Bushnell | 1 | | |
| William Lea | 16 | | |
| Mary Smith | 18 | | |

| | | |
|---|---|---|
| RICHARD FENN | 27 | certified by Alderman Richard Fenn |

| | | | |
|---|---|---|---|
| THOMAS SAVAGE | 27 | tailor of Taunton, county Somerset | Boston |

| | | | |
|---|---|---|---|
| RICHARD HARVIE | 22 | tailor | Salem |
| Mrs. Anne Harvie | 22 | | |

| | | | |
|---|---|---|---|
| FRANCIS PEABODY | 21 | husbandman | Ipswich |

| | | | |
|---|---|---|---|
| WILLIAM WILCOCKSON | 34 | weaver | Hartford |
| Mrs. Margaret Wilcockson | 24 | | |
| John Wilcockson | 2 | | |

| | | | |
|---|---|---|---|
| WILLIAM BEARDSLEY | 30 | | Concord and Stratford, Connecticut |
| Mrs. Mary Beardsley | 26 | | |
| Mary Beardsley | 4 | | |
| John Beardsley | 2 | | |
| Joseph Beardsley | ½ | | |

| | | | |
|---|---|---|---|
| ALLEN PERLEY | 27 | husbandman | Ipswich |

| | | | |
|---|---|---|---|
| WILLIAM FELLOE | 24 | shoemaker | Ipswich |

| | | | |
|---|---|---|---|
| FRANCIS BAKER | 24 | tailor | Boston |

The

The following passengers certified from Kingston, Surrey:

| | | | |
|---|---|---|---|
| PALMER TINGLEY | 21 | miller | Ipswich |
| William Buttrick | 20 | hostler | |
| THOMAS JEWELL | 27 | miller | Braintree |

The following passengers certified from Sudbury, Suffolk:

| | | | |
|---|---|---|---|
| RICHARD HAFFIELD | 54 | currier | Ipswich |
| Mrs. Martha Haffield | 42 | | |
| Mary Haffield | 18 | | |
| Sarah Haffield | 14 | | |
| Martha Haffield | 8 | | |
| Rachel Haffield | 6 | | |
| Ruth Haffield | 3 | | |
| Alice Smith | 40 | | |
| Elizabeth Cooper | 24 | | |
| John Smith | 13 | | |
| Job Hawkins | 15 | | |

The following passengers certified, but no place stated:

| | | | |
|---|---|---|---|
| Mrs. Eylin Hanford | 46 | of Fremington, county Devon | Scituate |
| Margaret Hanford | 16 | | |
| Elizabeth Hanford | 14 | | |
| Rodolphus Elmes | 15 | servant of Southwark, Surrey | Scituate |
| Thomas Stanley | 16 | servant | |
| Mrs. Sarah Pitney | 22 | (?) | Marshfield |
| Margaret Pitney | 22 | | |
| Sarah Pitney | 7 | | |
| Samuel Pitney | 1½ | | |
| Rachel Deane | 31 | | |

ELIZABETH of London, William Stagg, Master. She sailed from London in April and arrived at Boston in midsummer.
Most

Most of the passengers were certified by 'Ministers and Justices of the Parish' (not stated), with the exceptions named below.[1]

| | | | |
|---|---|---|---|
| CLEMENT BATES | 40 | tailor of Lydd, county Kent | Hingham |
| Mrs. Anne Bates | 40 | | |
| James Bates | 14 | | |
| Clement Bates | 12 | | |
| Rachel Bates | 8 | | |
| Joseph Bates | 5 | | |
| Benjamin Bates | 2 | | |
| John Wynchester | 19 | servant | |
| JERVICE GOULD | 30 | servant | Hingham |
| WILLIAM HOLDRED | 25 | certified from Saint Alphege, London | Ipswich |
| ROGER PRESTON | 21 | certified from Saint Alphege, London | Ipswich |
| Daniel Brodley | 20 | certified from Saint Alphege, London | Ipswich |
| JAMES HOSMER | 28 | clothier of Hawkhurst, county Kent | Concord |
| Mrs. Anne Hosmer | 27 | | |
| Mary Hosmer | 2 | | |
| Anne Hosmer | ¼ | | |
| Mary Dounard | 24 | servant | |
| Mary Martin | 19 | servant | |
| JOHN STONE | 40 | certified from Hawkhurst, county Kent | |
| EDWARD GOULD | 28 | certified from Hawkhurst, county Kent | Hingham |
| George Russell | 19 | certified from Hawkhurst, county Kent | |
| John Mussell | 15 | | |

WILLIAM WILD

[1] Public Record Office MSS., and Drake: *Founders*, 18, 19, 21, 24, 25, 26, 27.

| | | |
|---|---|---|
| WILLIAM WILD | 30 | Ipswich |
| Mrs. Alice Wild | 40 | |
| Peter Thorne | 20 | |
| John Wild | 17 | |
| | | |
| WILLIAM WHITRED | 36 carpenter | Ipswich |
| Mrs. Elizabeth Whitred | 30 | |
| Thomas Whitred | 10 | |
| | | |
| JOHN CLUFFE | 22 | |
| | | |
| SAMUEL HAYWARD | 22 carpenter | Boston |
| John Duke | 20 | |
| | | |
| JOHN BROWNE | 40 | Plymouth (?) |
| Sarah Walker | 17 servants to William Brasey, linen | |
| James Walker | 15 draper of Cheapside and John Brown, baker | |
| | | |
| THOMAS MILLETT | 30 certified by Minister of Saint Saviour's, South-wark, county Surrey | Dorchester |
| Mrs. Mary Millett | 29 | |
| Thomas Millett | 2 | |
| Ursula Greenway | 32 certified as above | |
| Henry Bull | 19 | |
| Joshua Wheat | 17 certified by Minister of Saint Saviour's, | |
| John Smith | 12 Southwark, county Surrey | |
| Ralph Chapman | 20 | |
| | | |
| RICHARD WALKER | 24 | Lynn (?) |
| William Walker | 15 | |
| | | |
| WILLIAM BEAMOND | 27 | Salem |
| John Beamond | 23 | Salem |
| | | |
| THOMAS LETTYNE | 23 Leighton (?) | Lynn |
| | | |
| JOHN JOHNSON | 23 | |
| | | |
| JAMES BATES | 53 husbandman of Lydd, county Kent | Dorchester |
| | | Mrs. Alice Bates |

| | | | |
|---|---|---|---|
| Mrs. Alice Bates | 52 | | |
| Lydia Bates | 20 | | |
| Margaret Bates | 12 | | |
| Mary Bates | 17 | | |
| James Bates | 9 | | |
| EDWARD BULLOCK | 32 | husbandman of Barkham, county Berks | Dorchester |
| ISAAC STEDMAN | 30 | of Biddenden, county Kent | Scituate |
| Mrs. Elizabeth Stedman | 26 | | |
| Nathaniel Stedman | 5 | | |
| Isaac Stedman | 1 | | |
| Robert Thornton | 11 | | Dorchester |
| Peter Gardner | 18 | | |
| Margaret Davies | 32 | | Boston |
| John Davies | 9 | | |
| Mary Davies | 4 | | |
| Elizabeth Davies | 1 | | |
| Dorothy Smith | 45 | | |
| Mary Smith | 15 | | |
| WILLIAM HUBBARD | 36 | see identical entry *Elizabeth and Anne*, 1635 | Wenham |
| John Hubbard | 10 | | |
| Rachel Biggs | 66 | widow of Cranbrooke, county Kent | Dorchester |
| Patience Foster | 40 | | |
| Hopestill Foster | 14 | | |
| FRANCIS WHITE | 24 | | |
| Joan Sellen | 50 | | Ipswich (?) |
| Anne Sellen | 7 | | |
| EDWARD LOOMIS | 27 | *see* Lummus | Ipswich |

INCREASE

INCREASE of London, Robert Lea, Master. She left England the latter part of April and arrived Boston the end of July.[1]

| | | | |
|---|---|---|---|
| GEORGE BACON | 43 | mason | Hingham |
| Samuel Bacon | 12 | | |
| Susan Bacon | 10 | | |
| John Bacon | 8 | | |
| | | | |
| THOMAS JOSSELYN | 43 | husbandman of Roxwell, Essex | Hingham |
| Mrs. Rebecca Josselyn | 43 | | |
| Rebecca Josselyn | 18 | | |
| Dorothy Josselyn | 11 | | |
| Nathaniel Josselyn | 8 | | |
| Elizabeth Josselyn | 6 | | |
| Mary Josselyn | 1 | | |
| Elizabeth Ward | 38 | servant | |
| | | | |
| WILLIAM ROSCOE | 41 | husbandman of Billerica, Essex | Cambridge |
| Mrs. Rebecca Roscoe | 40 | | |
| Sarah Roscoe | 9 | | |
| Mary Roscoe | 7 | | |
| Samuel Roscoe | 5 | | |
| William Roscoe | 1 | | |
| | | | |
| THOMAS PAGE | 29 | tailor; certified from All Saints' Stayning, Mark Lane, London | Saco, Maine |
| Mrs. Elizabeth Page | 28 | | |
| Thomas Page, Jr. | 2 | | |
| Catherine Page | 1 | | |
| Edward Sparks | 22 | servant | |
| Catherine Taylor | 24 | servant | |
| | | | |
| SAMUEL ANDREWS | 37 | from London | Falmouth, Maine |
| Mrs. Jane Andrews | 30 | | |
| | | | Jane Andrews |

[1] Public Record Office MSS., and Drake: *Founders*, 20, 22, 24, 25, 26.

| | | |
|---|---|---|
| Jane Andrews | 3 | |
| Elizabeth Andrews | 2 | |
| ROBERT NANNEY | 22 | servant |
| ROBERT SANKEY | 30 | servant |
| JAMES GIBBONS | 21 | servant |
| | | |
| THOMAS BLODGETT | 30 | glover, from Suffolk      Cambridge |
| Mrs. Susan Blodgett | 37 | |
| Daniel Blodgett | 4 | |
| Samuel Blodgett | 1½ | |
| | | |
| THOMAS CHITTENDEN | 51 | linen-weaver of Hawkhurst,    Scituate |
| | | Kent |
| Mrs. Rebecca | | |
|     Chittenden | 40 | |
| Isaac Chittenden | 10 | |
| Henry Chittenden | 6 | |
| | | |
| SAMUEL MORSE | 50 | husbandman         Dedham |
| Mrs. Elizabeth | | |
|     Morse | 48 | |
| Joseph Morse | 20 | |
| Elizabeth Daniell | 2 | |
| | | |
| PHILEMON DALTON | 45 | linen-     Hampton, New Hampshire |
| | | weaver |
| Mrs. Hannah Dalton | 35 | |
| Samuel Dalton | 5 | |
| William White | 14 | servant |
| | | |
| JOHN DAVIS | 29 | joiner           Boston |
| | | |
| MATTHEW MARVIN | 45 | husbandman of Bentley    Hartford |
| | | Magna, Essex |
| Mrs. Elizabeth | | |
|     Marvin | 31 | |
| Matthew Marvin | 8 | |
| Mary Marvin | 6 | |
| Sarah Marvin | 3 | |
| Hannah Marvin | ½ | |
| John Warner | 30 | servant |
| Isaac More | 13 | servant |

SAMUEL IRELAND

| | | |
|---|---|---|
| SAMUEL IRELAND | 32 | carpenter |
| Mrs. Mary Ireland | 30 | |
| Martha Ireland | ½ | |

| | | | |
|---|---|---|---|
| WILLIAM PAYNE | 37 | husbandman of Lavenham, Suffolk | Salem |
| Mrs. Anne Payne | 40 | | |
| Susan Payne | 11 | | |
| William Payne | 10 | | |
| Anna Payne | 5 | | |
| John Payne | 3 | | |
| Daniel Payne | ¼ | | |

| | | | |
|---|---|---|---|
| SIMON STONE | 50 | husbandman of Bromley Magna, Essex | Watertown |
| Mrs. Joan Stone | 38 | | |
| Francis Stone | 16 | | |
| Anne Stone | 11 | | |
| Simon Stone, Jr. | 4 | | |
| Mary Stone | 3 | | |
| John Stone | 1 mo. | | |

| | | | |
|---|---|---|---|
| SIMON AYERS | 48 | chirugeon of Lavenham, Suffolk | Watertown |
| Mrs. Dorothy Ayers | 38 | | |
| Mary Ayers | 15 | | |
| Thomas Ayers | 13 | | |
| Simon Ayers, Jr. | 11 | | |
| Rebecca Ayers | 9 | | |
| Christian Ayers | 7 | | |
| Anna Ayers | 5 | | |
| Benjamin Ayers | 3 | | |
| Sarah Ayers | ¼ | | |

| | | | |
|---|---|---|---|
| THOMAS KILBOURNE | 55 | husbandman of Wood Ditton, Cambridge | Wethersfield |
| Mrs. Frances Kilbourne | 50 | | |
| Margaret Kilbourne | 23 | | |
| Lydia Kilbourne | 22 | | |
| | | | Mary Kilbourne |

| | | |
|---|---|---|
| Mary Kilbourne | 16 | |
| Frances Kilbourne | 12 | |
| John Kilbourne | 10 | |

WILLIAM BUCK      50 plow-wright      Cambridge
    Roger Buck      18

ABRAHAM FLEMING      40 husbandman

JOHN FOKAR      21 husbandman

THOMAS PARRISH      22 clothier      Watertown

WILLIAM HOUGHTON      22 butcher

JAMES BITTON      27

WILLIAM POTTER      25

STEPHEN UPSON      23 sawyer

| | | |
|---|---|---|
| Henry Cross | 20 | carpenter |
| James Roger | 20 | |
| Richard Nun | 19 | |
| Thomas Barrett | 16 | |
| John Hackwell | 18 | |
| John Wyndell | 16 | |
| Isaac Worden | 18 | |
| Nathaniel Wood | 12 | |
| Elizabeth Wood | 30 | |
| Elizabeth Beard | 24 | |
| Aymes Gladwell | 16 | |
| Phebe Pearce | 18 | |
| Mary Teller | 16 | |
| Jane Rawlins | 30 | |
| Elizabeth Streaton | 19 | |

JAMES, John May, Master. She sailed for New England the latter part of July and arrived at Boston the last week in September.

September. All passengers were certified by the 'Minister' of their conformity, and as 'no Subsidy men.' [1]

| | | | |
|---|---|---|---|
| THOMAS EWER | 40 | tailor, perhaps of Hertfordshire | Charlestown |
| Mrs. Sarah Ewer | 28 | | |
| Elizabeth Ewer | 4 | | |
| Thomas Ewer | 1½ | | |
| Sarah Beale | 28 | | |
| Elizabeth Newman | 24 | | |
| John Scudder | 16 | | Charlestown |
| WILLIAM BALLARD | 32 | husbandman of Bradwell, county Suffolk | Lynn |
| Mrs. Elizabeth Ballard | 26 | | |
| Hester Ballard | 2 | | |
| John Ballard | 1 | | |
| Alice Jones | 26 | | |
| Elizabeth Goffe | 26 | | |
| EDMOND BRIDGES | 23 | | Lynn |
| MICHAEL MILNER | 23 | | Lynn |
| THOMAS TERRY | 28 | | Southold, Long Island |
| Richard Terry | 17 | | |
| ROBERT TERRY | 25 | | Southold, Long Island |
| THOMAS MARSHALL | 22 | | Boston |
| William Hooper | 18 | | |
| EDMOND JOHNSON | 23 | | Hampton, New Hampshire |
| SAMUEL BENNETT | 24 | | Lynn |
| RICHARD PALMER | 29 | | |
| ANTHONY BESSEY | 26 | | Sandwich |
| EDWARD GARDINER | 25 | | Cambridge |
| William Colbron | 16 | | |
| | | | HENRY BULL |

[1] Public Record Office MSS., and Drake: *Founders*, 31, 39.

| | | |
|---|---|---|
| HENRY BULL | 25 | Newport, Rhode Island |
| Solomon Martin | 16 shipwright | Gloucester |
| WILLIAM HILL | 70 wheelwright | |
| NICHOLAS BUTTRY | 33 | Cambridge |
| Mrs. Martha Buttry | 28 | |
| Grace Buttry | 1 | |
| JOHN HART | 40 shoemaker | Salem |
| Mrs. Mary Hart | 31 | |
| HENRY TYBBOTT | 39 shoemaker | Dover, New Hampshire |
| Mrs. Elizabeth Tybbott | 39 | |
| Jeremy Tybbott | 4 | |
| Samuel Tybbott | 2 | |
| Remembrance Tybbott | 28 | |
| NICHOLAS GOODHUE | 60 clothworker | probably Ipswich |
| Mrs. Jane Goodhue | 58 | |
| JOHN JOHNSON | 26 | probably Ipswich |
| Mrs. Susan Johnson | 24 | |
| Elizabeth Johnson | 3 | |
| Thomas Johnson | 1½ | |
| RALPH FARNHAM | 32 barber | Ipswich |
| Mrs. Alice Farnham | 28 | |
| Mary Farnham | 7 | |
| Thomas Farnham | 4 | |
| Ralph Farnham | 2 | |

BATCHELOR, Thomas Webb, Master, of twenty-five tons, sailed for New England August 11 and arrived November 28. 'Here arrived,' wrote Winthrop, 'a small Norsey Bark, sent by the Lords Say, etc., with one Gardiner, an expert engineer, or work base, and provisions of all sorts, to begin a fort at the

the mouth of Connecticut. Her passingers twelve men, two women and goods, all safe.' [1]

| | | |
|---|---|---|
| LYON GARDINER | 36 probably of London | Long Island, New York |
| Mrs. Mary Gardiner | 34 | |
| Elizabeth Coles | 23 | |
| | | |
| WILLIAM JOPE | 40 | |

ELIZABETH AND ANNE, Roger Cooper, Master. She sailed about the middle of May and arrived at Boston in Midsummer, with one hundred and two passengers. [2]

| | | |
|---|---|---|
| Mrs. Marjorie Washburn | 49 | of Evesham, county Worcester Plymouth |
| John Washburn | 14 | |
| Phillip Washburn | 11 | |
| | | |
| ROBERT HAWKINS | 25 husbandman | Charlestown |
| Mrs. Mary Hawkins | 24 | |
| | | |
| JOHN WHITNEY | 35 | Watertown |
| Mrs. Ellen Whitney | 30 | |
| John Whitney | 11 | |
| Richard Whitney | 9 | |
| Nathaniel Whitney | 8 | |
| Thomas Whitney | 6 | |
| Jonathan Whitney | 1 | |
| | | |
| John Palmerley | 20 | |
| Richard Martin | 12 | |
| | | |
| Abigail Eaton | 35 | Watertown |
| Mary Eaton | 4 | |
| Thomas Eaton | 1 | |

WILLIAM HUBBARD

[1] *Journal*, I, 165–66.
[2] Public Record Office MSS., and Drake: *Founders*, 20, 22, 24, 27, 28, 29, 30.

| | | | |
|---|---|---|---|
| WILLIAM HUBBARD | 35 | | Salem |
| Thomas Hubbard | 10 | | |
| Nicholas Sension | 13 | | |
| HENRY JACKSON | 29 | | Watertown |
| JOHN JACKSON | 27 | | |
| Sarah Cartrack | 24 | | |
| Mildred Cartrack | 2 | | |
| Jane Dammand | 9 | | |
| Mary Broomer | 10 | | |
| Thomas Alsopp | 20 | | |
| Joseph Alsopp | 14 | | |
| Percy King | 24 | maidservant | |
| THOMAS HODSALL | 47 | | |
| ALEXANDER BAKER | 28 | | Gloucester |
| Mrs. Elizabeth Baker | 23 | | |
| Elizabeth Baker | 3 | | |
| Christian Baker | 1 | | |
| SAMUEL BAKER | 30 | | |
| CLEMENT CHAPLIN | 48 | of Thetford, county Norfolk | Cambridge |
| WILLIAM SWAYNE | 50 | | Watertown |
| RICHARD BROCK | 31 | carpenter | |
| EDWARD SALE | 24 | | |
| Daniel Preston | 13 | | |
| Richard Goard | 17 | | |
| THOMAS LORD | 50 | smith, of Towcester, Northants | Hartford |
| Mrs. Dorothy Lord | 46 | | |
| Thomas Lord | 16 | | |
| Anne Lord | 14 | | |
| William Lord | 12 | | |
| John Lord | 10 | | |
| | | | Robert Lord |

| | | | |
|---|---|---|---|
| Robert Lord | 9 | | |
| Amy Lord | 6 | | |
| Dorothy Lord | 4 | | |
| JAMES COBBETT | 23 | | |
| JOSIAS COBBETT | 21 | | |
| JOSEPH FABER | 26 | | |
| William Samond | 19 | | |
| JOHN HOLLOWAY | 21 | | |
| Jane Bennett | 16 | | |
| WILLIAM REEVE | 22 | | |
| CHRISTOPHER STANLEY | 32 | tailor, perhaps of London | Boston |
| Mrs. Susanna Stanley | 31 | | |
| HENRY WILKINSON | 25 | tallow chandler | Ipswich |
| Robert Haws | 19 | soap boiler | Roxbury |
| SAMUEL HULL | 25 | | |
| William Swynden | 20 | | |
| JOHN HALSEY | 24 | | |
| VINCENT POTTER | 21 | | Boston |
| William Adams | 15 | | |
| HENRY CURTIS | 27 | | Watertown |
| JOHN WYLIE | 25 | | Reading |
| JOHN THOMPSON | 22 | | |
| EDMOND WESTON | 30 | | Duxbury |
| Gamaliel Beamont | 12 | | Dorchester |
| THOMAS WHITTEN | 36 | of Benenden, county Kent | Plymouth |
| Mrs. Audrey Whitten | 45 | | |
| Jeremy Whitten | 8 | | |
| Nicholas Morecock | 14 | | |
| | | | Bennet Morecock |

| | | | |
|---|---|---|---|
| Bennet Morecock | 16 | | |
| Mary Morecock | 10 | | |
| GEORGE ORRIS | 21 | | Boston |
| Elizabeth Fabin | 16 | (*see* Faber, above) | |
| ROBERT JEFFRIES | 30 | | Charlestown |
| Mary Jeffries | 27 | | |
| Thomas Jeffries | 7 | | |
| Elizabeth Jeffries | 6 | | |
| Mary Jeffries | 3 | | |
| Hannah Day | 20 | | |
| Susan Brown | 21 | | |
| ROBERT CARR | 21 | tailor | |
| Caleb Carr | 11 | | |
| RICHARD WHITE | 30 | carpenter | Sudbury |
| THOMAS DANE | 32 | carpenter | Concord |
| WILLIAM HILLIARD | 21 | carpenter | Duxbury |
| WILLIAM COURSER | 26 | shoemaker | Boston |
| GEORGE WYLDE | 37 | husbandman | |
| GEORGE PARKER | 23 | carpenter | perhaps York, Maine |
| JOHN BORDEN | 28 | of Benenden county Kent | Watertown |
| Joan Borden | 23 | | |
| Matthew Borden | 5 | | |
| Elizabeth Borden | 3 | | |
| RICHARD SAMPSON | 28 | tailor | |
| ROBERT STANDY | 22 | | |
| John Oldham | 12 | 'near kinsman' of John Oldham | Watertown |
| Thomas Oldham | 10 | | |

HOPEWELL

HOPEWELL of London, William Bundock, Master. She sailed early in April from London and arrived at Boston in June.[1]

| | | | |
|---|---|---|---|
| JOHN COOPER | 41 | of Olney, county Bucks | Lynn |
| Wybroe Cooper | 42 | | |
| Mary Cooper | 13 | | |
| John Cooper | 10 | | |
| Thomas Cooper | 7 | | |
| Martha Cooper | 5 | | |
| Philip Phillips | | servant | |
| | | | |
| EDMOND FARRINGTON | 47 | of Olney, county Bucks, miller | Lynn |
| Elizabeth Farrington | 49 | | |
| Sarah Farrington | 14 | | |
| Matthew Farrington | 12 | | |
| John Farrington | 11 | | |
| Elizabeth Farrington | 8 | | |
| | | | |
| WILLIAM PARRYER | 36 | of Olney, county Bucks | Ipswich |
| Alice Parryer | 37 | | |
| Mary Parryer | 7 | | |
| Sarah Parryer | 5 | | |
| Katherine | 1½ | | |
| | | | |
| GEORGE GRIGGS | 42 | of Lavenden, county Bucks | Boston |
| Alice Griggs | 42 | | |
| Thomas Griggs | 15 | | |
| William Griggs | 14 | | |
| Elizabeth Griggs | 10 | | |
| Mary Griggs | 6 | | |
| James Griggs | 2 | | |
| | | | |
| PHILIP KIRTLAND | 21 | of Sherrington, county Bucks | Lynn |
| Nathaniel Kirtland | 19 | | |
| | | | |
| JOHN ASTWOOD | 26 | | New Haven |
| Martha Carter | 27 | | |
| Mary Elliott | 13 | | |

JOHN PEAT

[1] Public Records Office MSS., and Drake: *Founders*, 15, 17, 19.

| | | |
|---|---|---|
| JOHN PEAT | 38 husbandman of Duffield, | Stratford |
| | county Derby | |
| ISAAC DESBROUGH | 18 of Eltisley, county Cambridge | |
| GEORGE WOODWARD | 35 fishmonger of Saint Botolph's, | |
| | Billingsgate, London | |
| JOHN RUGGLES | 44 shoemaker of Nazing, | Roxbury |
| | county Essex, | |
| Barbara Ruggles | 30 | |
| John Ruggles | 10 (nephew) | |
| John Ruggles | 7 | |
| Elizabeth Eliot | 30 of Nazing, county Essex | Roxbury |
| Elizabeth Eliot | 8 | |
| Sarah Eliot | 6 | |
| Lydia Eliot | 4 | |
| Philip Eliot | 2 | |
| GILES PAYSON | 26 of Nazing, county Essex | Roxbury |
| Isaac Morris | 9 | |
| LAWRENCE WHITTE-MORE | 63 husbandman of Stanstead | Roxbury |
| | Abbots, county Herts | |
| Mrs. Elizabeth Whittemore | 57 | |
| Elizabeth Turner | 20 | |
| ROBERT DAY | 30 of Stanstead Abbots, | Cambridge |
| | county Herts | |
| William Peacock | 12 | |
| ROBERT TITUS | 35 husbandman of Saint | Weymouth |
| | Katherine, Tower, London | |
| Mrs. Hannah Titus | 31 | |
| John Titus | 9 | |
| Edmund Titus | 5 | |
| THOMAS PELL | 22 tailor | New Haven |
| JOHN BUSHNELL | 21 glazier | Salem |
| James Burgis | 14 | |

Alexander Thwaites

| | | |
|---|---|---|
| Alexander Thwaites | 20 | Concord |
| John Abbott | 16 | |
| Mary Abbott | 15 | |
| John Bellows | 12 | |
| John Johnes | 18 | |
| Christian Luddington | 18 | |
| Mary Coke | 14 | |
| Mary Peake | 15 | |

REBECCA, John Hodges, Master. She sailed from London in April and arrived at Boston June 8, with the following passengers.[1]

| | | |
|---|---|---|
| PETER UNDERWOOD | 22 | |
| Isabel Craddock | 30 | |
| JACOB WALSH | 32 | |
| GEORGE WOODWARD | 35 | (also in the Hopewell, *q.v.*) |
| Elizabeth Winckall | 52 | |
| John Winckall | 13 | |
| WILLIAM SWAYNE | 16 | Hampton, N. H. |
| FRANCIS SWAYNE | 14 | Hampton, N. H. |

ANGEL GABRIEL of Bristol, two hundred and forty tons, ...... Taylor, Master. Sailed for New England in June and was wrecked at Pemaquid in August, but no lives were lost.[2]

| | | |
|---|---|---|
| RALPH BLAISDELL | of Lancashire | York, Maine |
| Mrs. Elizabeth Blaisdell | | |
| Henry Blaisdell | | |
| HENRY SIMPSON | | York, Maine |
| | | GEORGE |

[1] Public Record Office MSS., and Drake: *Founders*, 20.
[2] Wallace: *History of Canaan, New Hampshire*, 504.

GEORGE of Bristol left that port September 28 and arrived at Boston November 7, following.[1]

| | | |
|---|---|---|
| ROBERT HULL | of Market Harborough, county Leicester, chandler | Boston |
| Mrs. Elizabeth Hull | | |
| John Hull | | |

ABIGAIL of London, Richard Hackwell, Master. She listed passengers for New England from June 4 until July 24, and sailed from Plymouth, as her last port of departure, about August 1, with two hundred and twenty persons aboard and many cattle. She arrived at Boston about October 8, infected with smallpox. Among those coming in this ship, but not listed, were Sir Henry Vane, son and heir of Sir Henry Vane, Comptroller of the King's Household, traveling incognito; the Reverend Hugh Peter, pastor of the English Church at Rotterdam, and the Reverend John Wilson, who was returning to Boston, with his wife, her first appearance in New England.[2]

| | | | |
|---|---|---|---|
| ROBERT MEARES | 43 | husbandman | Boston |
| Mrs. Elizabeth Meares | 30 | | |
| Samuel Meares | 6 | | |
| John Meares | ¼ | | |
| THOMAS BUTTOLPH | 32 | glover | Boston |
| Mrs. Anne Buttolph | 24 | | |
| RALPH MASON | 35 | carpenter of Saint Olave's Southwark | Boston |
| Mrs. Anne Mason | 35 | | |
| Richard Mason | 5 | | |
| | | | Samuel Mason |

[1] Hull: *Diary*, in American Antiquarian Society, *Proceedings*.
[2] Public Record Office MSS., and Drake: *Founders*, 28, 31–38.

| | | | |
|---|---|---|---|
| Samuel Mason | 3 | | |
| Susan Mason | 1 | | |
| JOHN WINTHROP | 27 | | |
| Mrs. Elizabeth Winthrop | 19 | | |
| Deane Winthrop | 11 | | |
| Matthew Abdy | 15 | fisherman | Boston |
| Edward Belcher | 8 | | Boston |
| Elizabeth Epps | 13 | | |
| Mary Lyne | 6 | | |
| GEORGE BURDEN | 24 | tanner | Boston |
| EDWARD RAINSFORD | 26 | merchant | Boston |
| NATHANIEL TILLEY | 32 | of Little Minories, London | Boston |
| WILLIAM TILLEY | 28 | of Little Minories, London | Boston |
| RALPH ROOT | 50 | | Boston |
| Mary Root | 15 | | |
| Robert Sharpe | 20 | | Braintree |
| RALPH SHEPHERD | 29 | tailor | Dedham |
| Mrs. Thanks Shepherd | 23 | | |
| Sarah Shepherd | 3 | | |
| JOHN HOUGHTON | 4 | (*sic.*) of Eaton Bray, county Bedford | Dedham |
| EDWARD WHITE | 42 | of Cranbrook, county Kent | Dorchester |
| Mrs. Martha White | 39 | | |
| Martha White | 10 | | |
| Mary White | 8 | | |
| JOSEPH FLUDD | 45 | baker | Dorchester |
| Mrs. Jane Fludd | 35 | | |
| Elizabeth Fludd | 9 | | |
| Obadiah Fludd | 4 | | |
| Joseph Fludd | ½ | | |

EDMOND MUNNINGS

| | | | |
|---|---|---|---|
| EDMOND MUNNINGS | 40 | of Denge, county Essex | Dorchester |
| Mrs. Mary Munnings | 30 | | |
| Mary Munnings | 9 | | |
| Anna Munnings | 6 | | |
| Mahalalcel Munnings | 3 | | |
| THOMAS JONES | 40 | | Dorchester |
| Mrs. Ellen Jones | 36 | | |
| Isaac Jones | 8 | | |
| Hester Jones | 6 | | |
| Thomas Jones | 3 | | |
| Sarah Jones | ¼ | | |
| HENRY BULLOCK | 40 | of Saint Lawrence, county Essex | Charlestown |
| Mrs. Susan Bullock | 42 | | |
| Henry Bullock | 8 | | |
| Mary Bullock | 6 | | |
| Thomas Bullock | 2 | | |
| THOMAS KNOWER | 33 | of London, clothier | Charlestown |
| Sarah Knower | 7 | | |
| NOEL KNOWER | 29 | of London | Charlestown |
| PHILIP DRINKER | 39 | potter | Charlestown |
| Mrs. Elizabeth Drinker | 32 | | |
| Edward Drinker | 12 | | |
| John Drinker | 8 | | |
| GEORGE HEPBORNE | 43 | glover of Southwark, county Surrey | Charlestown |
| Mrs. Anne Hepborne | 46 | | |
| Rebecca Hepborne | 10 | | |
| Anna Hepborne | 4 | | |
| JOSEPH BOREBANK | 24 | servant | |
| Joan Jordan | 16 | servant | |
| WILLIAM FULLER | 25 | | Ipswich |
| | | | Joseph Fuller |

| | | | |
|---|---|---|---|
| Joseph Fuller | 15 | | |
| Robert Whitman | 20 | of Little Minories, London | Ipswich |
| John West | 11 | | Ipswich |
| John Emerson | 20 | | Scituate |
| | | | |
| RICHARD CARR | 29 | | Salisbury |
| | | | |
| HUGH BURT | 35 | of Dorking, county Surrey | Lynn |
| Mrs. Anne Burt | 32 | | |
| Hugh Burt | 15 | | |
| Edward Burt | 8 | | |
| William Bassett | 9 | son of Mrs. Burt by a previous marriage | |
| | | | |
| EDWARD IRESON | 32 | perhaps from Buckenham, county Norfolk | Lynn |
| Mrs. Elizabeth Ireson | 27 | | |
| | | | |
| HENRY COLLINS | 29 | starchmaker, certified at Stepney | Lynn |
| Mrs. Anne Collins | 30 | | |
| Henry Collins | 5 | | |
| John Collins | 3 | | |
| Margery Collins | 1 | | |
| | | | |
| DENNIS GEERE | 30 | certified by the minister of Islesworth, county Middlesex, but came from Ovingdean, county Sussex | Lynn |
| Mrs. Elizabeth Geere | 22 | | |
| Elizabeth Geere | 3 | | |
| Sarah Geere | 2 | | |
| Elizabeth Tusolie | 55 | | |
| Anne Pankhurst | 16 | cousin of Geere | |
| Constance Woods | 12 | | |
| Thomas Brane | 40 | servant | |
| Thomas Launder | 22 | servant | |
| | | | |
| EDMUND FREEMAN | 34 | gentleman of Pulborough, county Sussex | Lynn |
| Mrs. Elizabeth Freeman | 35 | | |
| Alice Freeman | 17 | | |
| | | Edward Freeman | |

Edward Freeman 15
Elizabeth Freeman 12
John Freeman 8

WILLIAM ALMY 34 of South Kilworth, county    Lynn
                       Leicester

Mrs. Audrey Almy 32
Agnes Almy 8
Christopher Almy 3

CHRISTOPHER FOSTER 32 husbandman of Ewell, county   Lynn
                       Surrey

Mrs. Frances Foster 25
Rebecca Foster 5
Nathaniel Foster 2
Joseph Foster 1
Alice Stevens 22 (probably sister of Mrs. Foster)
Thomas Stevens 12

JOHN DEACON 28 blacksmith                Lynn
  Mrs. Alice Deacon 30

HUGH ALLEY 27 certified at Stepney       Lynn

JOSHUA GRIFFITH 25 certified from Stepney     Lynn
  Richard Woodman 9                        Lynn

RALPH WALLIS 40 husbandman          Malden
  George Wallis 15

JOHN ALLEN 30 of Haverhill, Suffolk    Plymouth
  Mrs. Anne Allen 30
  Ezra Covell 15

RICHARD ADAMS 29 shoemaker of Northampton,   Salem
                    county Northants

Mrs. Susan Adams 26
Henry Sumner 15 certified from Northampton  Woburn
Elizabeth Sumner 18

JOHN HARBERT 23 shoemaker of Northampton,  Salem
                    county Northants

                                  RICHARD GRAVES

| | | | |
|---|---|---|---|
| RICHARD GRAVES | 23 | | Salem |
| John Cooke | 17 | | Salem |
| Robert Driver | 8 | (*sic.*), probably 43 tailor | Salem |
| John Mere | 3 | mo. | |
| JOHN FREEMAN | 35 | | Sudbury |
| Mrs. Mary Freeman | 30 | | |
| John Freeman | 9 | | |
| Cicely Freeman | 4 | | |
| JASPER ARNOLD | 40 | certified from Shoreditch, London | |
| Mrs. Anne Arnold | 39 | | |
| WILLIAM POTTER | 27 | husbandman | Watertown |
| Mrs. Frances Potter | 26 | | |
| Joseph Potter | ½ | | |
| JOHN ROOKMAN | 45 | | |
| Mrs. Elizabeth Rook-man | 31 | | |
| John Rookman | 9 | | |
| JOHN COKE | 27 | | |
| EDWARD FOUNTAIN | 28 | | |
| JOHN FOX | 35 | | |
| Richard Fox | 15 | | |
| THOMAS FREEMAN | 24 | | |
| WALTER GUTSALL | 23 | | |
| JOHN HOLLIOCK | 28 | | |
| CHARLES JONES | 21 | certified from Little Minories, London | |
| John Jones | 15 | | |
| WILLIAM KING | 28 | | |
| WILLIAM MARSHALL | 40 | | |
| GEORGE RUM (?) | 25 | | |
| JOSEPH STANLEY | 34 | | |
| JOSEPH TERRY | 32 | | |

George Drewry

| | | |
|---|---|---|
| George Drewry | 19 | of East Grinstead, Sussex |
| James Dodd | 16 | |
| Thomas Goad | 15 | |
| Peter Kettell | 10 | |
| Edward Martin | 19 | |
| William Paine | 15 | |
| John Paine | 14 | |
| John Stroud | 15 | |
| Thomas Thompson | 18 | |
| William Yates | 14 | |
| Agnes Alcock | 18 | |
| Lydia Browne | | certified from Little Minories, London |
| Ruth Bushell | 23 | |
| Margaret Devotion | 9 | |
| Elizabeth Ellis | 16 | |
| Elizabeth Harding | 12 | certified from Little Minories, London |
| Susan Hathaway | 34 | |
| Elinor Hillman | 33 | |
| Mary Jones | 30 | |
| Rebecca Price | 14 | |
| Margaret Tucker | 23 | |
| Joan Wall | 19 | |
| Anne Williams | 10 | |

DEFENCE of London, Edward Bostock, Master. She sailed from London about the last of July and arrived at Boston October 8, with about one hundred passengers.

| | | | |
|---|---|---|---|
| ROBERT LONG | 45 | of Dunstable, county Bedford, innholder | Charlestown |
| Mrs. Elizabeth Long | 30 | | |
| Michael Long | 20 | | |
| Sarah Long | 18 | | |
| Robert Long | 16 | | |
| Elizabeth Long | 12 | | |
| Anne Long | 10 | | |
| | | | Mary Long |

| | |
|---|---|
| Mary Long | 9 |
| Rebecca Long | 8 |
| John Long | 8 |
| Zachary Long | 4 |
| Joshua Long | ¾ |

JOHN GOULD      25 of Towcester, county     Charlestown
                              Northants

Mrs. Grace Gould    25

ADAM MOTT       39 of Cambridge, county     Hingham
                              Cambridge, tailor

| | |
|---|---|
| Mrs. Sarah Mott | 31 |
| John Mott | 14 |
| Adam Mott | 12 |
| Jonathan Mott | 9 |
| Elizabeth Mott | 6 |
| Mary Mott | 4 |

JOHN SHEPARD      36 (pseudonym for the Reverend Thomas
                              Shepard)

| | |
|---|---|
| Mrs. Margaret Shepard | 31 |
| Thomas Shepard | ½ |

Thomas Boylston      20 of Fenchurch Street,     Charlestown
                              London

ROGER HARLAKENDEN    23 of Earl's Colne, county     Cambridge
                              Essex

| | | |
|---|---|---|
| Mrs. Elizabeth Harlakenden | 18 | |
| Mabel Harlakenden | 22 | |
| Anne Wood | 23 | |
| Samuel Shepard | 22 | |
| Joseph Cooke | 27 | |
| George Cooke | 25 | |
| William French | 30 | servants |
| Mrs. Elizabeth French | 32 | |
| Robert ...... | | |
| Sarah Simes | 30 | |

                                      Mrs. Elizabeth French

| | | | |
|---|---|---|---|
| Mrs. Elizabeth French | 30 | | Cambridge |
| Francis French | 10 | | |
| Elizabeth French | 6 | | |
| Mary French | 2½ | | |
| John French | ½ | | |
| JOHN JACKSON | 30 | Birching Lane, London | |
| JAMES FITCH | 30 | | Boston |
| Mrs. Abigail Fitch | 24 | | |
| John Fitch | 14 | | |
| RICHARD PARK | 33 | miller | Cambridge |
| Mrs. Margery Park | 30 | | |
| HENRY DEWHURST | 35 | | |
| Robert Hill | 20 | servant to Matthew Cradock | Medford |
| WILLIAM HUBBARD | 40 | husbandman of Little Clacton, Essex | Ipswich |
| Mrs. Judith Hubbard | 25 | | |
| John Hubbard | 15 | | |
| William Hubbard | 13 | | |
| Nathaniel Hubbard | 6 | | |
| Richard Hubbard | 4 | | |
| Martha Hubbard | 22 | | |
| Mary Hubbard | 20 | | |
| ROBERT COLBORNE | 28 | | Ipswich |
| Edward Colborne | 17 | | |
| WILLIAM READE | 48 | | Boston |
| Mrs. Mabel Reade | 30 | | |
| George Reade | 6 | | |
| Ralph Reade | 5 | | |
| Justus Reade | 1½ | | |
| ROBERT KEAYNE | 40 | merchant of London | Boston |
| Mrs. Anne Keayne | 38 | | |
| | | | Benjamin Keayne |

| | | | |
|---|---|---|---|
| Benjamin Keayne | 16 | | |
| Penelope Darno | 29 | servant | |
| WILLIAM WILLIAMSON | 25 | | |
| Mrs. Mary William-<br>son | 23 | | |
| JASPER GUNN | 29 | | Milford, Connecticut |
| Mrs. Anne Gunn | 25 | | |
| Phebe Maulder | 7 | | |
| THOMAS DONN | 25 | | |
| JOHN JENKINS | 26 | | |
| JOHN BURTES | 29 | | |
| WILLIAM SAWKYN | 25 | | |
| Mrs. Sarah Knight | 50 | | |
| Dorothy Knight | 24 | | |
| Susannah Fare-<br>brother | 25 | | |
| Elizabeth Fenwick | 25 | | |
| Dorothy Adams | 24 | | |
| Francis Nutbrowne | 16 | | |
| Martha Banes | 20 | | |
| Elizabeth Steere | 18 | | |
| Mary Bentley | 20 | | |
| Simon Rogers | 20 | shoemaker | Concord |

The following distinguished persons came in this ship, although their names are not on the official passenger list.[1] It is certain that they came under assumed names, owing to the rigorous inspection of emigrant ships to New England.

| | | |
|---|---|---|
| *Rev.* THOMAS SHEPARD | of Towcester, county<br>Northants | Cambridge |
| | Mrs. Margaret Shepard | |

[1] Winthrop: *Journal*, 1, 160.

Mrs. Margaret Shepard
Thomas Shepard

| | | |
|---|---|---|
| *Rev.* JOHN WILSON | returning from England | Boston |
| *Rev.* HUGH PETER | of Fowey, county Cornwall | Salem |
| *Rev.* JOHN NORTON | of Bishops Stortford, county Herts | Ipswich |
| Mrs. Mary Norton | | |

*Rev.* JOHN JONES                             Concord
   Mrs. Sarah Jones   34            Fairfield, Conn.
   Sarah Jones       15 ⎫
   John Jones       11 ⎪
   Ruth Jones        7 ⎬ his children
   Theophilus Jones   3 ⎪
   Rebecca Jones    2 ⎪
   Elizabeth Jones   ½ ⎭

TRUELOVE, John Gibbs, Master. She sailed in September, probably, from London and arrived at Boston late in November.[1]

| | | |
|---|---|---|
| THOMAS BURCHARD   40 laborer | | Roxbury |
|   Mrs. Mary Burchard 38 | | |
|   Elizabeth Burchard  13 | | |
|   Mary Burchard     12 | | |
|   Sarah Burchard    9 | | |
|   Susan Burchard    8 | | |
|   John Burchard     7 | | |
|   Anne Burchard   1½ | | |

EDWARD HOWE      60 husbandman of Berk-     Lynn
                      hampstead, county Herts
  Mrs. Elizabeth
    Howe         50
                                    Jeremy Howe

[1] Public Record Office MSS., and Drake: *Founders*, 42.

| | | | |
|---|---|---|---|
| Jeremy Howe | 21 | | |
| Sarah Howe | 12 | | |
| Ephraim Howe | 9 | | |
| Isaac Howe | 7 | | |
| William Howe | 6 | | |
| ZACHARIAH WHITMAN | 40 | of Lee, county Bucks | Weymouth. |
| Mrs. Sarah Whit- | | | Removed to |
| man | 25 | | Stratford, |
| Zachariah Whitman | 2½ | | Connecticut |
| Rebecca Fenner | 25 | | |
| Thomas Tibbalds | 20 | | |
| John Stream | 14 | | |
| Thomas Sterte | 15 | | |
| RALPH TOMPKINS | 50 | husbandman | Dorchester |
| Mrs. Katherine | | | |
| Tompkins | | | |
| Samuel Tompkins | 22 | | |
| Elizabeth Tompkins | 18 | | |
| Mary Tompkins | 14 | | |
| RICHARD HAWES | 29 | of Great Missenden, Bucks | Dorchester |
| Mrs. Anne Hawes | 26 | | |
| Anne Hawes | 2½ | | |
| Obadiah Hawes | ½ | | |
| WILLIAM PRESTON | 44 | of Giggleswick, county York | Dorchester and New Haven |
| Mrs. Mary Preston | 34 | | |
| Elizabeth Preston | 11 | | |
| Sarah Preston | 8 | | |
| Mary Preston | 6 | | |
| John Preston | 3 | | |
| WILLIAM BEERESTO | 23 | | Dedham |
| GEORGE BEERESTO | 21 | | Dedham |
| WILLIAM BENTLEY | 47 | | |
| John Bentley | 17 | | |
| Alice Bentley | 15 | | |
| | | | PETER PLACE |

| PETER PLACE | 20 | | Boston |
| RALPH ELLINWOOD | 28 | | Salem |
| GEORGE TAYLOR | 31 | | Lynn |
| RICHARD SWAYNE | 34 | | |
| ROBERT BROWNE | 24 | | |
| JOHN SEDGWICK | 24 | | |
| JEREMY BLACKWELL | 18 | probably of Lincoln (City) | |
| Lester Gunter | 13 | | |
| THOMAS STOCKTON | 21 | | |
| George Morey | 16 | | |
| THOMAS BLOWER | 50 | | |
| EDWARD JEFFRIES | 24 | | |
| JOHN SIMPSON | 30 | | |
| THOMAS BRIGHTON | 31 | | |
| THOMAS RUMBALL | 22 | | Stratford, Connecticut |
| EDWARD PARRIE | 24 | | |
| Roger Broome | 17 | | |
| John Done | 16 | | |
| WILLIAM JOES | 28 | (perhaps error for Jones or Jose) | |
| Elizabeth Jenkins | 27 | | |
| Margaret Killinghall | 20 | | |
| Sarah Haile | 11 | | |
| Jane Walston | 19 | | |
| Dorothy Lowe | 13 | | |

## PIED COW.

PIED COW. Nothing is known of this vessel, the time of her departure or her arrival, except what is given below. [1]

| | | |
|---|---|---|
| WILLIAM HARRISON | 55 certified by Sir Edward Spencer, 'resident near Bramford' (county Suffolk) | |
| John Baldwin | | |
| William Baldwin | | |
| ROBERT BILLS | 32 husbandman | Charlestown |

HOPEWELL of London, Thomas Babb, Master. She sailed about the middle of September and arrived at Boston in the latter part of November. [2]

| | | | |
|---|---|---|---|
| THOMAS TREDWELL | 30 | certified at Saint Giles's, Cripplegate, London | Dorchester |
| Mrs. Mary Tredwell | 30 | | |
| Thomas Tredwell | 1 | | |
| Thomas Blackley | 20 | | |
| HENRY MAUDSLEY | 24 | | Dorchester |
| WILLIAM NORTON | 25 | | Ipswich |
| THOMAS TURNER | 43 | | Hingham |
| ROBERT PENNAIRD | 21 | | |
| Thomas Pennaird | 10 | | |
| WILLIAM WOOD | 27 | husbandman | Lynn |
| Mrs. Elizabeth Wood | 24 | | |
| JOHN WOOD | 26 | | Salem |
| THOMAS JOHNSON | 25 | | |
| THOMAS BULL | 25 | | |
| | | | Mary Hubbard |

[1] Public Record Office MSS., and Drake: *Founders*, 38, 41.

[2] Public Record Office MSS., and *N.E. Gen. Register* for October, 1848.

| | | | |
|---|---|---|---|
| Mary Hubbard | 24 | | |
| John Kerbie | 12 | | |
| John Thomas | 14 | | |
| Isaac Robinson | 15 | | |
| Anne Williamson | 18 | | |
| William Lyon | 14 | | |
| Grace Stokes | 20 | | |
| Robert Chambers | 13 | | |
| THOMAS BULL | 25 | | |
| Joseph Miller | 15 | | |
| Richard Hutley | 15 | | |
| John Prior | 15 | | Duxbury |
| Daniel Prior | 13 | | Scituate |
| John Marshall | 14 | | |
| Mary Clark | 16 | | |
| Joan Cleeven | 18 | | |
| Joan Grave | 30 | | |
| Mary Grave | 26 | | |
| Edmond Chipper- field | 20 | | |
| ROBERT EDWARDS | 22 | | |
| ROBERT EDGE | 25 | | York, Maine |
| WALTER LLOYD | 27 | | |
| Ellen Leaves | 17 | | |
| Alice Albon | 25 | | |
| Barbara Rose | 20 | | |
| John Foster | 14 | | |
| Gabriel Reed | 18 | | |
| JOHN WEEKS | 26 | tanner | perhaps Plymouth |
| Mrs. Mary Weeks | 28 | | |
| Anne Weeks | 1 | | |
| Mary Withie | 62 | | |
| Robert Withie | 20 | | |
| Susan Withie | 18 | | |
| Mary Withie | 16 | | |

ROBERT BAYLIE

| | | | |
|---|---|---|---|
| ROBERT BAYLIE | 23 | | |
| SAMUEL YOUNGLOVE | 30 | | Ipswich |
| Mrs. Margaret Younglove | 28 | | |
| Samuel Younglove | 1 | | |
| ANDREW HULL | 29 | | |
| Mrs. Katherine Hull | 23 | | |
| ROGER TOOTHAKER | 23 | | Plymouth |
| Mrs. Margaret Toothaker | 28 | | |
| Roger Toothaker | 1 | | |
| ISAAC HEATH | 50 | harness-maker of Little Amwell, Herts | Roxbury |
| Mrs. Elizabeth Heath | 40 | | |
| Elizabeth Heath | 5 | | |
| Martha Heath | 30 | | |
| ANTHONY FREEMAN | 22 | | |
| Twyford West | 19 | servant | Plymouth |
| Henry Ticknall | 15 | | |

BLESSING, John Leicester, Master. She sailed in June with the following passengers 'to be transported to New England' and arrived at Boston in August.[1]

| | | | |
|---|---|---|---|
| WILLIAM VASSALL | 42 | of Stepney, county Middlesex, merchant | Scituate |
| Mrs. Anne Vassall | 42 | | |
| Judith Vassall | 16 | | |
| Frances Vassall | 12 | | |
| John Vassall | 10 | | |
| Anne Vassall | 6 | | |
| | | | Margaret Vassall |

[1] Public Record Office MSS.

| | | | |
|---|---|---|---|
| Margaret Vassall | 2 | | |
| Mary Vassall | 1 | | |
| William Brooke | 20 | servant | Marshfield |
| Gilbert Brooke | 14 | servant | Marshfield |
| THOMAS KING | 31 | of Cold Norton, Essex | Scituate |
| Susan King | 32 | | |
| Thomasine Munson | 14 | servant | Scituate |
| JOHN STOCKBRIDGE | 27 | | Scituate |
| Mrs. Anne Stockbridge | 21 | | |
| NICHOLAS ROBINSON | 30 | | Cambridge |
| Mrs. Elizabeth Robinson | 32 | | |
| Katherine Robinson | 12 | | |
| Mary Robinson | 7 | | |
| John Robinson | 5 | | |
| Sarah Robinson | 1½ | | |
| ROBERT SAYWELL | 30 | | Boston |
| Mrs. Susan Saywell | 25 | | |
| James Saywell | 1 | | |
| Nathaniel Byham | 14 | | Marshfield |
| Richard More | 20 | | |
| John Morey | 19 | | |
| John Briggs | 20 | | Watertown |
| Nicholas Long | 19 | | |
| John Hathaway | 18 | | Yarmouth |
| Henry Beck | 18 | | Dover, New Hampshire |
| Edward Ingraham | 18 | | Salem |
| John Manifold | 17 | | |
| John Fitch | 14 | | |
| Richard Sexton | 14 | | Windsor |
| Elizabeth Holley | 30 | | |
| Sarah Tinkler | 15 | | |
| Mary Hubbard | 24 | | |
| Mary Sprall | 20 | | |
| Christian Buck | 26 | | |

WILLIAM COPE

| | | | |
|---|---|---|---|
| WILLIAM COPE | 26 | | |
| RICHARD COPE | 24 | | |
| ROBERT TURNER | 24 | | Boston |
| ROBERT ONION | 26 | | Roxbury |
| RICHARD HOLLINGS-<br>WORTH | 40 [1] | | Salem |
| Mrs. Susan Hollings-<br>worth | 30 | | |
| William Hollings-<br>worth | 7 | | |
| Richard Hollings-<br>worth | 4 | | |
| Elizabeth Hollings-<br>worth | 3 | | |
| Susan Hollingsworth | 2 | | |
| Christian Hunter | 20 [1] | | |
| Elizabeth Hunter | 18 | | |
| Thomas Hunter | 14 | | |
| William Hunter | 11 | | |
| Thomas Trentum | 14 | | |
| Thomas Biggs | 13 | | |
| JOHN JACKSON | 40 | fisherman | Cambridge |
| Mrs. Margaret Jack-<br>son | 36 | | |
| John Jackson | 2 | | |
| BARNABY DAVIS | 36 | | Charlestown |
| Mrs. Susan Davis | 16 | | |
| ROBERT LEWIS | 28 | | Salem |
| Mrs. Elizabeth<br>Lewis | 22 | | |
| JOHN BURULES | 26 | (probably Burrell) | |

1636

[1] William Hollingsworth testified that his father came with twelve persons in 1635, and the last six named in his family are probably those who are found in Salem afterward.

1636

HECTOR. No information is available about this ship except that she arrived sometime in May.[1]


...... 'Divers of the ships this spring out of the Downs came
in five weeks,' but no information is available as to names of
the vessels or passengers.[2]


...... A ship arrived November 10, from London, 'Full of
Passengers, men, women and children.' [3]


...... ......On November 17, two ships arrived from
London, names unknown, 'full of passengers.' One of them
had been twenty-six weeks from the Thames, and eighteen
weeks from land to land. 'Their beer all spent and leaked
out a month before their arrival, so as they were forced to
stinking water (and that very little) mixed with sack or vine-
gar, and their other provisions very short and bad. Yet,
through the great providence of the Lord, they came safe on
shore, and most of them sound and well liking. One of the
ships was overset in the night by a sudden gust, and lay so for
half an hour, yet righted herself.' [4]

| | | |
|---|---|---|
| *Rev.* NATHANIEL ROGERS | of Haverhill, county Suffolk | Ipswich |
| Mrs. Margaret Rogers | | |
| Nathaniel Rogers | of Haverhill, county Suffolk | Ipswich |
| Samuel Rogers | | |
| | *Rev.* RALPH PARTRIDGE | |

[1] Winthrop: *Journal*, I, 181.    [2] *Ibid.*, 181.    [3] *Ibid.*, 199.    [4] *Ibid.*, 200

*Rev.* RALPH PARTRIDGE    of Lenham, county Kent    Duxbury
Mrs. Patience Partridge
Elizabeth Partridge
Mary Partridge


GEORGE of Bristol, arrived at Plymouth, December 27, laden with cattle and passengers, under stress of weather, 'having spent her mainmast about Cape Cod.'[1] No information as to names of the emigrants.


## 1637

June 3. 'Two ships arrived here out of England (Mr. Peirce was [Master of] one).'[2]


June 20. 'Three ships arrived here from Ipswich with three hundred and sixty passengers.'[3]


June 26. 'There arrived two ships from London, the *Hector* and the (blank). In these came Mr. Davenport and another minister, and Mr. Eaton and Mr. Hopkins, two merchants of London, men of fair estate and of great esteem for religion and wisdom in outward affairs.'

In the *Hector* came also the Lord Ley, son and heir of the Earl of Marlborough.[4]

*Rev.* JOHN DAVENPORT

[1] Winthrop: *Journal*, I, 208.    [2] *Ibid.*, 221.    [3] *Ibid.*, 222.    [4] *Ibid.*, 223.

| | |
|---|---|
| *Rev.* JOHN DAVENPORT | New Haven |
| EDWARD HOPKINS | New Haven |
| THEOPHILUS EATON | New Haven |
| *Rev.* JOHN HARVARD (?) | It is possible that the 'other Minister' was the famous John Harvard as he arrived here this summer |

MARY ANNE of Yarmouth, William Goose, Master. She sailed from Ipswich in May and arrived at Boston June 20.[1]

| THOMAS PAINE | 50 | weaver of Wrentham, Suffolk | Salem |
|---|---|---|---|
| Mrs. Elizabeth Paine | 53 | | |
| Thomas Paine, Jr. | | | |
| John Paine | | | |
| Mary Paine | | | |
| Elizabeth Paine | | | |
| Dorothy Paine | | | |
| Sarah Paine | | | |
| Margaret Neave | 58 | widow, of Great Yarmouth, Norfolk | Salem |
| Rachel Dixon | | | |
| BENJAMIN COOPER | 50 | husbandman of Brampton, Suffolk | Salem |
| Mrs. Elizabeth Cooper | 48 | | |
| Lawrence Cooper | | | |
| Mary Cooper | | | |
| Rebecca Cooper | | | |
| Benjamin Cooper, Jr. | | | |
| Frances Tillingham | 32 | | |
| Esther Cooper | 48 | | |
| John Killin | | | |
| Philemon Dickerson | | servant | Salem |
| ABRAHAM TOPPAN | | | |

[1] Winthrop: *Journal*, I, 222; Wyman: *Charlestown*, I, 563; and original list in Public Records Office.

| | | | |
|---|---|---|---|
| ABRAHAM TOPPAN | 31 | cooper of Great Yarmouth, Norfolk | Newbury |
| Mrs. Susanna Toppan | 30 | | |
| Peter Toppan | | | |
| Elizabeth Toppan | | | |
| Anne Goodin | 18 | servant | |
| | | | |
| WILLIAM THOMAS | 26 | of Great Comberton, Worcester | |
| | | | |
| JOHN THURSTON | 30 | husbandman of Wrentham, Suffolk | Salem |
| Mrs. Margaret Thurston | 32 | | |
| Thomas Thurston | | | |
| John Thurston | | | |
| Lucy Poyett | 23 | spinster | |
| | | | |
| JOHN BURROWE | 48 | cooper of Great Yarmouth, Norfolk | Salem |
| Mrs. Anne Burrowe | 40 | | |
| | | | |
| WILLIAM GAULT | 29 | cordwainer of Great Yarmouth, Norfolk | Salem |
| AUGUSTINE CA...... | | | |
| Mrs. Alice Ca...... | 40 | | |
| | | | |
| JOHN DARRELL | | | |
| Mrs. Joan Ames | 50 | widow of Great Yarmouth, Norfolk | Salem |
| Ruth Ames | 18 | | |
| William Ames | | | |
| John Ames | | | |
| | | | |
| JOHN GEDNEY | | of Norwich, Norfolk | Salem |
| Mrs. Sarah Gedney | 25 | | |
| Lydia Gedney | | | |
| Hannah Gedney | | | |
| John Gedney | | | |
| William Walker | | servant | |
| ...... Burgess | 26 | servant | |

SAMUEL GREENFIELD

| | | | |
|---|---|---|---|
| SAMUEL GREENFIELD | 27 | weaver of Norwich, Norfolk | Salem |
| Mrs. Barbara Green-<br>field | 25 | | |
| Mary Greenfield | | | |
| Barbara Greenfield | | | |
| John Teed | 19 | servant | |
| THOMAS JONES | 25 | butcher of Elzing,<br>Norfolk | Charlestown |
| THOMAS OLIVER | 36 | calender of Norwich, Norfolk | Salem |
| Mrs. Mary Oliver | 34 | | |
| Thomas Oliver, Jr. | | | |
| John Oliver | | | |
| Thomas Doged | 30 | servant | |
| Mary Sape | 12 | servant | |
| WILLIAM COCKRAM | 28 | mariner of Southold,<br>Suffolk | Hingham |
| Mrs. Christian Cock-<br>ram | 26 | | |
| William Cockram, Jr. | | | |
| ...... Cockram | | | |
| JOHN CUTLER ¹ | | | Hingham |
| Mrs. Mary Cutler | | | |
| ...... Cutler | | | |
| ...... Cutler | | | |
| ...... Cutler | | | |
| ...... Cutler | | | |
| ...... Cutler | | | |
| ...... Cutler | | | |
| ...... Cutler | | | |
| ...... ...... | | (servant) | |
| HENRY TUTHILL ¹ | | of Saxlingham, Norfolk | Hingham |
| Mrs. ...... Tuthill | | | |
| ISAAC WRIGHT ¹ | | | |
| JOHN TOWER ¹ | | | Hingham |

JOHN AND DOROTHY

¹ These four families are taken from Daniel Cushing's Record. (Drake: *Founders*, 84.)

JOHN AND DOROTHY of Ipswich, William Andrews, Master.

ROSE of Yarmouth, William Andrews, Jr., Master.

The following named passengers sailed in these two ships from Ipswich, and arrived June 8 at Boston.[1] It is not possible to allocate them to either ship and they are combined in this way.[2]

| | | | |
|---|---|---|---|
| JOHN BAKER | 39 | grocer of Norwich, Norfolk | Charlestown |
| Mrs. Elizabeth Baker | 31 | | |
| Elizabeth Baker | | | |
| Thomas Baker | | | |
| John Baker, Jr. | | | |
| Mary Alxarson | 24 | | |
| Anne Alxarson | 20 | | |
| Bridget Boulle | 32 | | |
| NICHOLAS BUSBY | 50 | weaver of Norwich, Norfolk | Watertown |
| Mrs. Bridget Busby | 53 | | |
| Nicholas Busby | | | |
| John Busby | | | |
| Abraham Busby | | | |
| Sarah Busby | | | |
| MICHAEL METCALF | 45 | weaver of Norwich, Norfolk | Dedham |
| Mrs. Sarah Metcalf | 39 | | |
| Mary Metcalf | 19 | | |
| Michael Metcalf, Jr. | 17 | | |
| John Metcalf | 15 | | |
| Sarah Metcalf | 13 | | |
| Elizabeth Metcalf | 11 | | |
| | | | Martha Metcalf |

[1] Winthrop: *Journal*, 1, 222.      [2] Public Record Office MSS.

| | | | |
|---|---|---|---|
| Martha Metcalf | 9 | | |
| Thomas Metcalf | 7 | | |
| Jane Metcalf | 5 | | |
| Rebecca Metcalf | 2 | | |
| Thomas Comber-bach | 16 | servant | |
| SAMUEL DIX | 43 | joiner of Norwich, Norfolk | |
| Mrs. Joan Dix | 38 | | |
| Priscilla Dix | | | |
| Abigail Dix | | | |
| William Storey | 23 | servant | |
| Daniel Lindsey | 18 | servant | |
| HENRY SKERRY | 31 | cordwainer of Great Yar-mouth, Norfolk | Salem |
| Mrs. Elizabeth Skerry | 25 | | |
| Henry Skerry, Jr. | | | |
| Edmund Towne | 18 | apprentice | |
| FRANCIS LAWES | | of Carleton Rode, Norfolk | Salem |
| Mrs. Lydia Lawes | 49 | | |
| Mary Lawes | | | |
| Samuel Lincoln | 18 | servant | |
| Anne Smith | 19 | servant | |
| JOHN MOULTON | 38 | husbandman of Ormsby, Norfolk | Newbury, Hampton, N.H. |
| Mrs. Anne Moulton | 38 | | |
| Henry Moulton | | | |
| Mercy Moulton | | | |
| Anne Moulton | | | |
| Jane Moulton | | | |
| Bridget Moulton | | | |
| Adam Goodens | 20 | servant | |
| Alice Eden | 18 | | |
| Mrs. Mary Moulton | 30 | widow | |
| Miriam Moulton | 23 | | |
| Ruth Moulton | 20 | | |
| John Marston | 20 | servant | |

THOMAS MOULTON

| | | | |
|---|---|---|---|
| THOMAS MOULTON | 31 | husbandman of Ormsby, Norfolk | Hampton, N.H., York, Me. |
| RICHARD CARVER | 60 | husbandman of Scratby, Norfolk | Watertown |
| Mrs. Grace Carver | 40 | | |
| Elizabeth Carver | 18 | twin | |
| Susanna Carver | 18 | twin | |
| Isaac Hart | 22 | servant | |
| Thomas Flagge | 21 | servant | |
| Merible Underwood | 20 | servant | |
| ROBERT PAGE | 33 | husbandman of Ormsby, Norfolk | Salem |
| Mrs. Lucy Page | 30 | | |
| Frances Page | | | |
| Margaret Page | | | |
| Susanna Page | | | |
| JOHN PEARCE | 49 | weaver of Norwich, Norfolk | Watertown |
| Mrs. Elizabeth Pearce | 36 | | |
| John Pearce | | | |
| Barbara Pearce | | | |
| Elizabeth Pearce | | | |
| Judith Pearce | | | |
| John Gedney | 19 | servant | |
| WILLIAM LUDKIN | 33 | locksmith of Norwich, Norfolk | Hingham |
| Mrs. Elizabeth Ludkin | 34 | | |
| Esther Ludkin | | | |
| (illegible)...... | 28 | cordwainer | |
| ...... ...... | | | |
| Samuel ...... | | | |
| John ...... | | | |
| Elizabeth ...... | | | |
| Deborah ...... | | | |
| Anne Williams | 15 | | |

WILLIAM NICKERSON

WILLIAM NICKERSON    33   weaver of Norwich, Norfolk    Boston
Mrs. Anne Nickerson 28
Nicholas Nickerson
Robert Nickerson
Elizabeth Nickerson
Anne Nickerson
William Moulton     20   servant
Anne Wadd         15   servant

HENRY DOW         29   husbandman of Ormsby,    Watertown
                        Norfolk

Mrs. Joan Dow      30
Thomas Dow        6
Henry Dow, Jr.      3
Anne Manning      17   servant
Ellen Robinson

WILLIAM WILLIAMS    40   of Great Yarmouth,     Watertown
                        Norfolk

Mrs. Alice Williams   38
Abraham Williams
Elizabeth Williams   31   spinster
Katherine Roby     68   widow

RICHARD LEEDS      32   mariner of Great Yar-     Dedham
                        mouth, Norfolk

Mrs. Joan Leeds     23

HENRY SMITH        30   husbandman of New      Dedham
                        Buckenham, Norfolk
Mrs. Elizabeth Smith 34
John Smith
Seth Smith

JOHN ROPER         26   carpenter of New Bucken-   Dedham
                        ham, Norfolk

Mrs. Alice Roper    23
Alice Roper
Elizabeth Roper

                                       HERCULES

HERCULES of Sandwich, John Witherley, Master. When this ship sailed from Sandwich is not known, but the following list of passengers 'for the American Plantations,' in the corporation records of Sandwich, is 'certified under the seal of the office of Mayoralty, 9 June, 1637.' All these passengers settled in New England. Winthrop states, under date of June 3, that 'Two ships arrived here out of England (Mr. Peirce was one),' and the *Hercules* may be the other.[1]

| | | |
|---|---|---|
| THOMAS STARR<br>  Mrs. Susan Starr | of Canterbury, yeoman | Dorchester |
| EDWARD JOHNSON<br>  Mrs. Susan Johnson<br>  Edward Johnson<br>  George Johnson<br>  Martha Johnson<br>  Matthew Johnson<br>  John Johnson<br>  Susan Johnson<br>  William Johnson<br>  John Farley<br>  John England | of Canterbury, joiner | Charlestown |
| NICHOLAS BUTLER<br>  Mrs. Joyce Butler<br>  John Butler<br>  Henry Butler<br>  Lydia Butler<br>  Thomas Butler<br>  John Pope<br>  John Gill<br>  Richard Jenkins<br>  Simon Athearn | of Ashford, yeoman | Dorchester |
| SAMUEL HALL<br>  Mrs. Joan Hall<br>  Edward Page | of Canterbury, yeoman | |
| | | Joan Granger |

[1] *Journal*, I, 221; Boys: *History of Sandwich*, 1786–92.

Joan Granger
Grace Granger

HENRY BACHELOR            of Dover, brewer            Ipswich
  Mrs. Martha Bachelor
  John Buck
  Susan Buck
  Samuel Taylor

JOSEPH BACHELOR           of Canterbury, tailor       Salem
  Mrs. Elizabeth Bachelor
  . . . . . . Bachelor
  Thomas Granger
  Edward Harsnet

HENRY RICHARDSON          of Canterbury, carpenter
  Mrs. Mary Richardson
  . . . . . . Richardson
  . . . . . . Richardson
  . . . . . . Richardson
  . . . . . . Richardson
  . . . . . . Richardson

JARVIS BOYKET             of Thannington,            Charlestown
                            carpenter
  Stephen Granger

JOHN BACHELOR             of Canterbury, tailor       Salem

NATHANIEL OVELL           of Dover, cordwainer
  Thomas Granger

THOMAS CALL               of Faversham, hus-         Charlestown
                            bandman
  Mrs. Bennet Call
  Thomas Call
  John Call
  Mary Call

WILLIAM EATON             of Staple, husbandman      Watertown
  Mrs. Martha Eaton
  John Eaton

. . . . . . . . . . . .

. . . . . .  . . . . . .
. . . . . .  . . . . . .
Jonas Eaton

| | | |
|---|---|---|
| JOSEPH COLEMAN | of Sandwich, shoemaker | |
| Mrs. Sarah Coleman | | |
| . . . . . . Coleman | | |
| . . . . . . Coleman | | |
| . . . . . . Coleman | | |
| . . . . . . Coleman | | |
| MATTHEW SMITH | of Sandwich, cord- wainer | Charlestown |
| Mrs. Jane Smith | | |
| Matthew Smith | | |
| . . . . . . Smith | | |
| . . . . . . Smith | | |
| . . . . . . Smith | | |
| MARMADUKE PEIRCE | of Sandwich, tailor | Salem |
| Mrs. Mary Peirce | | |
| John Hooke | | |

## 1638

Governor Winthrop had ceased to record the separate arrivals of passenger ships and lumped them all together. About September 1 he made the following record: 'There came over this summer twenty ships, and at least three thousand persons, so as they were forced to look out new plantations. One was begun at Merrimack, and another four or five miles above Concord, and another at Winicowett.'[1] This last named place became later Hampton, New Hampshire.[2] Of these twenty ships not half are known by name, but the following have been identified as coming this year:

CASTLE

[1] *Journal*, I, 274.      [2] *Mass. Col. Rec.*, I, 271.

CASTLE of London, sailed in April for New England.[1]


SUSAN AND ELLEN, Edward Payne, Master, sailed from London April 11 and arrived July 17 this year.[2]


...... 'a ship of Barnstaple' arrived September 21 with eighty passengers, 'near all Western people.'[3]

Rev. MARMADUKE MATTHEWS 32        Yarmouth, Cape Cod
Mrs. Katherine Matthews


DILIGENT, of Ipswich, John Martin, Master. She sailed from Ipswich, Suffolk, in June and arrived August 10 at Boston, with about one hundred passengers, principally from Hingham, Norfolk, destined for Hingham, Massachusetts.[4]

| | | |
|---|---|---|
| Rev. ROBERT PECK | of Hingham, county Norfolk | Hingham |
| Mrs. ...... Peck | | |
| Anne Peck | | |
| Joseph Peck | | |
| JOSEPH PECK | of Hingham, county Norfolk | Hingham |
| Mrs. ...... Peck | | |
| EDWARD GILMAN | of Hingham, county Norfolk | Hingham |
| Mrs. Mary Gilman | | |
| Edward Gilman | | |
| | | Moses Gilman |

[1] *Lechford Note Book*, 77.        [2] *Ibid.*, 91.
[3] Winthrop: *Journal*, 1, 277.        [4] Cushing MSS.

Moses Gilman
Lydia Gilman
Sarah Gilman
John Gilman

| | | |
|---|---|---|
| JOHN FOLSOM | of Hingham, county Norfolk | Hingham |

Mrs. Mary Folsom
John Folsom

| | | |
|---|---|---|
| *Mrs.* CHRISTIAN CHAMBERLAIN | of Hingham, county Norfolk | Hingham |
| HENRY CHAMBERLAIN | of Hingham, county Norfolk | Hingham |

Mrs. ...... Chamberlain
...... Chamberlain
...... Chamberlain

| | | |
|---|---|---|
| STEPHEN GATES | of Norwich, Norfolk | Hingham |

Mrs. Anne Gates
Elizabeth Gates
Mary Gates

| | | |
|---|---|---|
| GEORGE KNIGHTS | of Barrow, Norfolk | Hingham |

Mrs. ...... Knights
...... Knights

| | | |
|---|---|---|
| THOMAS COOPER | of Hingham, county Norfolk | Hingham |

Mrs. Cooper
...... Cooper
...... Cooper

| | | |
|---|---|---|
| FRANCIS JAMES | of Hingham, county Norfolk | Hingham |

Mrs. Elizabeth James

| | | |
|---|---|---|
| MATTHEW HAWKE | of Cambridge, England | Hingham |

Mrs. Margaret Hawke

| | | |
|---|---|---|
| MATTHEW CUSHING | of Hingham, county Norfolk | Hingham |

Mrs. Nazareth Cushing

Mrs. Nazareth Cushing
Daniel Cushing
Jeremiah Cushing
Matthew Cushing
John Cushing
Deborah Cushing

| | | |
|---|---|---|
| JOHN TUFTS | of Hingham, county Norfolk | Hingham |
| ROBERT SKOULDING | of Norwich, county Norfolk | Hingham |

Elizabeth Sayer
Mary Sayer

| | | |
|---|---|---|
| JOHN FEARING | of Cambridge, England | Hingham |
| PHILIP JAMES | of Hingham, county Norfolk | Hingham |

Mrs. Jane James
...... James
...... James
...... James
...... James

| | | |
|---|---|---|
| STEPHEN PAINE | of Great Ellingham, Norfolk | Hingham |

Mrs. Rose Paine
...... Paine
...... Paine
...... Paine
...... Paine

| | | |
|---|---|---|
| JOHN SUTTON | of Attleborough, Norfolk | Hingham |

Mrs. Elizabeth Sutton
Hannah Sutton
John Sutton, Jr.
Nathaniel Sutton
Elizabeth Sutton

*Mrs.* JOAN LINCOLN

                                        STEPHEN LINCOLN

| | | |
|---|---|---|
| STEPHEN LINCOLN<br>Mrs. ...... Lincoln<br>Stephen Lincoln, Jr. | of Wymondham, Norfolk | Hingham |
| SAMUEL PACKER<br>Mrs. Elizabeth Packer<br>...... Packer | of Wymondham, Norfolk | Hingham |
| HENRY SMITH<br>Mrs. Judith Smith<br>John Smith<br>Henry Smith<br>Daniel Smith<br>Judith Smith<br>Elizabeth Smith | of Hempnall, Norfolk | Hingham |
| BOZOUN ALLEN<br>Mrs. Anne Allen | of King's Lynn, Norfolk | Hingham |
| WILLIAM RIPLEY<br>Mrs. ...... Ripley<br>Mary Ripley<br>John Ripley<br>Abraham Ripley<br>Sarah Ripley | of Wymondham, Norfolk | Hingham |
| THOMAS SUCKLIN | of Hingham, Norfolk | Hingham |
| RICHARD BAXTER | of Hingham, Norfolk | Hingham |
| WILLIAM PITTS | of Hingham, Norfolk | Hingham |
| EDWARD MITCHELL | of Hingham, Norfolk | Hingham |
| JAMES BUCK | of Hingham, Norfolk | Hingham |
| JOHN MORFIELD | of Hingham, Norfolk | Hingham |
| THOMAS LINCOLN | of Hingham, Norfolk | Hingham |
| JEREMIAH MOORE<br>And about 20 servants | of Wymondham, Norfolk | Hingham |

CONFIDENCE,

CONFIDENCE, of London, two hundred tons, John Gibson, Master. She sailed from Southampton the last of April,'by vertue of the Lord Treasurers warrant of the 11th of April, 1638.'[1]

| | | | |
|---|---|---|---|
| WALTER HAYNES | 55 | linen weaver of Sutton Mansfield, Wilts | Sudbury |
| Mrs. Elizabeth Haynes | | | |
| John Haynes | | | |
| Josias Haynes | | | |
| Suffrance Haynes | | | |
| Mary Haynes | | | |
| John Blandford | 27 | servant | |
| John Riddet | 26 | servant | |
| Richard Biddle-combe | 16 | servant | |
| PETER NOYES | 47 | of Penton, county Hants, yeoman | Watertown |
| Thomas Noyes | 15 | | |
| Elizabeth Noyes | | | |
| Robert Davis | 30 | servant | |
| Margaret Davis | 26 | servant | |
| John Rutter | 22 | servant | |
| NICHOLAS GUY | 50 | of Upton Gray, county Hants, carpenter | Watertown |
| Mrs. Jane Guy | 30 | | |
| Mary Guy | | | |
| Joseph Taintor | 25 | servant | |
| Robert Bayley | 23 | servant | |
| JOHN BENT | 35 | of Penton, Hants, husbandman | Sudbury |
| Mrs. Martha Bent | | | |
| Robert Bent | 10 | | |
| Agnes Bent | 8 | | |
| William Bent | 6 | | |
| Peter Bent | 4 | | |
| John Bent | 2 | | |

ROGER PORTER

[1] Colonial Papers, America and West Indies, v, 375.

| | | | |
|---|---|---|---|
| ROGER PORTER | 55 | of Long Sutton, Hants | Watertown |
| Joan Porter | | | |
| Susan Porter | | | |
| Mary Porter | | | |
| Rose Porter | | | |
| JOHN SANDERS | 25 | of Langford, Wilts, husbandman | Salisbury |
| Mrs. Sarah Sanders | | | |
| John Cole | 40 | | |
| Roger Eastman | 15 | servant | |
| Richard Blake | 16 | servant | |
| William Cottle | 12 | servant | |
| Robert King | 24 | servant | |
| JOHN ROLFE | 50 | of Melchitt Park, Wilts, husbandman | Salisbury |
| Mrs. Anne Rolfe | | | |
| Thomas Whittle | 18 | servant | |
| JOHN GOODENOWE | 42 | of Semley, county Wilts, husbandman | Sudbury |
| Mrs. Jane Goodenowe | | | |
| Lydia Goodenowe | | | |
| Jane Goodenowe | | | |
| EDMUND GOODENOWE | 27 | of Donhead, county Wilts, husbandman | Sudbury |
| Mrs. Anne Goodenowe | | | |
| John Goodenowe | 3 | | |
| Thomas Goodenowe | 1 | | |
| Richard Sanger | 18 | servant | |
| THOMAS GOODENOWE | 30 | of Shaftesbury, county Dorset | Sudbury |
| Mrs. Jane Goodenowe | | | |
| Ursula Goodenowe | | | |
| Thomas Goodenowe | 1 | | |
| EDMUND KERLEY | 22 | of Ashmore, county Dorset, husbandman | |
| William Kerley | | | |

| | | | |
|---|---|---|---|
| William Kerley | | husbandman | Sudbury |
| Edmund Morris | | of Kington Magna, county Dorset | |

STEPHEN KENT — 27 of Nether Wallop, county Newbury Hants

| | | |
|---|---|---|
| Mrs. Margery Kent | 26 | |
| George Church | 16 | servant |
| Hugh March | 20 | servant |
| Anthony Sadler | 9 | servant |
| Nicholas Wallington | | 'a poor boy' |
| Rebecca Kent | 16 | servant |

JOHN STEPHENS — 31 of Caversham, county Newbury Oxford, husbandman

| | | |
|---|---|---|
| Mrs. Elizabeth Stephens | | |
| Mrs. Alice Stephens | | mother |
| William Stephens | 21 | of Caversham, county Oxford, husbandman |
| John Lougie | 16 | servant |
| Grace Lougie | | servant |

THOMAS JONES — 36 of Caversham, county Oxford, tailor

| | | |
|---|---|---|
| Mrs. Anne Jones | | |
| ...... Jones | 8 | |
| ...... Jones | 6 | |
| ...... Jones | 4 | |
| ...... Jones | 2 | |
| William Baunsh | 24 | servant |
| Jude Donley | | servant |

| | | |
|---|---|---|
| Mrs. Martha Wilder | | of Shiplake, county Oxford, spinster |
| Mary Wilder | | daughter |
| Augustine Bearce | 20 | |
| Martha Keene | 60 | |
| Elizabeth Keene | 13 | |
| Martha Keene | | |
| Josias Keene | | |
| John Keene | 17 | |
| Sarah Keene | | |

JOHN BENSON

| | | |
|---|---|---|
| JOHN BENSON | 30 of Caversham, county Oxford, husbandman | Hingham |
| Mrs. Mary Benson | | |
| John Benson | 3 | |
| Mary Benson | 1 | |
| WILLIAM ILSLEY | 26 of Nether Wallop, county Hants, shoemaker | Newbury |
| Mrs. Barbara Ilsley | | |
| Philip Davie | 12 servant | |
| JOHN ILSLEY | 24 of Nether Wallop, county Hants, shoemaker | Salisbury |
| JOSEPH PARKER | 24 of Newbury, county Berks, tanner | Newbury |
| *Mrs.* SARAH OSGOOD | of Wherwell, county Hants, spinster | Newbury |
| Sarah Osgood | 9 | |
| John Osgood | 7 | |
| Mary Osgood | 5 | |
| Elizabeth Osgood | 3 | |
| William Osgood | } 'children under xj years' | |
| William Jones | | |
| Margery Parke | servant | |
| JOHN LUDWELL | 50 | |
| Henry Hangert | 40 servant | |
| David Wheeler | 11 servant | |
| RICHARD BIDGOOD | of Romsey, county Hants, merchant | Boston |

BEVIS of Southampton, one hundred and fifty tons, Robert Batten, Master. Probably sailed in May, 'by vertue of the Lord Treasurers warrant of the second of May, wch was after

after the restraynt and they some dayes gone to sea Before
the Kinges Mates Proclamation Came into Southampton.' [1]

No record of her arrival.

| | | | |
|---|---|---|---|
| JOHN FRYE | 37 | of Basing, county Hants, wheelwright | Newbury |
| Mrs. Anne Frye | | | |
| John Frye | | | |
| Sarah Frye | | | |
| Benjamin Frye | | | |
| | | | |
| RICHARD AUSTIN | 40 | of Bishopstoke, county Hants, tailor | Charlestown (?) |
| Mrs. ...... Austin | | | |
| ...... Austin | | | |
| ...... Austin | | | |
| Robert Knight | | carpenter, his servant | |
| | | | |
| CHRISTOPHER BATT | 37 | of Salisbury, county Wilts, tanner | Newbury |
| Mrs. Anne Batt | 37 | | |
| Anne Batt | 8 | | |
| Jane Batt | 7 | | |
| Christopher Batt | 5 | | |
| Thomas Batt | 3 | | |
| Elizabeth Batt | 2 | | |
| Dorothy Batt | | sister of Christopher | |
| Thomas Good | 24 | servant | |
| Elizabeth Blackstone | 22 | servant | |
| Rebecca Pond | 18 | | |
| | | | |
| WILLIAM CARPENTER | 62 | of Wherwell, county Hants, carpenter | Weymouth |
| | | | |
| WILLIAM CARPENTER, JR. | 33 | of Wherwell, county Hants, carpenter | Weymouth |
| Mrs. Abigail Carpenter | 32 | | |
| ...... Carpenter | | | |
| ...... Carpenter | | | |
| | | | ...... Carpenter |

[1] Drake: *Founders*, 60.

| | | | |
|---|---|---|---|
| . . . . . . Carpenter | | | |
| . . . . . . Carpenter | | | |
| Thomas Banshott | 14 | servant | |
| *Mrs.* AGNES LITTLE- | | | |
| FIELD | 38 | | Wells, Maine |
| John Littlefield | 14 | | |
| Elizabeth Littlefield | 11 | | |
| Mary Littlefield | 8 | | |
| Thomas Littlefield | 5 | | |
| Anne Littlefield | 5 | | |
| Francis Littlefield | 2 | | |
| John Knight | | carpenter, servant | |
| Hugh Durdal | | servant | Newport |
| HENRY BILEY | 26 | of Salisbury, county Wilts, tanner | Salisbury |
| Mary Biley | 22 | sister | |
| Thomas Reeves | | servant | Roxbury |
| RICHARD DUMMER | 40 | of Bishopstoke, county Hants, gentleman | Newbury |
| Mrs. Alice Dummer | 35 | | |
| Thomas Dummer | 19 | | |
| Joan Dummer | 19 | | |
| Jane Dummer | 10 | | |
| Dorothy Dummer | 6 | | |
| Richard Dummer | 4 | | |
| Thomas Dummer | 2 | | |
| STEPHEN DUMMER | | of Bishopstoke, county Hants, husbandman | Newbury |
| John Hutchinson | 30 | servant, carpenter | |
| Francis Alcock | 26 | servant | |
| Adam Mott | 19 | servant, tailor | |
| William Wakefield | 22 | servant | |
| Anne Wakefield | 20 | servant | |
| Samuel Poor | 18 | servant | |
| Daniel Poor | 14 | servant | |
| Alice Poor | 20 | servant | |
| Nathaniel Parker | 20 | servant, of London, baker | |
| Richard Bayley | 15 | servant | |

MARTIN.

MARTIN. The voyage of this ship is only known through the death of one of its passengers, and the settlement of his estate by depositions of witnesses as to the will. She arrived in Boston Harbor before July 13.

| | | |
|---|---|---|
| SYLVESTER BALDWIN | of Aston Clinton, county Bucks | |
| Mrs. Sarah Baldwin | | |
| Richard Baldwin | | |
| Sarah Baldwin | | |
| | | |
| JAMES WEEDEN | of Chesham, county Bucks | Newport, Rhode Island |
| Mrs. Phillippa Weeden | | |
| John Weeden | | |
| William Weeden | | |
| Anna Weeden | | |
| Martha Weeden | | |
| | | |
| CHAD BROWN | | Providence |
| Mrs. Elizabeth Brown | | |
| John Brown | | |

## 1639

JONATHAN. The facts concerning this ship are taken from local records, but it is not known when she departed or arrived. The passengers are believed to be from the county of Hampshire and it is supposed that she sailed from Southampton.[1]

| | | | |
|---|---|---|---|
| THOMAS GOULD | 32 | of Bovingdon, Herts | Charlestown |
| Mrs. Hannah Gould | | | |
| | | | |
| THOMAS BLANCHARD | | of Penton, county Hants | Charlestown |
| Mrs. Agnes Blanchard | | | |
| Thomas Blanchard, Jr. | | | |
| | | | George Blanchard |

[1] Middlesex Files.

George Blanchard
Nathaniel Blanchard
Mrs. Agnes Bent          mother of Mrs. Blanchard

PETER NOYES          48 (returning)                    Watertown

ISAAC WHEELER                                         Charlestown
Mrs. Frances Wheeler

RICHARD BARNES          of Penton, county Hants Charlestown

SAMUEL HYDE                                             Cambridge

THOMAS PLYMPTON                                           Sudbury
Elizabeth Plympton


BEAVER of London, George Mayne, Master, arrived June 22 at Boston with passengers.[1]


MARY ROSE of Bristol, two hundred tons, arrived at Boston from Bristol with one hundred and twenty passengers.[2]


## 1640

No further lists of passengers are available for the ships coming this year. The following named vessels were given license to transport emigrants to New England.[3]

NEPTUNE

[1] *Lechford Note Book,* 69.
[2] Middlesex Files.
[3] Colonial Papers, America and West Indies, 1, 30.

NEPTUNE of Bristol was licensed to carry one hundred and twenty-five passengers to New England.[1]


FELLOWSHIP of Bristol was licensed to carry two hundred and fifty passengers to New England.[2] She sailed about April.

SAMUEL WAKEMAN          (returning)


CHARLES of Bristol was licensed to carry two hundred and fifty passengers to New England.[3] Of this vessel Winthrop made the following record: 'A great ship called the *Charles*, of above 300 tons, brought passengers hither this year. The master was a plain, quiet man, but his company was very wicked, and did wrong the passengers much, and being at Pascataquack to take in clapboards with another ship wherein Mr. (Hugh) Peter by occasion preached one Lord's Day, the company of the *Charles* did use all the means they could to disturb the exercise by hooting and hallooing.'[4] After many delays she sailed from Bristol June 18 and one of the passengers testified that they 'were debarred of our beere & water before landing and if we had bin put to a long voyage we must needs have suffered much more than we did.'[5]

NATHANIEL PATTEN          of Crewkerne, Somerset          Dorchester
Mrs. Justine Patten

ST. JOHN,

---

[1] *History, Merchant Venturers,* 151.
[2] *Ibid.,* 151.          [3] *Ibid.,* 152.
[4] *Journal,* II, 20.          [5] *Lechford Note Book,* 180.

ST. JOHN, Stephen Goodyear, owner, was licensed to take two hundred and fifty passengers to New England. She probably sailed from Bristol.[1]

| STEPHEN GOODYEAR | | of Saint Gregory, London | New Haven, Connecticut |
|---|---|---|---|
| RICHARD RUSSELL | 29 | of Hereford, county Hereford | Charlestown |
| Mrs. Maude Russell | | | |
| Katherine Russell | | | |

WILLIAM AND JOHN of Bristol was licensed to carry sixty passengers to New England.[2]

HOPEWELL, probably of London (see under 1635), brought passengers this year destined for Connecticut.[3]

WILLIAM AND GEORGE of Bristol was licensed to carry one hundred and eighty passengers to New England.[4]

DESIRE 'of New England' was licensed to carry fifty passengers to New England.[5]

SPARROW

[1] *Lechford Note Book*, 176.
[2] *History, Merchant Venturers*, 152.
[3] Pope, *Pioneers*, 474.
[4] Colonial Papers, Public Record Office.     [5] *Ibid.*

SPARROW 'of New England,' fifty tons, was licensed to carry fifty passengers to New England.[1]

MERCHANT ADVENTURER of London, three hundred tons, was licensed to carry one hundred and eighty passengers to New England.[2]

SCIPIO of London, three hundred tons, was licensed to carry one hundred and eighty passengers to New England.[3]

GREEN LYON of Barnstaple, two hundred and forty tons, Mark Beaple, Master, arrived this year with passengers at Boston and loaded clapboards at Portsmouth on the return voyage.[4]

This compilation contains about 3600 passengers by name, while Hotten has only about 2100 listed for New England. Recalling the statement of Johnson, quoted in an earlier part of this book (page 12), that there were 298 ships which brought about 21,200 to New England 'to 1643,' it will be seen that the present compilation can account for the arrival of but 213 ships in all to 1641, and only 158 by name. Thus, only twenty per cent of the emigrants by name and the ships they came in have been recovered.

[1] Colonial Papers, Public Record Office.  [2] *Ibid.*  [3] *Ibid.*
[4] *Lechford Note Book*, 181.

# APPENDIX

## THE SHIP LYON, 1630

THERE is no known list of passengers coming on this ship, just before the arrival of the Winthrop Fleet (see page 85), and an attempt is here made to supply this lack from casual references and a process of elimination based on contemporary evidence. This synthetic list is offered as a contribution to the solution of this interesting question.

| | | |
|---|---|---|
| CHRISTOPHER LEVETT | (transient) | |
| ISAAC ALLERTON | (returning) | Plymouth |
| EDWARD ASHLEY | | Kennebec |
| THOMAS WRIGHT | | Kennebec |
| THOMAS PURCHASE | (returning) of Dorchester, Dorset | Pejepscot |
| JOHN MOORE | | Roxbury |
| JOHN HOLGRAVE | fisherman | Salem |
|   Mrs. Elizabeth Holgrave | | |
|   Joshua Holgrave | | |
|   Lydia Holgrave | | |
| FRANCIS DENT | of London (?) | Salem |
| JACOB BARNEY | of Braddenham, county Bucks | Salem |
| RALPH FOGG | | Plymouth |
| JOHN HARDY | | Salem |
| JOHN SIBLEY | of Bradpole, Dorset | Salem |

# INDEXES

# INDEX OF SURNAMES

Persons using this index with a view to obtaining a clue to the English origin of an ancestor (not located in this compilation) are advised to note the names of those settled in the same town with him and follow up those persons in the English parishes whence they came. This will give at least a definite locality to search instead of a general hunt throughout the forty counties of England.

Abbott, 66, 160
Abdy, 162
Abell, 66
Adams, 21, 50, 126, 156, 165, 170
Agar, 66
Albon, 175
Albury, 122
Alcock, 66, 167, 200
Alden, 25, 50
Alderton, 50
Aleworth, 66
Allen, Allyn, 98, 126, 127, 165, 194
Allerton, 48, 60, 62, 93, 207
Alley, 165
Allis, 99
Almy, 165
Alsopp, 155
Altham, 55
Alxarson, 184
Ames, 182
Andrew, Andrews, 66, 138, 148, 149, 183
Annable, 53
Anthony, 107
Antrobus, 141
Antrum, 137
Archer, 66
Armitage, 135
Arnold, 166
Ashby, 130
Ashley, 207
Aspinwall, 66
Astwood, 158
Athearn, 188
Atherson, 134
Atkinson, 23
Atwood, 132, 143
Audley, 66, 78

Austin, 115, 199
Avery, 118
Ayers, 150

Babb, 124, 174
Baber, 126
Bachiler, 19, 96, 189
Bacon, 148
Bailey, Baylie, Bayley, 176, 195, 200
Baker, 66, 143, 155, 184
Balch, 58
Baldwin, 174, 201
Ballard, 111, 152
Balston, 66
Bancroft, 98
Banes, 170
Bangs, 53
Banks, 11, 47, 50, 52, 55, 58, 65, 87, 104
Banshott, 200
Barber, 129
Barnard, 119, 122, 126
Barnes, 202
Barney, 207
Barrett, 151
Barsham, 66
Barstow, Beeresto, 172
Bartholomew, 114
Bartlett, 53, 66, 100, 112
Barton, 50
Baskom, 87
Bassett, 50, 129, 164
Bates, 145, 146, 147
Batt, 137, 199
Batten, 198
Batter, 137
Baunsh, 197
Baxter, 66, 194

Beale, 50, 152
Beamond, 146, 156
Beamsley, 66
Beaple, 205
Bearce, 197
Beard, 151
Beardsley, 143
Beck, 177
Becket, 55, 124
Beecher, 60, 66
Beeresto (*see* Barstow)
Beets, 121
Belcher, 66, 132, 162
Bellows, 160
Bendall, 67
Benham, 67
Benjamin, 101
Bennett, 115, 152, 156
Benson, 198
Bent, 195
Bentley, 170, 172
Besbeech, 116
Bessey, 152
Best, 117
Bicknell, 126
Biddlecombe, 195
Bidgood, 198
Biggs, 67, 147, 178
Biley, 200
Bill, 143, 174
Billington, 49
Bird, 132
Bitton, 152
Black, 61, 67
Blackley, 174
Blackstone, 56, 199
Blackwell, 173
Blaisdell, 160
Blake, 196
Blanchard, 201, 202
Blandford, 195
Blason, 134
Blinman, 20
Blodgett, 149
Bloomfield, 120
Blosse, 123
Blossom, 64
Blower, 173
Boggust, 67

Bolles, 29
Bolton, 56 — *footnote*
Bompasse, 51
Bonney, 115
Borden, 157
Borebank, 163
Bostock, 167
Boswell, 67, 130
Bosworth, 67
Boulle, 184
Bourne, 67
Bowman, 67
Boyden, 123
Boykett, 189
Boylston, 168
Brackenbury, 59
Bradford, 12, 25, 47, 52, 55, 58, 59, 60, 62,
  64, 86, 91, 92, 93
Bradshaw (*see* Bratcher)
Bradstreet, 67, 119, 120
Brand, 61, 67
Brane, 164
Brasey, 146
Bratcher, 67
Brease, 67
Brenton, 67
Brewer, 101
Brewster, 47, 50, 55
Bridges, 55, 152
Brigden, 117
Briggs, 51, 177
Brigham, 133
Bright, 64, 67
Brighton, 173
Britteridge, 50
Brock, 155
Brodley, 145
Brook(e), 92, 115, 134, 177
Broome, 173
Broomer, 134, 155
Browne, 23, 50, 63, 67, 68, 100, 112, 130,
  131, 136, 137, 138, 146, 157, 167, 173,
  201
Buck, 151, 177, 189, 194
Buckland, 68
Bugby, 68, 122
Bulgar, 68
Bulkeley, 134
Bull, 146, 153, 174, 175

Bullock, 147, 163
Bundick, Bundock, 91, 158
Burbank, 163
Burchard, Burcher, 55, 171
Burden, 162
Burdock, 102
Burgis, 159, 182
Burkett, 60
Burnell, 68
Burr, 68
Burrell, 178
Burroughs, Burrowes, 68, 132, 182
Bursley, 57
Burt(es), 164, 170
Burules (see Burrell)
Busby, 184
Bushell, 167
Bushnell, 143, 159
Buskett, 129
Butler, 23, 136, 188
Buttolph, 161
Button, 48
Buttrick, 133, 144
Buttry, 153
Byham, 177

Cable, 68
Cakebread, 68
Call, 189
Cannon, 51
Carman, 51
Carpenter, 133, 137, 199, 200
Carr, 157, 164
Carrington, 101
Carter, 48, 141, 158
Cartrack, 155
Carvanyell, 51
Carver, 47
Chadwick, 68
Chamberlain, 192
Chambers, 68, 175
Champion, 116
Chaplin, 155
Chapman, 146
Chappell, 129
Chase, 68
Chauner, 68
Cheesebrough, 68, 69
Cherrall, 130

Child, 69
Chilton, 49
Chipperfield, 175
Chittenden, 149
Chittwood, 141
Chubb, 87
Chubbock, 103
Church, 69, 197
Churchman, 100
Clapp, 87
Clarke, 50, 53, 69, 95, 100, 111, 121, 124, 143, 175
Claydon, 65
Cleeven, 175
Cleeves, 22, 92
Clement, 136
Clifford, 132
Clough, 69
Cluffe, 146
Cobbett, 69, 156
Cockayne, 29
Cockram, 183
Coddington, 69, 105
Coe, 123, 132
Cogan, 104
Cogswell, 99
Coke, 160, 166
Coker, 112
Colborne (*see* Colbron), 169
Colborn (*see* Colborne), 69, 152
Colby, 69
Cole, 71, 111, 116, 132, 196
Coleman, 190
Collins, 164
Colman, 136
Colt, 106
Comberbach, 185
Conant, 53, 55
Connor, 51
Converse, 71
Cooke, 49, 54, 71, 87, 166, 168
Cooper, 129, 132, 135, 139, 140, 144, 154, 158, 181, 192
Cope, 178
Corbin, 102
Corrington, 133
Cottle, 196
Cotton, 19, 35, 36, 105
Couchman, 115

Courser, 157
Cousins, 136
Covell, 165
Cowlishaw, 71
Cox, 62
Crabb, 71
Crackston, 48
Craddock, 160
Crafts, 71
Cranwell, 71
Cribb, 71, 129
Cromwell, 32
Crosby, 134
Cross, 119, 151
Crowe, 103
Crowther, 107
Crugott, 71
Curtis, 100, 137, 156
Cushing, 106, 192, 193
Cushman, 51
Cutler, 183
Cutting, 120, 121

Dade, 33
Dady, 71
Dalton, 35, 149
Dammand, 155
Dane, 157
Daniell, 149
Darno, 170
Darrell, 182
Davenport, 180, 181
Davie, 198
Davis, Davies, 107, 137, 140, 147, 149, 178, 195
Dawes, 142
Day, 120, 157, 159
Deacon, 165
Deane, 51, 144
Deekes, 71
Denny, 130
Denslow, 87
Dent, 207
Desbrough, 159
Devereux, 72
Devotion, 167
Dewhurst, 169
Dexter, 142
Dibble, 127

Dickerson, 181
Diffy, 72
Dillingham, 72
Dix, 53, 134, 185
Dixon, 72, 181
Dodd, 167
Dodge, 61
Doggett, 72, 183
Done, 173
Donley, 197
Donn, 170
Donnard, 145
Dorifall, 121
Dotey, 48
Dow, 187
Downing, 72
Drake, 10, 16, 24, 87, 110, 129, 130, 131, 140, 145, 148, 152, 154, 158, 160, 161, 174
Draper, 121
Drewry, 167
Drinker, 163
Driver, 166
Dudley, 26, 72
Duke, 146
Dummer, 96, 200
Duncan, Dunkin, 88, 117
Durdal, 200
Dutton, 72
Dyer, 87, 129

Eads, 61
Early, 107
Eastman, 196
Easton, 111
Eaton, 49, 154, 180, 181, 189, 190
Eden, 185
Edge, 175
Edmonds, 72
Edwards, 175
Eggleston, 72
Elford, 59
Ellinwood, 173
Elliott, Eliot, 19, 94, 107, 158, 159
Ellis, 72, 167
Elmes, 144
Elmore, 101, 102
Elston, 72
Emerson, 164

Emery, 138, 139
Endicott, 59
England, 188
English, 50
Epps, 162
Evered, 136
Ewell, 116
Ewer, 152

Faber, 156, 157
Fabin, 157
Faldoe, 143
Farebrother, 170
Farley, 188
Farnham, 153
Farrington, 158
Farrow, 140
Faunce, 53
Fawer, 135
Fayerweather, 72
Feake, 72
Fearing, 193
Felloe, 143
Fenn, 143
Fenner, 172
Fenwick, 170
Fever, 126
Ficher, 57
Field, 138
Fiennes, 7, 72
Fifield, 108
Finch, 73
Firman, 73, 121
Fitch, 169, 177
Fitzrandolph, 73
Flagg, 186
Flavell, 51, 54
Fleming, 151
Fletcher, 50
Flood, Fludd, 53, 162
Fogg, 207
Fokar, 151
Folsom, 192
Ford, 51, 88, 115, 127, 134
Foster, 108, 147, 165, 175
Foulfoot, 129
Fountain, 166
Fowle, 133
Fowler, 112

Fox, 73, 166
Foxwell, 73
Franklin, 111
Freeborn, 122
Freeman, 73, 164, 165, 166, 175
French, 73, 125, 168, 169
Frothingham, 69
Frye, 124, 199
Fuller, 48, 49, 54, 142, 163, 164

Gage, 69
Gager, 26, 69
Gallant, 115
Gallop, 88
Gamlin, 97
Gardiner, Gardner, 50, 58, 147, 152, 153, 154
Garnett, 124
Garrett, 69
Gates, 192
Gaudens, 59
Gault, 182
Gedney, 182, 186
Geere, 164
Gibbons, 57, 149
Gibbs, 59, 61, 86, 88, 103, 171
Gibson, 70, 195
Giddins, 141
Gilbert, 16, 24
Gill, 188
Gillett, 88, 111
Gilman, 191, 192
Gilson, 133
Giver, 70
Gladwell, 151
Glover, 70, 102, 121
Goad, 167
Goard, 155
Godbertson, 53
Goddard, 136
Godfrey, 112
Goffe, 70, 152
Goldstone, 120
Goldthwaite, 70
Good, 199
Goodale, 120
Goodenow, 196
Goodhue, 153
Gooding, Goodens, 182, 185

Goodman, 50
Goodspeed, 36
Goodwin, 101
Goodyear, 204
Goose, 181
Gordon, 133
Gorges, 16, 56
Gosnall, 70
Gosse, 70
Gott, 59
Gould, 145, 168, 201
Goulworth, 70
Grane, 128
Granger, 189
Grant, 98, 101, 106
Graves, Grave, 62, 63, 94, 95, 102, 136, 166, 175
Gray, 58
Greene, 98, 122, 134, 137, 141
Greenfield, 183
Greenhill, 108
Greenway, 88, 146
Gridley, 70
Griffith, 165
Griggs, 158
Gunn, 170
Gunter, 173
Gutsall, 166
Guy, 195

Hackwell, 151, 161
Haddon, 70
Haffield, 144
Haford, 141
Haile, 173
Hailton, 121
Haines (*see* Haynes), 114
Hale, 70
Halford, 130
Hall, 70, 188
Hallett, 36, 128
Halsey, 156
Hammond, 70, 124
Hanbury, 142
Handgert, 198
Hanford, 144
Hannum, 88
Harbert, 165
Harding, 70, 167

Hardy, 207
Harlakenden, 8, 35, 168
Harman, 63, 131
Harris, 71, 84, 96, 97, 116, 129
Harrison, 174
Harsnet, 189
Hart, 95, 97, 130, 153, 186
Harvard, 181
Harvie, 143
Harwood, 73, 129
Hastings, 120
Hatch, 116
Hathaway, 167, 177
Hatherley, 53, 92, 98, 102
Haward, 65
Hawes, 156, 172
Hawke, 73, 192
Hawkesworth, 130
Hawkins, 73, 132, 144, 154
Hawthorne, 74
Haynes (*see* Haines), 8, 106, 195
Hayward, 97, 122, 141, 146
Heale, 26
Heard, 53
Heath, 99, 176
Heaton, 114
Hepborne, 163
Herrick, 62
Hesselden, 74
Hewlett, 108
Heylei, 130
Heywood, 115
Hibbens, 111
Hicks, 51, 54
Higdon, 138
Higginson, 60, 61, 62, 63
Hill, 88, 89, 97, 104, 153, 169
Hilliard, 157
Hillman, 167
Hilton, 22, 51, 54
Hinckley, 116
Hitchcock, 133
Hoames, 74
Hobart, 18, 103, 139
Hoble, 128
Hodges, 160
Hodsall, 155
Hoffe, 74, 131
Holbeck, 48

Holbrook, 127
Holden, 122
Holdred, 145
Holgrave, 63, 207
Hollard, 128
Hollingsworth, 178
Hollinck, 166
Holloway, 156
Holman, 53, 89, 102, 130
Holmes (*see* Hoames), 116
Holt, 138
Hooke, 48, 190
Hooker, 18, 19, 24, 35, 36, 105
Hooper, 152
Hopkins, 48, 180, 181
Hopwood, 74
Horne, 74
Horsford, 104
Hosier, 74
Hoskins, 89
Hosmer, 145
Hotten, 10
Hough, 105
Houghton, 64, 151, 162
Howe, 171, 172
Howland, 47
Howlett, 74
Hoyt, 64
Hubbard, 147, 155, 169, 175, 177
Hudson, 74, 133
Hulbirt, 74
Hull, 89, 125, 156, 161, 176
Humphrey, 109, 110
Hunter, 178
Huntington, 103
Huson, 91
Hussey, 97
Huste, 128
Hutchins, 74
Hutchinson, 19, 21, 41, 113, 200
Hutley, 175
Hyde, 136, 202

Iggleden, 116
Ijons, 74
Ilsley, 198
Ingersoll, 65
Ingles, 136
Ingraham, 177

Ireland, 150
Ireson, 164
Isaac, 121

Jackson, 155, 169, 178
Jacob, 103, 112
James, 62, 74, 101, 192, 193
Jarman, 134
Jarvis, 74
Jeffries, Jeffreys, 57, 157, 173
Jenkins, 115, 170, 173, 188
Jenney, 55
Jennings, 116, 121
Jennison, 63
Jessop, 126
Jewell, 144
Johnes, 160
Johnson, 7, 12, 25, 57, 60, 74, 75, 146,
    152, 153, 174, 188
Jones, 25, 47, 75, 98, 117, 128, 132, 152,
    163, 166, 167, 171, 173, 183, 197, 198
Jope, 154
Jordan, 112, 163
Josselyn, 148
Jupe, 96

Keayne, 169, 170
Keene, 197
Kemp, 139
Kempton, 53
Kendrick, 135
Kent, 111, 197
Kerbie, 175
Kerley, 196, 197
Ketcherell, 116
Kettell, 167
Kidby, 75
Kiddey, 107
Kilbourne, 119, 150, 151
Killin, 181
Killinghall, 173
Kimball, 118
King, 108, 119, 127, 138, 155, 166, 177,
    196
Kingman, 112, 127
Kingsbury, 75
Kinham, 128
Kirk, 133
Kirtland, 158

Kitchen, 126, 128
Knapp, 75
Knight, 58, 138, 170, 192, 199, 200
Knower, 75, 76, 163
Knowles, 133

Ladd, 112
Lamb, 76
Lambert, 132
Langmore, 48
Lannin, 140
Lapham, 114
Large, 140
Laskin, 59
Latcome, 108
Latham, 47
Laud, 19, 33, 35, 128
Launder, 164
Laverick, 121
Lawes, 185
Lawrence, 141
Lawson, 76
Lea, 121, 143, 148
Leach, 59, 133, 143
Leake, 130
Learned, 76
Leatherland, 76
Leaves, 175
Leeds, 187
Legge, 76
Leicester, 176
Leigh, 8
Lettyne 146
Leverage, 107, 138
Leverett, 106
Levett, 56, 207
Levin, 97
Lewis, 92, 101, 116, 117, 178
Ley, 180
Lincoln, 185, 193, 194
Lindsey, 185
Lister, 48
Littlefield, 200
Littlehale, 112
Livermore, 124
Lloyd, 175
Lockwood, 76
Long, 53, 167, 168, 177
Loomis (*see* Lummus), 147

Lord, 155, 156
Lothrop, 19, 41, 113
Lougie, 197
Love, 116
Lovell, 89, 127, 128
Lowe, 173
Luddington, 160
Ludkin, 140, 186
Ludlow, 89
Ludwell, 198
Luff, 110
Lummus (*see* Loomis), 132, 147
Lunt, 111
Lush, 128
Lyford, Lieford, 57, 134
Lyman, 94
Lynde, 114
Lyne, 162
Lynn, 76
Lynton, 76
Lyon, 175

Madder, 24
Maddox, 140
Manifold, 177
Mannering, 97
Manning, 187
Mansfield, 124, 132
Mapes, 123
March, 197
Margesson, 50
Marlborough, 180
Marsh, 110
Marshall, 129, 152, 166, 175, 185
Martin, 48, 128, 145, 153, 154, 167, 191
Marvin, 149
Mason, 117, 123, 161, 162
Massey, 62
Masters, 76
Masterson, 64
Mather, 20, 135
Matson, 76
Matthews, 191
Maude, 135
Maudsley, 174
Maulder, 170
Maverick, 56, 89
May, 151
Mayhew, 77

Mayne, 202
Mayo, 97
Meares, 161
Meech, 64
Merriman, 96
Metcalf, 184, 185
Miles, 111
Miller, 77, 175
Millet, 77, 146
Mills, 77
Milner, 152
Minor, 61
Minter, 47
Mitchell, 53, 135, 194
Mixer, 119
Moody, 110
Moore, More, 29, 47, 89, 133, 141, 149, 177, 194, 207
Morden, 129
Morecock, 156, 157
Morey, 59, 77, 173, 177
Morfield, 194
Morgan, 51
Morley, 77
Morrill, 56, 100
Morris, 77, 141, 159, 197
Morrison, 23, 141
Morse, 136, 149
Morton, 51, 53, 55, 57, 62, 77
Mosier, 98
Mosse, 121
Mott, 168, 200
Moulton, 64, 77, 185, 186
Mousall, 77
Mullins, 48
Munnings, 119, 163
Munson, 121, 177
Munt, 77
Mussell, 145
Musselwhite, 138
Mussey, 111
Mygatt, 106

Nanney, 149
Nash, 77
Nealwy, 116
Neave, 181
Needham, 77
Newby, 111

Newcom, 142
Newell, 122
Newman, 111, 152
Newton, 53
Nichols, Nicolls, 78, 133
Nickerson, 187
Nicolas, 51
Noddle, 64
North, 131
Norton, 63, 64, 97, 171, 174
Nowell, 78
Noye, Noyes, de la, 51, 112, 195, 202
Nun, 151
Nutbrowne, 170

Odell, 36
Odlin, 78
Oldham, 54, 157
Oliver, 97, 183
Olmstead, 101
Olney, 141
Onge, 93
Onion, 178
Orris, 157
Osgood, 110, 198
Ovell, 189

Packer, 194
Page, 78, 148, 180, 186
Paine, Payne, 96, 131, 150, 167, 181, 193
Painter, 78
Palfrey, 58
Palmer, 51, 54, 55, 64, 78, 121, 152
Palmerley, 154
Palsford, 78
Palsgrave, 78
Pankhurst, 164
Pantry, 109
Parke, 78, 93, 169
Parker, 78, 111, 131, 132, 136, 157, 198, 200
Parkman, 104
Parrie, 173
Parrish, 151
Parryer, 158
Parsons, 126, 138
Partridge, 180
Patchen, 116
Patten, 8, 203

Patteson, 129
Patrick, 78
Payson, 159
Peabody, 143
Peacock, 159
Peake, 160
Pease, 123
Peat, 159
Peck, 191
Pelham, 78, 133
Pell, 159
Pemberton, 78, 79
Penn, 54, 79
Pennaird, 174
Penniman, 79
Pepys, 124
Perien, 115
Perkins, 93, 97
Perley, 143
Perry, 79
Peter, Peters, 19, 24, 35, 60, 161, 171, 203
Pettit, 79
Phelps, 90, 108
Phillips, 18, 79, 141, 158
Phippen, 141
Pickering, 79
Pickworth, 79
Pierce, Peirce, Pearce, 26, 52, 58, 62, 64, 79, 86, 92, 94, 99, 105, 121, 151, 186, 188, 190
Pike, 138, 198
Pinney, 90
Pithouse, 136
Pitney, 144
Pitt(s), 51, 194
Place, 173
Plaistow, 79
Plympton, 202
Podd, 132
Pollard, 79
Pomeroy, 90
Pond, 80, 199
Poole, 127
Poore, 200
Pope, 111, 188
Popham, 16
Porter, 80, 128, 196
Potter, 151, 156, 166
Poyett, 182

Pratt, 52, 54, 80
Prence, 51
Preston, 129, 145, 155, 172
Price, 167
Priest, 50
Pring, 16
Prior, 175
Proctor, 131
Prower, 48
Pucket, 59
Purchase, 104, 207
Pynchon, 80
Pynder, 132

Quincy, 106

Rainsford, 80, 162
Ralegh, 16, 24
Rand, 54
Randall, 104
Rasdell, 57
Ratcliff, 54, 80
Rawlins, 80, 151
Rayner, 118
Reade, Reed, 80, 126, 169, 175
Reeder, 80
Reading, 80
Reekes, 92
Reeves, 129, 156, 200
Revell, 81
Reynolds, 81, 112, 121
Richards, 90, 100, 115
Richardson, 81, 133, 189
Rickman, 63
Riddet, 195
Riddlesden, 132
Rider, 108
Ridley, 142
Rigdale, 49
Ripley, 194
Roberts, 99
Robinson, 64, 65, 115, 129, 175, 177, 187
Roby, 187
Rockett, 104
Rogers, 20, 49, 52, 60, 151, 170, 179
Rookman, 166
Root(es) 117, 162
Roper, 187
Roscoe, 148

Rose, 105, 121, 122, 137, 175
Rossiter, 26, 90
Rowton, 134
Royal, 61
Royce, 81
Ruggles, 81, 159
Rum, 166
Rumball, 173
Russell, 145, 204
Rutter, 195

Sadler, 197
Salter, 138
Samond, 156
Sampson, 81, 157
Sanborn, 94, 96
Sanders, Saunders, 141, 142, 196
Sanford, 81
Sanger, 196
Sankey, 149
Sale, Sales, 81, 155
Saltonstall, 7, 60, 81, 132
Sape, 183
Sargeant, 82
Savage, 143
Savery, 110
Sawkyn, 170
Saxton, 81
Sayer, Sayres, 110, 117, 193
Saywell, 177
Scoates, 138
Scott, 81, 118, 119
Scudder, 152
Seager, 138
Seaman, 81
Seaver, 110
Sedgwick, 173
Seely, 82
Sellen, 147
Sension, 155
Sexton, 177
Shafflin, 137
Sharpe, 62, 82, 162
Shelley, 99
Shepard, Shepherd, 35, 128, 162, 168, 170
Sherborne, 98
Sherin, 121
Sherman, 121
Sherwood, 123

Short, 111
Shut, 82
Sibley, 207
Simes, 168
Simonson, 51
Simpson, 82, 160, 173
Skelton, 62
Skerry, 185
Skolfield, 132
Skoulding, 193
Small, 137
Smalley, 96
Smart, 140
Smead, 82
Smith, Smyth, 22, 27, 61, 63, 82, 95, 96,
    103, 120, 133, 135, 137, 138, 142, 143,
    144, 146, 147, 185, 187, 190, 194
Snow, 54, 132
Soule, 47
Southcote, 90, 93
Southworth, 54, 55
Sparks, 148
Spelman, 30
Spencer, 111, 174
Sprague, 54, 61
Sprall, 177
Spring, 118
Stacie, 51
Stagg, 144
Standish, 48, 55
Standy, 157
Stanion, 142
Stanley, 109, 144, 156, 166
Starr, 117, 188
Stearns, 82
Stebbins, 123
Stedman, 147
Steele, 95
Steere, 170
Sterte, 172
Stevens, Stephens, 141, 165, 197
Steward, 52
Stickline, 64
Stileman, 82
Stilles, 129
Stockbridge, 177
Stockton, 173
Stokes, 175
Stone, 106, 145, 150

Storey, Story, 47, 185
Stoughton, 77, 82
Stowers, 64
Strange, 124
Stratton, 56
Stream, 172
Streaton, 151
Street, 131
Stroud, 167
Sucklin, 194
Sumner, 83, 165
Sutton, 114, 116, 193
Swaddon, 83
Swanson, 83
Swayne, 133, 143, 155, 160, 173
Sweet, 110
Swynden, 156
Sydlie, 133
Sylvester, 90
Symmes, 41, 113

Tabor, 126
Taintor, 195
Talcott, 99
Talmadge, 83
Taylor, 83, 133, 134, 148, 160, 173, 189
Teed, 183
Teller, 151
Tench, 52
Terry, 90, 152, 166
Thatcher, 138
Thomas, 96, 175, 182
Thompson, 48, 56, 156, 167
Thorne, 146
Thornton, 131, 147
Throckmorton, 93
Thurston, 182
Thwaites, 160
Thwing, 133
Tibbalds, 172
Ticknall, 176
Tilden, 54, 114
Tilley, 49, 58, 61, 91, 162
Tillingham, 181
Timewell, 83
Tingley, 144
Tinker, 49
Tinkler, 177
Titus, 159

Tomlins, 64, 83, 133
Tompkins, 172
Toothaker, 176
Toppan, 182
Totman, 100
Tower, 183
Towne, 185
Tracy, 54, 110
Trane, 134
Trask, 58, 110
Travers, 110
Tredwell, 174
Trelawny, 105
Trentum, 178
Trerice, 140
Trevor, 102
Tritton, 116
Tucker, 167
Tufts, 193
Turner, 49, 83, 159, 174, 178
Turvey, 117
Tusolie, 164
Tuttle, Tuthill, 141, 142, 183
Tybbott, 153
Tyndal, 83

Ufford, 99, 100
Underhill, 83
Underwood, 120, 160, 186
Upham, 128
Upsall, 91
Upson, 151

Vane, 8, 161
Vassall, 83, 176, 177
Veren, 137
Vincent, 113

Wadd, 187
Wade, 83, 100, 128
Wadsworth, 99
Wakefield, 200
Wakeman, 94, 203
Wales, 135
Walker, 83, 136, 146, 182
Wall, 83, 167
Wallace, Wallis, 160, 165
Wallen, 54
Wallington, 197

Walsh, 160
Walston, 173
Ward, 84, 148
Warham, 91
Warner, 95, 149
Warren, 49, 54, 55, 84
Washburn, 154
Waterbury, 84
Waterman, 64
Waters, 84
Watson, 99
Wattlin, 123
Way, 91, 104
Weaver, 84, 142
Webb, 61, 84, 136, 153
Weed, 84
Weeden, 132, 201
Weeks, 175
Weillust, 84
Weld, 96
Weldon, 84
Wells, 116, 132, 133, 143
West, 110, 164, 176
Weston, 30, 52, 55, 84, 156
Westwood, 121
Weymouth, 16
Wharton, 23
Wheat, 146
Wheeler, 112, 113, 136, 198, 202
Whetstone, 96
Whipple, 100
White, 48, 57, 87, 101, 112, 122, 129, 147, 149, 157, 162
Whitman, 164, 172
Whitmarsh, 126
Whitney, 154
Whitred, 146
Whittemore, 159
Whitten, 156
Wiggin, 107
Wignall, 63
Wilbore, 84
Wilcockson, 143
Wild, Wylde, 146, 157
Wilder, 47, 197

Wilkinson, 84, 156
Willard, 109
Willett, 65, 100
Williams, 42, 50, 84, 91, 93, 167, 186, 187
Williamson, 141, 170, 175
Wilsby, Wilby, 84, 132
Wilson, 18, 63, 85, 95, 161, 171
Wilton, 85
Winch, 123
Winckall, 160
Wines, 115
Wing, 85, 122
Winslow, 47, 50, 52, 57, 58, 96
Winter, 105
Winthrop, 7, 9, 12, 17, 18, 19, 21, 26, 28, 31, 36, 85, 91, 92, 93, 94, 95, 96, 98, 99, 102, 104, 105, 106, 107, 108, 109, 113, 114, 124, 125, 131, 135, 139, 153, 162
Witchfield, 100
Witherell, 115
Witherley, 114, 188
Withie, 175
Wolcott, 8, 91
Wolhouston, 142
Wollaston, 57
Wood, Woods, 85, 125, 151, 164, 168, 174
Woodbridge, 110
Woodbury, 58
Woodcock, 128
Woodford, 96
Woodman, 136, 165
Woodward, 117, 118, 159, 160
Woolrich, 85
Worden, 151
Wormwood, 85
Wrast, 141
Wright, 52, 85, 183, 207
Wylie, 156
Wyman, 181
Wynchester, 145
Wyndell, 151

Yates, 106, 167
Younglove, 176

# INDEX OF PLACE NAMES

## ENGLISH PARISHES

Alford, Lincolnshire, 113, 114
Allington, Dorset, 104
Amesbury, Wilts, 137
Ashen, Essex, 124
Ashfield, Notts, 73
Ashford, Kent, 64, 109, 115, 116, 188
Ashmore, Dorset, 196
Assington, Suffolk, 73
Aston Clinton, Bucks, 201
Attleboro, Norfolk, 193
Austerfield, Yorks, 47, 51
Aylesford, Kent, 115

Baddow, Gt., Essex, 123, 130
Barkham, Berks, 147
Barnstaple, Devon, 93, 97, 107, 191
Barrington, Somerset, 126
Barrow, Norfolk, 192
Basing, Hants, 199
Batcombe, Somerset, 125, 126, 128
Beaminster, Dorset, 90
Bedingham, Norfolk, 84
Belchamp Water, Essex, 124
Benenden, Kent, 156, 157
Bentley Magna, Essex, 149
Berkhampstead, Herts, 171
Bermondsey, Surrey, 76
Bethnal Green, Middlesex, 50
Bicester, Oxford, 83
Biddenden, Kent, 147
Billerica, Essex, 148
Binfield, Berks, 74
Birmingham, Warwick, 79
Bishopstoke, Hants, 96, 199, 200
Bishops Stortford, Herts, 20, 171
Bitteswell, Leicester, 72
Bocking, Essex, 100, 101
Boreham, Essex, 70
Boston, Lincoln, 19, 68, 69, 105, 106, 111
Bovingdon, Herts, 201
Boxford, Suffolk, 18, 123
Boxted, Essex, 67

Braddenham, Bucks, 207
Bradpole, Dorset, 207
Bradwell, Suffolk, 152
Braintree, Essex, 19, 57, 99
Bramford, Suffolk, 174
Brampton, Suffolk, 181
Brandeston, Suffolk, 123
Braunton, Devon, 98
Brenchley, Kent, 138
Brentwood, Essex, 69
Bridport, Dorset, 91
Bristol, Gloucester, 9, 13, 18, 31, 62, 86, 92, 93, 161, 202, 203
Broadway, Somerset, 125, 127
Bromfield, Essex, 80
Bromley Magna, Essex, 150
Buckenham, New Norfolk, 164, 187
Bures, St. Mary, Suffolk, 75, 78
Burnham, Essex, 122
Burstead, Great, Essex, 48, 50
Bury St. Edmunds, Suffolk, 67, 69, 70
Buxhall, Suffolk, 82

Cambridge, Cambridge, 53, 59, 64, 70, 150, 168, 192, 193
Canterbury, Kent, 78, 113, 117, 188, 189
Capel St. Mary, Suffolk, 119
Carleton Rode, Norfolk, 185
Caversham, Oxford, 138, 197, 198
Chaldon, Dorset, 109
Chart, Gt., Kent, 117
Chatham, Kent, 74
Chelmsford, Essex, 18, 69
Chesham, Bucks, 201
Chester, Cheshire, 22, 75
Chetnold, Dorset, 59
Chew Magna, Somerset, 61
Childhay, Dorset, 59
Chilthorne, Somerset, 91
Chinnoch, Middle, Somerset, 61
Chittingley, Sussex, 57
Clacton, Little, Essex, 169

Clapham, Bedford, 141
Clapham, Surrey, 53, 102
Claydon, Oxford, 121
Clipsham, Rutland, 75
Coggeshall, Essex, 82
Colchester, Essex, 53, 63, 74, 77
Combe St. Nicholas, Somerset, 90
Comberton, Gt., Worcester, 182
Combs, Suffolk, 76
Copford Hall, Essex, 106
Cranbrooke, Kent, 147, 162
Crewkerne, Somerset, 8, 89, 203

Dartmouth, Devon, 9, 47
Dedham, Essex, 119
Denge, Essex, 163
Dennington, Suffolk, 120
Denton, Lancashire, 61
Devizes, Wilts, 137
Dinder, Somerset, 128
Doncaster, Yorks, 47
Donhead, Wilts, 196
Dorchester, Dorset, 61, 88, 90, 91, 104, 207
Dorking, Surrey, 48, 97, 164
Dover, Kent, 114, 189
Downton, Wilts, 137
Drawlington, Warwick, 107
Drimpton, Dorset, 59
Droitwich, Worcester, 47
Duffield, Derby, 159
Dunmow, Essex, 82
Dunstable, Bedford, 114, 167

Earls Barton, Northants, 74
Eastwell, Kent, 117
Eaton Bray, Bedford, 162
Eckington, Worcester, 47
Edwardston, Suffolk, 67
Egerton, Kent, 19
Eling, Hants, 138
Ellingham, Gt., Norfolk, 193
Elmham, Suffolk, 120
Elmsett, Suffolk, 118
Elmswell, Suffolk, 121
Eltisley, Cambridge, 159
Elzing, Norfolk, 186
Ewell, Surrey, 165
Exeter, Devon, 88, 104, 124
Exning, Suffolk, 81

Fairstead, Essex, 95, 101
Falmouth, Cornwall, 3, 9
Faversham, Kent, 117, 189
Fitzhead, Somerset, 90
Folke, Dorset, 59
Fordington, Dorset, 61
Fowey, Cornwall, 171
Fremington, Devon, 144
Frome, Somerset, 127

Giggleswick, Yorks, 172
Glemsford, Suffolk, 81
Gravesend, Kent, 61, 62, 63, 64, 91, 106
Grinstead, East Sussex, 167
Groton, Suffolk, 67, 70, 71, 75, 80, 85, 94
Guilsborough, Northants, 66

Hackney, Middlesex, 68
Halifax, Yorks, 135
Halstead, Essex, 99
Hammersmith, Middlesex, 67
Hampstead, Middlesex, 107
Hampsworth, Yorks, 138
Hardingham, Norfolk, 103
Harptree, West, Somerset, 91
Harwich, Essex, 50
Harworth, Notts, 55
Hatfield, Broadoak, Essex, 68, 100
Haverhill, Suffolk, 83, 165, 179
Hawkdon, Suffolk, 67, 68
Hawkhurst, Kent, 145, 149
Heathfield, Sussex, 101
Heedon, Northumberland, 20, 35
Hemington, Leicester, 66
Hempnall, Norfolk, 194
Hereford, Hereford, 204
Hertford, Herts, 106
Highworth, Wilts, 110
Hilmorton, Warwick, 93
Hingham, Norfolk, 17, 103, 106, 140, 191, 192, 193, 194
Holderness, Yorks, 69
Holnest, Dorset, 59
Horncastle, Lincoln, 56
Hoxton, Middlesex, 54

Ipswich, Suffolk, 9, 33, 35, 108, 117, 121, 124, 180, 181, 184
Islesworth, Middlesex, 164

Kilworth, South Leicester, 165
King's Lynn, Norfolk, 194
Kingston on Hull, Yorks, 133
Kingston, Surrey, 144
Kington Magna, Dorset, 197
Knutsford, Chester, 62

Langford, Wilts, 138, 196
Lavenden, Bucks, 158
Lavenham, Suffolk, 77, 81, 93, 124, 150
Lawford, Suffolk, 122
Lee, Bucks, 172
Leighton, Salop, 146
Lincoln, Lincoln, 173
Lindsey, Suffolk, 122
Littleham, Devon, 124
Liverpool, Lancaster, 20
London, 9, 14, 17, 18, 19, 29, 30, 31, 35,
    47, 48, 49, 50, 51, 52, 55, 63, 64, 67,
    70, 72, 74, 75, 76, 77, 78, 80, 81, 82,
    83, 85, 94, 96, 97, 98, 99, 100, 101,
    102, 105, 107, 129, 137, 140, 148, 154,
    156, 158, 160, 163, 167, 169, 200,
    204
  All Saints, Barking, 51
  All Saints, Stayning, 148
  Birching Lane, 169
  Blackwall, 3
  Cheapside, 146
  Clifford's Inn, 57
  Duke's Place, 53, 54
  Little Minories, 162, 164, 166, 167
  St. Alphege, 145
  St. Andrew Undershaft, 82
  St. Anne, Blackfriars, 73
  St. Giles, Cripplegate, 174
  St. Giles in the Field, 31
  St. James, Clerkenwell, 51
  St. Katherine, Tower, 159
  St. Lawrence, Jewry, 53
  St. Mary, Bow, 116
  St. Peter, 51
  Shoreditch, 166
  Stepney, 51, 54, 66, 85, 86, 140, 164,
    165
  Wapping, 140
  Whitechapel, 70, 86
Lydd, Kent, 145, 146
Lyme Regis, Dorset, 88, 104

Maiden Bradley, Wilts, 89
Maidstone, Kent, 115
Maldon, Essex, 123
Malford, Wilts, 136
Manchester, Lancashire, 66, 83
Maplestead, Gt., Essex, 83
Market Harborough, Leicester, 161
Marlborough, Wilts, 110, 112, 136, 137
Martock, Somerset, 59
Melchitt Park, Wilts, 196
Mersey, Essex, 71
Millbrook, Bedford, 129
Missenden, Gt., Bucks, 172
Mohuns Ottery, Devon, 90
Monk Soham, Suffolk, 55
Mosterton, Dorset, 88

Navistock, Essex, 71
Nayland, Suffolk, 73, 84
Nazing, Essex, 19, 66, 94, 95, 100, 159
Netherbury, Dorset, 128
Nether Wallop, Hants, 197, 198
Newbourne, Suffolk, 99
Newbury, Berks, 198
Newton Stacey, Hants, 83, 96
Northbourne, Kent, 117
Northleigh, Cornwall, 56
Northleigh, Devon, 125
Northwich, Chester, 51
Norwich, Norfolk, 55, 103, 182, 183, 184,
    185, 186, 187, 192, 193
Nottingham, Notts, 71

Olney, Bucks, 158
Ongar, High, Essex, 81, 94
Ormsby, Norfolk, 185, 186, 187
Ovingdean, Sussex, 164

Panfield, Essex, 53
Penton, Hants, 195, 201, 202
Pitminster, Somerset, 90
Plaitford, Wilts, 137
Plymouth, Devon, 6, 9, 47, 56, 87, 104,
    161
Polstead, Suffolk, 69
Poole, Dorset, 56
Prittlewell, Essex, 83
Pulborough, Sussex, 164
Purleigh, Essex, 53

Rainhill, Lancashire, 70
Ramsden Crays, Essex, 79
Rattlesden, Suffolk, 118, 119
Rayleigh, Essex, 64
Raynham, Norfolk, 79
Reading, Berks, 136
Redenhall, Norfolk, 48
Ringstead, Northants, 142
Rolvenden, Kent, 51
Romsey, Hants, 138, 139, 198
Rowley, Yorks, 19
Roxwell, Essex, 74, 82, 106, 148

Saffron Walden, Essex, 70, 79
St. Albans, Herts, 141
St. Lawrence, Essex, 163
Salisbury, Wilts, 112, 137, 138, 199, 200
Saltford, Somerset, 126
Sandwich, Kent, 9, 50, 64, 115, 116, 117, 188, 190
Sandy, Bedford, 65
Saxlingham, Norfolk, 183
Scratby, Norfolk, 186
Scrooby, Notts, 47
Semley, Wilts, 196
Settrington, Yorks, 72
Shaftsbury, Dorset, 196
Sharpenhoe, Bedford, 63
Shenfield, Essex, 71, 73
Sherrington, Bucks, 158
Shiplake, Oxford, 197
Shrewsbury, Salop, 92
Sidmouth, Devon, 104
Simsbury, Dorset, 88, 128
Southampton, Hants, 9, 47, 95, 107, 110, 135, 138, 195, 198, 199
Southold, Suffolk, 139, 183
Southwark, Surrey, 51, 53, 54, 55, 67, 83, 144, 146, 161, 163
Spalding in the Moor, Yorks, 134
Stanstead Abbots, Herts, 159
Stanton, Wilts, 110
Staple, Kent, 189
Staplehurst, Kent, 108, 109
Stoke Nayland, Suffolk, 72, 82
Sutton, Bedford, 65

Sutton, Long Hants, 196
Sutton Mansfield, Wilts, 195
Swyre, Dorset, 89

Taunton, Somerset, 143
Tenterden, Kent, 114, 115, 116
Terling, Essex, 96
Thannington, Kent, 189
Thetford, Norfolk, 155
Thurlow, Little, Suffolk, 124
Tilton, Leicester, 105
Tisbury, Wilts, 77
Tolland, Somerset, 91
Towcester, Northants, 155, 168, 170
Toxteth, Lancaster, 135

Upcerne, Dorset, 59
Upminster, Essex, 97
Upton Gray, Hants, 195
Upway, Dorset, 61

Wanstead, Essex, 71
Weald, Kent, 19
Wendover, Bucks, 70
Westmill, Herts, 81
Weymouth, Dorset, 58, 59, 104, 125, 126
Wherwell, Hants, 19, 198, 199
Wickford, Essex, 80
Widford, Essex, 79
Wight, Isle of, 9, 60, 85
Wigsthorpe, Northants, 106
Woodbridge, Suffolk, 71
Wood Ditton, Cambridge, 119
Woolwich, Kent, 94
Wotton under Edge, Gloucester, 48
Wrentham, Suffolk, 182
Writtle, Essex, 80
Wymondham, Norfolk, 194

Yardley, Northants, 72
Yarmouth, Norfolk, 9, 23, 35, 50, 54, 65, 100, 102, 181, 182, 187

## OTHER PLACES

Leyden, Holland, 51, 53, 64, 65
Loughall, Armagh, Ireland, 57

## NEW ENGLAND TOWNS

Agamenticus, Me., 40

Boston, Mass., 8, 40, 42, 43, 56, 63, 64, 66, 67, 68, 69, 70, 71, 72, 74, 75, 77, 78, 79, 80, 81, 82, 83, 84, 85, 86, 93, 94, 95, 98, 99, 102, 104, 105, 106, 108, 113, 114, 117, 122, 124, 125, 129, 132, 135, 136, 138, 142, 143, 144, 146, 147, 148, 149, 151, 152, 154, 156, 157, 158, 160, 161, 162, 169, 171, 173, 174, 177, 178, 198, 205
Braintree, Mass., 141, 144, 162

Cambridge, Mass., 20, 43, 66, 70, 72, 73, 79, 84, 95, 98, 99, 100, 101, 105, 106, 109, 115, 116, 117, 118, 120, 121, 122, 133, 134, 148, 149, 151, 152, 153, 155, 159, 168, 169, 170, 177, 178
Cape Ann, Mass., 40, 58
Cape Cod, Mass., 47, 50
Casco Bay, Me., 56, 92, 94, 98
Charlestown, Mass., 61, 62, 63, 64, 66, 67, 69, 70, 71, 74, 75, 76, 77, 78, 79, 81, 83, 84, 85, 92, 98, 100, 101, 103, 107, 113, 114, 115, 116, 117, 131, 135, 137, 140, 152, 154, 157, 163, 167, 168, 178, 183, 184, 188, 189, 190, 201, 204
Concord, Mass., 143, 145, 157, 160, 171

Damariscove, Me., 52, 55
Dedham, Mass., 68, 84, 121, 149, 162, 172, 184, 187
Dorchester, Mass., 6, 9, 20, 67, 68, 70, 72, 74, 79, 80, 82, 83, 87, 100, 104, 124, 128, 135, 146, 147, 162, 163, 172, 174, 188, 203
Dover, N.H., 107, 153, 177
Duxbury, Mass., 156, 157, 175

Fairfield, Ct., 68, 171
Falmouth, Me., 148

Gloucester, Mass., 153, 155

Hampton, N.H., 97, 108, 149, 152, 186
Hartford, Ct., 19, 108, 143, 149, 155
Hingham, Mass., 18, 68, 78, 139, 140, 145,

148, 168, 174, 183, 191, 192, 193, 194, 198

Ipswich, Mass., 73, 108, 110, 111, 112, 114, 119, 120, 130, 131, 132, 135, 138, 141, 143, 144, 145, 146, 147, 153, 156, 158, 163, 164, 169, 171, 174, 176, 179, 189
Isles of Shoals, Me., 40, 134

Kennebec, Me., 207
Kittery, Me., 139

Long Island, N.Y., 154
Lynn, Mass., 64, 76, 83, 132, 133, 134, 135, 146, 152, 158, 164, 165, 171, 173, 174

Marblehead, Mass., 115
Malden, Mass., 165
Marshfield, Mass., 20, 144, 177
Martha's Vineyard, Mass., 72, 77
Medford, Mass., 169
Milford, Ct., 170
Monhegan, Me., 40

Nantasket, Mass., 87, 94
Newbury, Mass., 110, 111, 112, 121, 136, 137, 138, 139, 182, 185, 197, 198, 200
New Haven, Ct., 129, 158, 159, 172, 204
Newport, R.I., 69, 138, 153, 200, 201
Northampton, Mass., 74, 100, 130, 165

Pejepscot, Me., 207
Pemaquid, Me., 42, 109, 160
Piscataqua, N.H., 102, 134, 203
Plymouth, Mass., 6, 22, 50, 52, 55, 57, 58, 59, 60, 62, 64, 65, 86, 91, 93, 96, 98, 100, 102, 110, 124, 137, 146, 154, 156, 165, 175, 176, 207
Portland, Me., 22
Portsmouth, N.H., 98, 205
Portsmouth, R.I., 107, 122
Providence, R.I., 201

Reading, Mass., 156
Rehoboth, Mass., 68

Richmond Island, Me., 105
Rowley, Mass., 20, 132
Roxbury, Mass., 19, 66, 68, 70, 71, 76, 80, 82, 93, 94, 96, 97, 99, 100, 101, 103, 110, 122, 156, 159, 171, 176, 178, 200, 207

Sabino, Me., 4
Saco, Me., 92, 93, 148
Salem, Mass., 59, 61, 62, 63, 64, 65, 66, 70, 74, 75, 77, 79, 82, 86, 93, 102, 106, 109, 110, 111, 114, 117, 120, 123, 127, 129, 134, 137, 138, 139, 140, 141, 143, 146, 150, 153, 155, 159, 165, 166, 171, 173, 174, 177, 178, 182, 183, 185, 189, 190, 207
Salisbury, Mass., 69, 70, 112, 130, 164, 196, 198, 200
Sandwich, Mass., 116, 152
Saugus, Mass., 96, 97
Scituate, Mass., 19, 73, 96, 102, 113, 114, 116, 123, 126, 135, 144, 147, 149, 164, 175, 176, 177
Southold, L.I., 123, 152
Springfield, Mass., 96, 99, 123

Stratford, Ct., 143, 159, 172, 173
Sudbury, Mass., 157, 166, 195, 196, 197

Topsfield, Mass., 137

Virginia, 3, 4, 23, 28, 29, 30, 106

Wallingford, Ct., 96
Watertown, Mass., 66, 67, 68, 69, 70, 72, 73, 74, 75, 76, 77, 78, 79, 81, 82, 83, 84, 93, 106, 117, 118, 119, 120, 121, 122, 123, 124, 132, 133, 150, 154, 155, 156, 157, 166, 177, 184, 187, 189, 195, 196
Wells, Me., 200
Wenham, Mass., 147
Wethersfield, Ct., 119, 120, 121, 150
Weymouth, Mass., 56, 125, 127, 128, 159, 172
Windsor, Ct., 72, 104, 129, 177
Woburn, Mass., 165

Yarmouth, Mass., 138, 177, 191
York, Me., 57, 72, 125, 157, 160, 175

# INDEX OF SHIPS

Abigail, 59, 161
Ambrose, 65
Angel Gabriel, 160
Anne, 52, 86
Arbella, 4, 5, 7, 25, 26, 28, 41, 65, 85, 86

Batchelor, 153
Beaver, 202
Bevis, 198
Bird, 106
Blessing, 176

Castle, 191
Charity, 57
Charles, 65, 97, 203
Christian, 129, 139
Clement and Job, 108
Confidence, 195

Defence, 35, 167
Desire, 130, 204
Diligent, 191
Discovery, 3

Elizabeth, 117, 139, 144
Elizabeth and Anne, 139, 147, 154
Elizabeth Bonaventure, 102, 108

Fellowship, 203
Fortune, 22, 50, 53, 55
Four Sisters, 63
Francis, 121
Friendship, 92, 93

George, 161, 180
George Bonaventure, 62
Gift, 92
Gift of God, 3
Goodspeed, 3
Great Hope, 131
Green Lyon, 205
Griffin, 6, 41, 105, 113

Handmaid, 91
Hector, 179
Hercules, 107, 114, 188
Hopewell, 8, 65, 124, 139, 158, 174, 204

Increase, 139, 148

Jacob, 58
James, 98, 106, 131, 134, 135, 139, 151
Jewel, 65
John and Dorothy, 184
Jonas, 107
Jonathan, 56

Katherine, 56

Little James, 55
Love, 130
Lyon, 19, 26, 42, 62, 85, 86, 92, 94, 99
Lyon's Whelp, 61

Marmaduke, 59
Martin, 201
Mary Anne, 181
Mary and Jane, 105
Mary and John, 3, 6, 85, 87, 110
Mary Rose, 202
Mayflower, 4, 5, 9, 10, 12, 23, 24, 26, 29, 31, 32, 41, 47, 54, 64, 65, 86
Merchant Adventurer, 205

Neptune, 108, 203

Pied Cow, 174
Planter, 108, 139, 140
Pleasure, 60
Plough, 94
Prophet Daniel, 56

Rebecca, 125, 139, 160
Reformation, 108
Regard, 124
Rose, 187

St. John, 204
Sarah Constant, 3
Scipio, 205
Seabridge, 31
Sea Flower, 108
Sparrow, 52, 205
Speedwell, 47
Success, 65
Susan and Ellen, 131, 191
Swan, 52
Swift, 92

Talbot, 60, 65
Thomas and William, 91
Trial, 65

Truelove, 108, 171

Unity, 57, 58

Welcome, 104
Whale, 65, 95
White Angel, 60, 93
William, 102
William and Francis, 65, 96
William and George, 204
William and Jane, 102
William and John, 204

Yorke Bonaventure, 56

Zouch Phenix, 58